"The strangest crimes
in this volume fall largely into one of two categories. In the personal crime it is the criminal
who wears the mantle of strangeness, but the
impersonal crime is strange in itself—in its conception and execution. Although this collection
covers a wide range of time and space, it does
not claim to be comprehensive, but merely
selective. There are enough strange crimes in
history to fill a score or more of similar volumes.

"In making the selection the author's aim has
been to seek variety not only in the nature of
the crime itself, but also in the particular
aspect of 'strangeness' involved—which may
lie in the deed or the doer or the done-to; or in
the circumstances of detection and trial; or in
some abstract element or principle strange to
the concept of justice as it is envisaged
throughout the civilized world."

—From the Introduction by C. E. Maine

THE WORLD'S STRANGEST CRIMES
was originally published by
Hart Publishing Company, Inc.

THE WORLD'S
STRANGEST
CRIMES

C. E. MAINE

PUBLISHED BY POCKET BOOKS NEW YORK

THE WORLD'S STRANGEST CRIMES

Hart edition published 1967

Pocket Book edition published March, 1970

Standard Book Number: 671–75461–0.
Copyright, ©, 1967, by C. E. Maine. All rights reserved.
This *Pocket Book* is published by arrangement with Hart Publishing
Company, Inc.

Printed in the U.S.A.

CONTENTS

INTRODUCTION

WHAT does the word "strange" mean in the context of crime? In one sense, all crimes are strange in that they signify a departure from normal and rational standards of behaviour, but a great deal of crime follows a familiar basic pattern so that the strangeness becomes lost in the familiarity. In another sense, there are no strange crimes at all, but only strange people whose anti-social motivations and odd eccentricities result in bizarre and sometimes criminal behaviour. The key word is behaviour, and if one digs beneath the surface of an unusual crime the apparent strangeness tends to recede to its point of origin in the distorted mind of the one who behaves— or misbehaves.

Crime can be personal or impersonal, although most crimes are of the personal type—the conflict between one individual and another, or against society as a whole, from fraud to arson, and mutiny to murder. The impersonal crime is less common; the identity of the criminal may be relatively unimportant for he represents an organization, faction or government and is working for a cause and not for personal motives. This type of crime frequently has a political basis and the individuals concerned do not matter—for example, the theft of the Coronation Stone from Westminster Abbey by Scottish Nationalists on Christmas morning 1950, or the massive forgery of British bank-notes by the Germans during the last war.

There are, of course, the border-line cases: the seizure of the Portuguese passenger liner *Santa Maria* in mid-ocean by an anti-Salazar rebel as a kind of unilateral declaration of independence against the Portuguese government may have been politically motivated, but the incident was really the expression of the single-minded and perhaps fanatical determination of one man rather than the tactical manoeuvre of an organized revolutionary movement. Similarly, political assassination is seldom impersonal because of the curious psychopathic mentality of the assassin. Impersonal crimes are generally committed by normal people; the reverse is true in the case of personal crimes.

The strange crimes outlined in this volume fall largely into one or the other of these two categories. In the personal crime it is the criminal who wears the mantle of strangeness, but the impersonal crime is strange in itself—in its conception and execution. Although this collection covers a wide range of time and space, it does not claim to be comprehensive, but merely selective. There are enough strange crimes in history to fill a score or more of similar volumes.

In making the selection the author's aim has been to seek variety not only in the nature of the crime itself but also in the particular aspect of "strangeness" involved—which may lie in the deed or the doer or the done-to; or in the circumstances of detection and trial; or in some abstract element or principle strange to the concept of justice as it is envisaged throughout the civilized world.

Strange crimes continue to happen, of course—there is no end to them. Among the most recent, which are too contemporary and well known to the public to justify inclusion in this present volume, are the theft of the Goya portrait from the National Gallery and the subsequent ransom attempts, and the sensational theft of the football World Cup. Both, fortunately, had happy endings.

The author is deeply indebted to many people for advice and references which facilitated the selection and compilation of material and case histories for this volume—in particular, Major James Haswell of the Army Legal Service, Mr. Robert Chapman of the *Sunday Express*, Mr. John F. Burke and Mr. Christopher S. Youd and other author colleagues of the Crime Writers' Association. The author would also like to pay tribute to the unfailing efficiency of the staff of the British Museum Newspaper Library at Colindale.

January, 1967

C. E. MAINE

THE WORLD'S
STRANGEST
CRIMES

Chapter 1

THE STONE OF DESTINY

THE Coronation Stone—alternatively known as Lia Fail, the Stone of Destiny, or simply the Stone of Scone—is housed beneath the seat of the Coronation Chair in the Chapel of St Edward the Confessor in Westminster Abbey. It is not an elegant object; it takes the form of a roughly rectangular block of coarse red-grey sandstone weighing some four hundred and fifty-eight pounds—about four hundredweight. Its dimensions are 26½ by 16½ inches and it is 11 inches thick.

The upper surface is indented by a rectangular hollow which is marked with a crudely chiselled Latin cross. On either side of the stone is embedded an iron ring, so placed as to allow a strong pole to be passed through the rings to facilitate carriage. The Stone of Destiny was brought to Westminster from Scotland in 1295 by King Edward I, who had the Coronation Chair specially made to contain it.

In that chair, with the stone set underneath, all of King Edward's successors have been crowned—with the exception of the two Marys. It is a very old and hallowed relic, and the stone itself, though worthless in terms of material, is of priceless historical value, and it has been the cause of much dissension over the centuries between the Scots and the English.

Early on Christmas morning in 1950 the night watchman in Westminster Abbey made his usual tour of inspection just after midnight. All was well. The last service had been in the late afternoon of Christmas Eve, and since then the Abbey had been in darkness and deserted. All over Britain families were attending to the Christmas ritual of filling stockings and placing presents under the Christmas tree. But at the next inspection, at about six o'clock in the morning, the night watchman, passing through St Edward's Chapel, was astonished to observe that the Coronation Stone had vanished from its box-like space beneath the seat of the Coronation chair.

The stone had certainly been there at midnight, but in the intervening period it had been forcibly wrenched from the chair, splintering the wood of one of the legs in the process. It had then apparently been dragged round the full length of the altar and across the south transept to Poets' Corner, where a padlocked door had been forced open. From there the stone had presumably been carried to Millbank, opposite the Houses of Parliament, and taken away in a waiting car.

Although the thieves had certainly broken out of the Abbey, there was no evidence that they had broken in. It seemed likely that they had attended the last service on the afternoon of Christmas Eve, which had ended at 4.15 p.m., and had then quietly and successfully concealed themselves behind tombs and pillars in the darkened chapel. The whole difficult operation had been accomplished in silence and complete secrecy. The four-hundredweight Stone of Destiny had calmly been taken from Westminster Abbey, and not a soul in the early hours of that Christmas morning had noticed anything unusual taking place in the vicinity of Westminster.

For the newspapers it was a frustrating time, for of course they did not publish at all on Christmas Day or Boxing Day, and the announcement of the sensational theft was the exclusive preserve of radio and television. Forty-eight hours went by before the press could get their headlines into print and on the streets. And although the police worked intensively over the two days of Christmas, there had been virtually no developments and no leads. The newspapers had to build up their terse, retrospective reports of the crime with potted histories of the Stone of Scone and hurried thumbnail sketches of the Scottish Nationalist movement, which was suspected to be behind the plot.

So far as the history of the Stone of Scone was concerned, the newspapers were fairly unanimous in their several ways. Legend identified the Stone of Scone with Jacob's Pillow, the sacred stone of Ireland, and the Chair of St Columbia. The stone, it was said, had been found by Jacob when journeying from Beersheba to Haran in the Holy Land, and was the hard pillow on which he lay when he saw the angels of God ascending and descending the ladder of Bethel.

During a long and devious history, in which the stone was at one time in the possession of the Pharaoh who was drowned in the Red Sea, it arrived in Ireland. Simon the Wolf was believed to have been crowned while sitting on it on the Hill of Tara. In A.D. 498 the stone made its final sea voyage from Ireland to Scotland, where it was installed in the Abbey of Dunstaffnage. There it was used as the Coronation Stone of all the Scottish kings until the ninth century.

So much is legend—and the stone emerges into actual historical record around the thirteenth century. It had then been moved from Dunstaffnage to the Abbey of Scone by King Kenneth II of Scotland to commemorate his victory over the Picts in the year of A.D. 840.

In 1295, King Edward I of England seized the stone as a trophy of war, and since then it has always been at Westminster embodied in the specially made Coronation Chair. The only time the stone has ever been removed from the Abbey was for the installation of Oliver Cromwell as Lord Protector. During the Second World War the chair itself was removed for safe keeping to Gloucester Cathedral, but the stone was kept in the Abbey and buried in the Islip Chapel. A map showing its precise location was sent to the Canadian Government—just in case Britain lost the war. In the event, the precaution was not necessary.

The news of the theft of the Coronation Stone was received with a sense of profound shock in England, and jubilation in some parts of Scotland. *The Times* leader on 27 December, 1950, said: "It is to be hoped, for the honour of the Scottish Nationalist movement, that no one remotely connected with it may be found responsible for this coarse and vulgar crime."

Miss Wendy Wood, however, a prominent and militant

Scottish Nationalist, thought it "the best news I have heard in years". She celebrated the occasion at her home by flying the Scottish flag of the lion rampant—and this at a time when it had not even been established that the Scottish Nationalists were involved in the removal of the stone.

The Dean of Westminster, Mr A. C. Don, said in a broadcast that the disappearance of the stone was "the most devastating thing which could have happened. It is the most precious relic we have, and we shall never be happy until it is returned to us". He added that the King (George VI) was greatly distressed by this act of sacrilege. Finally, the Dean urged the public to co-operate; if they had any information they should get in touch with the police—"or let me know and I will go to the ends of the earth to fetch it back."

The fact was that for centuries Scottish patriots had been campaigning vigorously for the return of the Stone of Scone to Scotland. It was regarded as an ancient symbol of Scottish nationality, even though it had originally come from Ireland. Edward III actually went so far as to agree to its return in 1328, but there was a great outcry from the people of London and he decided to abandon the idea. The dispute began to quieten down when James IV of Scotland ascended the English throne to become James I of England, and in theory the Act of Union in 1707 between England and Scotland should have terminated the argument completely—but it continued nevertheless, and goes on to this day.

One curious and perhaps characteristic result of the theft was that in the few days after Christmas thousands of sightseers who would normally never have bothered to visit Westminster Abbey to see the Coronation Stone went there in droves to stare at the empty space under the chair where the stone had been.

Police investigations at first made little progress. There were one or two tangible but not very helpful clues. Near the damaged chair in the Abbey the police had found a crowbar, which had obviously been used to prise the stone from its setting and to force the exit door. They also found a man's wrist-watch. However, neither article proved to be helpful in identifying the owners.

The police also tried to trace the owner of an Anglia car which had been seen parked outside the Abbey at about 5.15 a.m. on Christmas morning. There was every reason to believe that this was the car which had been used by the raiders. A police constable had noticed the car and, not suspicious, but merely making a routine check, had questioned the man and the woman sitting in the front seat. Their answers, given in a Scottish accent, had been satisfactory and the incident had passed by without being recorded. The policeman could be forgiven for not deducing that a Scots couple in an Anglia outside Westminster Abbey early on Christmas morning were part of an organized plot to steal the Coronation Stone!

As a matter of routine the Serpentine was dragged by the police, and there was some excitement when a big heavy stone was located with grapples, but it turned out to be a concrete block of little antiquity—and a false alarm.

Miss Wendy Wood, the Scottish Nationalist, announced that she was initiating legal action to make sure that the stone remained in Scotland. It had not yet been officially stated that the stone was in Scotland at all, but Miss Wood may have had her own private sources of information. She said: "All this talk about thieves is rubbish. The stone was only retrieved."

And in *The Times*, where indignant correspondence quickly materialized, one writer observed: "The plain fact is that the stone was filched from the Irish by the Scots, and filched from the Scots by the English. Do those who now talk of restoring the stone to its rightful resting place mean to transport it across the Irish Sea to Tara?"

On 29 December, four days after the theft, the first positive indication came that the Stone of Scone was in Scotland, and had been stolen by Scottish Nationalists, as had been suspected. It took the form of a petition to King George VI. One copy of the petition was sent to the police, and another to the Scottish *Daily Record*.

The document promised that "His Majesty's petitioners will most readily return the stone to the safe-keeping of His Majesty's Officers if His Majesty will but graciously assure them that in all time coming the stone will remain in Scotland in such of His Majesty's properties, or otherwise, as shall be deemed fitting by him.

"That such assurance will in no way preclude the use of the stone in any coronation of any of His Majesty's successors, whether in England or Scotland.

"That His Majesty's humble petitioners are prepared to submit to His Majesty's Ministers or their representatives, proof that they are people able, willing and eager to restore the Stone of Destiny to the keeping of His Majesty's Officers."

The petition added: "In witness of the good faith of His Majesty's petitioners, the following information concerning a watch left in Westminster Abbey on 25 December is appended. (1) The main-spring of the watch was recently repaired. (2) The bar holding the right-hand wrist strap had recently broken and been soldered." The petition was unsigned.

On examining the watch, the police were able to confirm that the strap had broken away from the shoulder and had at some time been repaired. Scratched inside the back cover of the watch was the inscription "JGC 148". This appeared to be the usual type of watchmaker's or repairer's identification mark—but the interesting thing was whether the watch repairer concerned, if traced, would be able to identify the owner of the watch from his records.

A few weeks later a Mr James Griffiths, a watchmaker of Guernsey, told the police that he thought the mark engraved on the back of the watch was his. "JGC 148" signified "James Griffiths, cleaned January 1948". This seemed reasonable enough, and the watch had almost certainly passed through his hands—but it had happened some three years previously, but he had no written record of the owner, nor could he recall him after such an interval of time. So this particular lead proved to be fruitless.

Another curious incident was the discovery on 7 January, 1951 (almost a fortnight after the theft), of a small oak plaque with a damaged frame on a bombed site in Tufton Street, Westminster, near the Abbey. The surface of the plaque bore an inscription which briefly outlined the history of the Coronation Chair, and proved in fact to be the actual plaque which was normally displayed on the chair for the information of visitors. The obvious assumption was that the plaque had been inadvertently taken along with the stone and had either fallen or been thrown from the car when the raiders had been making their escape. It was an interesting "clue", but yielded no useful results.

Throughout January the police concentrated their search in Scotland, and there is little doubt that they very quickly formed a short list of likely suspects, but for policy reasons no positive action was taken. The most important task was to recover the stone itself. Once that had been accomplished, the matter of bringing the raiders to justice could be considered in a more political light. Meanwhile, patriotic Scots continued to make unconditional demands which appeared to be based on the principle that "possession is nine-tenths of the law". A speaker of the Scottish National Congress declared that the missing Stone of Destiny would not be delivered up "except to a Scottish Prime Minister elected by the Scottish people as their representative". It is difficult to believe that such spokesmen were not well aware of the fate and whereabouts of the stone, and also the identity of those who had taken it; how else could they have assumed the right to impose such conditions? What they did not fully realize was that they were attempting to use the stone to change the Constitution of the United Kingdom itself, and authority—i.e., the Establishment —was not amenable to such pressure.

Needless to say, during the many weeks of police investigation, Scotland Yard was offered the services of telepathists, clairvoyants, water diviners and spiritualistic mediums—to the extent that the Yard went so far as to deny press reports that it had officially engaged a Dutch clairvoyant. This incident was the subject of a question in the House of Commons, to which Mr Chuter Ede, then Home Secretary, replied: "The gentleman in question whose activities were given publicity, not by the police, was one of a number of selected persons who were given facilities to visit Westminster Abbey to examine clues. He was not invited by the police, his expenses were not met from public funds, and no results have accrued." (Loud laughter in the House.)

Nothing very much happened until the end of January when an anonymous caller telephoned a newspaper office in Edinburgh to announce that a sheet of paper bearing news of the stone had been nailed to the door of St Giles Cathedral in the city. Reporters were immediately sent to the spot, to discover a piece of paper lying on the cathedral steps, where it had evidently fallen from the door to which it had been originally pinned. The paper bore a typewritten statement from the holders of the Stone of Destiny, and its phrasing appeared to indicate some doubt and change of heart.

In effect, the message asked the Scottish people for instructions regarding the disposal of the stone—which was clearly becoming an embarrassment as police pincers closed in and any possibility of negotiation at government level on its future became more and more utterly remote.

The message said that "in the face of imprisonment we reaffirm our resolution to retain this ancient symbol of Scottish nationality in our country unless it be the clearly demonstrated will of the Scottish people that the stone be handed back to the Church of England." The notice further called on the Scottish National Assembly at its next meeting to decide the future resting place of the stone. The decision would be honoured and the proper action taken.

To establish the *bona fide* character of the communication, information was added which called for specialized knowledge which only the raiders could have possessed—as in the case of the first petition. The addendum stated: "On the night of 23 December one of our number was ejected from Westminster Abbey by the watchman half an hour after the Abbey was closed." The name and London address of the person concerned was given. This was checked by the police and found to be true enough, although the "person concerned" was no longer available in London for questioning.

It was also stated that the nail used to pin the document to the door of St Giles Cathedral "was recently removed from the fabric of Westminster Abbey". Whether the police were able to verify this is not recorded. Nevertheless, it was not doubted that the typewritten sheet of paper was a genuine communication from the people illegally in possession of the stone, who now seemed anxious to shed their responsibilities.

Miss Wendy Wood had meanwhile been very busily researching among all the available archives and consulting eminent men of law ("too eminent to allow their names to be used", she said) and claimed that she had collected irrefutable proof that Scotland had exclusive right to ownership of the Stone of Scone.

Scotland Yard detectives went quietly and patiently about their task and gradually closed in on the raiders. By the middle of March they knew the identity of the four suspects, but for political reasons took no immediate action, apart from interrogation. Their terms of reference were to locate and retrieve the stone—not to make arrests that might result in an Anglo-Scottish war. It seems likely in retrospect that the offenders were told that if they delivered up the stone to authority, in a proper ceremonial way to appease Scottish

Scottish Nationalist was remotely connected with "this coarse and vulgar crime", commented on 12 April that "the most ancient and honourable part of the Scottish regalia—for such is how the Nationalists describe it—has been treated like a sack of coals, and yesterday was taken into Arbroath Abbey in the back of a motor-car. It was later removed to police headquarters and 'locked in a cell'—a shameful and dishonourable resting place." Disapproval was being spread in all directions, even against the police who, in imprisoning the stone, were merely safeguarding it against second thoughts on the part of those who had surrendered it, or even more militant attempt to re-possess it by other less law-abiding Nationalists.

The Times, in fact, took a rather sympathetic view of the Scottish plea for self-government, but thought that any progress which might have been made at Westminster had been seriously jeopardized by the stone "prank". (Escapade might have been a better word.) A *Times* leader observed that "so long as the Scottish demand for self-government is shrouded in a heavy mist of folklore and legend, so long as the arguments for it come no nearer the present than Bannockburn and Flodden, there will be little sympathy for it in London. If, however, it can be shown that the demand is related to the political and economic facts of today, the Scottish case will in the end prevail by reason of its justice and practicability."

Identification of the stone was carried out by the Clerk of Works of Westminster Abbey, who travelled to Scotland to perform his task. He confirmed that it was the original and genuine Stone of Destiny.

The next step was to take the stone back to Westminster, but for obvious reasons this was an operation which had to be carried out in secrecy and with the utmost security. And the Scottish National Congress issued a solemn warning that if the stone was returned to London a further deterioration in Anglo-Scottish relations would result.

With a certain unintentional irony the Stone of Destiny, which had been removed from Westminster Abbey on Christmas morning, was delivered back there on Friday, 13 April, allegedly the Devil's birthday. But presumably superstition played no part in the selection of the date, though some Scottish Nationalists may have been gratified.

The Stone of Destiny made its long journey south in a police car escorted by two other police cars. There was no publicity, and no incident. Even the shouting was over. The police convoy arrived at Westminster Abbey at about 8 p.m. A circle of policemen formed round the cars after they had driven in to the Abbey precincts, and the gates were locked. There was no need for the heavy security. The Scots, having surrendered with dignity their cherished Stone of Destiny, were too proud a people to invite anti-climax by any further demonstration or intrigue. The secret operation of smuggling the stone back into England was successfully carried out, but one wonders whether it needed to be so secret.

The question of further police action against the Nationalists who had removed the stone in the first place hung fire for nearly a week. The position was that the police had in fact identified the four persons concerned in the "prank" (as *The Times* defined it), and had obtained admissions from three of them. But after due reflection it was felt that these "vulgar acts of vandalism which have caused great distress and offence in both England and Scotland" did not, in the public interest, merit criminal proceedings. The four culprits were never named.

The matter was allowed to die a natural death. Newspapers, without a "D notice", showed a curious reluctance to publish any further correspondence on the subject.

Whether the four Scottish "heroes" ever received their silver medals from the Scottish National Congress is not recorded.

Chapter 2

HAYDN'S HEAD

FRANZ JOSEF HAYDN was born in 1732 and died in 1809. He was a celebrated composer and is regarded today as "the father of modern instrumental music"—so much so that Beethoven took lessons in him. He lived in Austria, and his father, who was a wheelwright by trade, was also the organist of the local village church. Haydn composed more than a hundred symphonies, plus oratorios, masses, concertos, quartets and songs, and was therefore a very prominent musical genius—which accounts for the mysterious things which happened to Haydn's head after he died. He had patrons, of course, as all significant composers did in those days. He became Capellmeister to Prince Paul Esterhazy, and later to his brother Prince Nicholas. At the time of his death his patron was Prince Anton Esterhazy, who had a secretary named Josef Karl Rosenbaum, and Rosenbaum was to play a key part in the strange things which happened to Haydn's head in the century and a half which followed his death.

At the time when Haydn died, Austria was being invaded by the French. Enemy troops were fighting their way into

Vienna. His burial was therefore a rush job with little pomp or ceremony. He was interred in a churchyard at Hundsthurm, near Vienna, where he had lived.

Two nights later, while the French were still bombarding the capital, four men carrying spades and a lantern stole into the cemetery, dug open Haydn's grave—not a difficult task, as it had only recently been filled in and the soil was still loose—and took the lid off the coffin. This was not just an ordinary body-snatching expedition; the raiders merely wanted a particular piece of Haydn's body. They cut off the head of the corpse and carefully wrapped it up, after which they closed the coffin and filled in the grave again. Then they departed as quietly as they had come, taking the severed head with them. In due course the head was delivered to a man named Johan Peter, who was the superintendent of two prisons in Vienna.

This grisly decapitation of the dead body of the celebrated composer had been arranged by Peter for an unusual purpose. His hobby was phrenology, and he took this hobby very seriously indeed. In order to make practical "scientific" tests of the theories of Dr. Gall, the deviser of phrenology, Peter had for some time been collecting the skulls of identifiable dead people so that, by means of meticulous measurement of the cranial structure, he could relate bone shape to the talents and propensities of the owner of the skull when he or she had been alive. As a prison executive, Peter encountered little difficulty in obtaining an adequate supply of run-of-the-mill heads of executed prisoners who, if they possessed any "bumps of knowledge" at all, undoubtedly wore them on that part of the cranium devoted to murder and crime. The death of Haydn in the confusion of war offered an ideal opportunity to acquire a really worthwhile subject for his pseudo-scientific phrenological tests. Haydn's head had been cut off in order to find out if he possessed a "bump of music".

The raid on the grave and the desecration of the corpse had been by no means a clandestine operation, although it had been performed secretly. It was "semi-official" in that the raiding party had been led by the sexton of the church himself, who had been handsomely bribed by Peter. To lend tone to the excursion, the sexton had been accompanied by two minor government officials and none other than Josef Rosenbaum, the secretary of Prince Esterhazy, Haydn's patron. No doubt they had all been bribed—but the Prince knew nothing of what was happening.

Johan Peter "processed" the head very carefully, reducing it to a skull and making a multitude of precise measurements. When he had completed his studies, he issued a formal and fatuous report to Rosenbaum in which he stated that he had found "the bump of music fully developed".

The project had been successfully completed, and the only remaining problem was what to do with Haydn's skull, which having served its purpose was now an embarrassment, even to a collector of skulls. To return it to the grave was impracticable, quite apart from the additional risk and further bribes involved, and in any case such a move would not mitigate the seriousness of the original offence if ever it came to light. Peter, therefore, kept the skull hidden in a silk-lined box until the war was over. He then gave the gruesome relic to Josef Rosenbaum who, apart from his own interest in music, and Haydn in particular through his association with him as Prince Esterhazy's secretary, had a wife who enthusiastically used music as a social catalyst to organize regular musical soirées at her home, events which were always highly successful and well attended.

Haydn's skull was seized upon by Mrs Rosenbaum in high delight as just the thing to make a bizarre and exciting focal point—and indeed talking point—for her musical evenings. But it had to be tastefully exhibited. So she commissioned a craftsman to make a handsome glass and ebony display case in which Haydn's skull could repose with dignity, like a Victorian stuffed bird. It was not only a success—it was a sensation. Mrs Rosenbaum's musical parties became even more popular. Although the news must have spread around that Haydn's head was in the Rosenbaums' home, it never seemed to reach the ears of authority, or, for that matter, Prince Esterhazy.

On the contrary, the Prince, as Haydn's patron, had already made up his mind that the composer's remains deserved a much nobler resting place than the humble wooden coffin buried in the churchyard at Hundsthurm, and he planned to have the body exhumed, transferred to a more worthy casket and re-interred in the church at Eisenstadt on the Prince's estate, where Haydn had served his patron for over thirty long and illustrious years.

The wheels were set in motion with the commissioning of an ornate bronze coffin which was duly manufactured and delivered to the Esterhazy palace at Eisenstadt, near the Hungarian border. It was stored in a passage near the kitchens, and there it stayed as years rolled by, forgotten by all but the kitchen staff, who found it a macabre encumbrance in their daily comings and goings. The Prince was a busy man, and had many other matters to occupy his mind.

In 1820—eleven years after Haydn's death—the Duke of Cambridge visited Austria and stayed as a guest of the Prince at the Eisenstadt palace. To celebrate the occasion, the Prince arranged for a full performance by a large orchestra of Haydn's "The Creation" in his private opera house. It was this event, highly praised by the Duke, which reminded the Prince of his plans to re-inter Haydn's remains—and of the fact that the bronze casket which had been specially made by skilled craftsmen had been gathering dust in the palace basement for much longer than he cared to recall. Possibly ashamed of the unintended delay in his plans, he now put the rest of the arrangements into effect without further delay. Instructions were sent to Vienna for Haydn's coffin to be dis-interred and delivered to Eisenstadt, where the skeleton would be transferred to the magnificent bronze casket and buried in the palace church.

This was done—but when the coffin was opened it was discovered, to everybody's outraged horror, that the skull was missing from the skeleton. Somebody had stolen Haydn's head! The police were immediately called, and the Prince offered a handsome reward for the return of the skull.

The principals originally involved in the head-snatching episode were, of course, disconcerted by this unexpected development. After all, eleven years had gone by since Haydn's death, and if it hadn't been for this grandiose scheme of re-interment, nobody would ever have known that the skull was missing. Even so, while a great fuss was inevitable, it seemed to be going too far to call in the police and offer a reward for a few bones stolen many years ago.

Johan Peter was the first to panic, for it was he who had organized the head-snatching expedition in the first place, and his known interest in phrenology made him a natural suspect. He called on the Rosenbaums and urged them to return the skull to Prince Esterhazy. Josef Rosenbaum, who because of his former connection with the Prince had no wish to be involved with the police, thought this was a sensible idea—though not without some apprehension and misgivings. Mrs Rosenbaum, however, stubbornly refused to part with her status symbol. How could she ever hold another musical soirée without Haydn's skull as the centrepiece of attraction? She became hysterical, not realizing that she could hardly continue to display the skull when it was the object of a police investigation. Mrs Rosenbaum's dominant personality was such that the skull stayed put, but was hidden away until the pursuit had died down.

Peter, possibly with one eye on the reward, then tipped off the police that the Rosenbaums had a skull which they claimed was Haydn's. Subsequent police inquiries drew a blank, but the police suspected that the Rosenbaums knew more about the missing head than they were admitting. They reported back to the Prince, and he in a very positive manner ordered Josef Rosenbaum to find and return the head or be thrown into prison.

Even then Mrs Rosenbaum flatly refused to hand over the cherished skull. Josef, caught in the pincer pressure exerted by his neurotic wife and the angry Prince, resorted to a subterfuge. He obtained a skull from a mortuary in Vienna and dispatched it to the Prince with an apologetic letter of explanation. The Prince, however, was not so gullible as Josef had hoped; he had the skull professionally examined by an expert and it was adjudged to be that of a young man of not more than twenty years of age.

The skull was returned to Josef. As his wife would still not give up the original, he obtained another skull, this time of the correct age group and of comparable appearance to the one in the glass and ebony case, and sent it to Eisenstadt. This one, after expert scrutiny, was accepted as genuine. It was ceremoniously added to Haydn's skeleton and the bronze coffin was then interred in the Eisenstadt church.

This might have been the end of the story, but was not—there were still one hundred and thirty-four years to go before Haydn's actual skull was reunited with the rest of his bones. Meanwhile, the skull stayed with the Rosenbaums, though it no longer formed the focal point of musical evenings. Years went by. Mrs Rosenbaum died, and then, when Josef Rosenbaum was dying he sent for Johan Peter and presented to him the glass and ebony case containing the controversial relic.

Peter was not very happy about this particular legacy, but he recognized the irony of the situation and accepted it with good grace. It was a case of casting bread upon the waters. The skull went once more into hiding, and it was not until he too had reached the point of death that he directed that it should be bequeathed to the Vienna Conservatory of Music. But he left no written instructions to this effect, and when he died his wife gave it to their family doctor, who in turn handed over to the Society of the Friends of Music in Vienna, Anatomy. The year was 1852, and Haydn had been dead some forty-three years.

In due course, because Josef Rosenbaum had signified his wish that the skull should go to a music institution, it was handed over to the Society of the Friends of Music in Vienna, and remained there until the early 1900s. The time-scale was changing; one has to think now in terms of a museum exhibit, where years become decades and decades become centuries in an effortless eternity. But as the twentieth century was born, there were many who saw in Haydn's skull a commercial money-spinner. Tourism was developing into an industry, and even members of the Friends of Music thought that the skull could profitably be exhibited to augment the funds of the Society. But other claimants, also with a view to attracting tourists, were beginning to appear.

In the end there were two main contenders. The first claimant was the local government of Burgenland, in which Eisenstadt was situated, which stated quite uncompromisingly that Haydn's skull should be added to the mortal remains of the great composer which were buried in 1820 in the Eisenstadt church. The spurious skull supplied by the very late Josef Rosenbaum would, of course, be discarded. So far as the Friends of Music were concerned, this seemed to be not only reasonable, but desirable. They were nothing if not a responsible organization. They agreed.

But it was not quite so simple. The Vienna council raised objections and invoked the law, so far as they could. They wanted the skull to be permanently displayed in a glass case in the Vienna historical museum—and they received a great deal of influential support. The basic issue was whether Haydn's much abused skull should be finally laid to rest with his bones in the bronze coffin at Eisenstadt, or whether it should be exhibited to tourists and the curious in a museum. It was, fundamentally, a question of taste.

The issue dragged on for decades—through two world wars. The Esterhazy family continued to press their claim, and in 1932 Prince Paul Esterhazy announced that he would donate an elegant mausoleum for Haydn, to be built in the Eisenstadt church—but only on condition that the skull and skeleton were reunited.

Legal arguments and discussion went on and on like a tedious game of chess—and then came the Second World War. A curious result of the war was that, after the surrender of Germany, the two parts of Haydn's skeleton became separated by a political as well as a physical barrier. His skeleton was buried in what was now the Soviet Zone of Austria, while his skull was still in the International Zone of Vienna. Haydn, though he was not aware of it, was involved in the Cold War.

But Haydn was soon to be at peace with himself. In 1946, when the war was over, the Society of the Friends of Music became active once more, and decided to resolve the long-standing problem of what to do with Haydn's skull once and for all. They put pressure on the new Vienna Council to renounce their claim to the skull, so that it could be returned to its rightful place in the bronze coffin in the mountain church at Eisenstadt.

After a great deal of persuasion, the Vienna local authority reached agreement with the Friends of Music in principle. All that remained was for the Society to negotiate and arrange matters with the local government of Burgenland, which embraced Eisenstadt. The result was predictable. The Soviet administration gave its assent—but it took eight years for the final act to be accomplished.

Finally, in the summer of 1954, the skull of Haydn, the great Austrian composer, was formally handed over to Burgenland officials to be put with the skeleton to which it belonged. At Eisenstadt, Haydn was exhumed for the last time, and his remains, united and complete for the first time in one hundred and forty-five years, were lowered in their bronze coffin into their final resting place.

Chapter 3

THE PEOPLE EATERS

FROM time to time in the course of human history natural depravity plumbs new depths—and not only during wars. The Sawney Beane case in the early seventeenth century concerned a family that lived in a cave and chose murder, cannibalism and incest as its way of life. For twenty-five years this family, rejecting all accepted standards of human behaviour and morality, carried on a vicious guerilla war against humanity. Even a medieval world accustomed to torture and violence was horrified.

Because over the years a large family was ultimately involved, most of whom had been born and raised in fantastic conditions under which they accepted such an existence as normal, taking their standards from the criminal behaviour of their parents, the case raises some interesting legal and moral issues. Retribution when it finally came was quick and merciless, but for many of the forty-eight Beanes who were duly put to death it may have been unjust.

The story itself is simple enough, though scarcely credible, and has been well authenticated. Sawney Beane was a Scot,

20

born within a few miles of Edinburgh in the reign of James VI of Scotland, who was also James I of England. His father worked on the land, and Sawney was no doubt brought up to follow the same hard-working but honourable career. But Sawney soon discovered that honest work of any kind was not his natural métier. At a very early age he began to exhibit what would today be regarded as delinquent traits. He was lazy, cunning and vicious, and resentful of authority of any kind.

As soon as he was old enough to look after himself he decided to leave home and live on his wits. They were to serve him very well for many years. He took with him a young woman of an equally irresponsible and evil disposition, and they went to set up "home" together on the Scottish coast by Galloway.

Home turned out to be a cave in a cliff by the sea, with a strip of yellow sand as a forecourt when the tide was out. It was a gigantic cave, penetrating more than a mile into the solid rock of the rather wild hinterland, with many tortuous windings and side passages. A short way from the entrance of the cave all was in complete darkness. Twice a day at high tide several hundred yards of the cave's entrance passage were flooded, which formed a deterrent to intruders. In this dark damp hole they decided to make their home. It seemed unlikely that they would ever be discovered.

In practice, the cave proved to be a lair rather than a home, and from this lair Sawney Beane launched a reign of terror which was to last for a quarter of a century. It was Sawney's plan to live on the proceeds of robbery, and it proved to be a simple enough matter to ambush travellers on the lonely narrow roads connecting nearby villages. In order to ensure that he could never be identified and tracked down, Sawney made a point of murdering his victims.

His principal requirement was money with which he could buy food at the village shops and markets, but he also stole jewellery, watches, clothing and any other articles of practical or potential value. He was shrewd enough not to attempt to sell valuables which might be recognized; these were simply stock-piled in the cave as unrealizable assets.

Although the stock-pile grew, the money gained from robbery and murder was not sufficient to maintain even the Sawney Beane's modest standard of living. People in that wild part of Scotland were not in the habit of carrying a great deal of money on their persons. Sawney's problem, as a committed troglodyte, was how to obtain enough food when money was in short supply and any attempt to sell stolen valuables taken from murdered victims might send him to the gallows. He chose the simple answer. Why waste the bodies of the people he had killed? Why not eat them?

This he and his wife proceeded to do. After an ambush on a nearby coastal road he dragged the body back to the cave. There, deep in the Scottish bedrock, in the pallid light of a tallow candle, he and his wife disembowelled and dismembered his victim. The limbs and edible flesh were dried, salted and pickled, and hung on improvised hooks around the walls of the cave to start a larder of human meat on which they were to survive, indeed thrive, for more than two decades. The bones were stacked in another part of the cave system.

Naturally, these abductions created intense alarm in the area. The succession of murders had been terrifying enough, but the complete disappearance of people travelling alone along the country roads was demoralizing. Although determined efforts were made to find the bodies of the victims and their killer, Sawney was never discovered. The cave was too deep and complex for facile exploration. Nobody suspected that the unseen marauder of Galloway could possibly live in a cave which twice a day was flooded with water. And nobody imagined for a moment that the missing people were, in fact, being eaten.

The Sawney way of life settled down into a pattern. His wife began to produce children, who were brought up in the cave. The family were by no means confined to the cave. Now that the food problem had been satisfactorily solved, the money stolen from victims could be used to buy other essentials. From time to time they were able to venture cautiously and discreetly into nearby towns and villages on shopping expeditions. At no time did they arouse suspicion. In themselves they were unremarkable people, as is the case with most murderers, and they were never challenged or identified.

On the desolate foreshore in front of the cave the children of the Beane family no doubt saw the light of day, and played and exercised and built up their strength while father or mother kept a look-out for intruders—perhaps as potential fodder for the larder.

The killing and cannibalism became habit. It was survival, it was normal, it was a job. Under these incredible conditions Sawney and his wife produced a family of fourteen children, and as they grew up the children in turn, by incest, produced a second generation of eight grandsons and fourteen granddaughters. In such a manner must the earliest cavemen have existed and reproduced their kind, though even they did not eat each other.

It is astonishing that with so many children and, eventually, adolescents milling around in and close to the cave somebody did not observe this strange phenomenon and investigate. The chances are that they did, from time to time—that they investigated too closely and were murdered and eaten. The Sawney children were no doubt brought up to regard other humans as food.

The young Sawneys received no education, except in the arts of primitive speech, murder and cannibal cuisine. They developed as a self-contained expanding colony of beasts of prey, with their communal appetite growing ever bigger and more insatiable. As the children became adults they were encouraged to join in the kidnappings and killings. The Sawney gang swelled its ranks to a formidable size. Murder and abduction became refined by years of skill and experience into a science, if not an art.

Despite the alarming increase in the number of Sawney mouths which had to be fed, the family were seldom short of human flesh in the larder. Sometimes, having too much food in store, they were obliged to discard portions of it as putrefaction set in despite the salting and pickling. Thus it happened that from time to time at remote distances from the cave, in open country or washed up on the beach, curiously preserved but decaying human remains would be discovered. Since these grisly objects consisted of severed limbs and lumps of dried flesh, they were never identified, nor was it possible to estimate when death had taken place, but it soon became obvious to authority that they were connected with the long list of missing people. And authority, at first disbelieving, began to realize with gathering horror the true nature of what was happening. Murder and dismemberment were one thing, but the salting and pickling of human flesh implied something far more sinister.

The efforts made to trace the missing persons and hunt

down their killers resulted in some unfortunate arrests and executions of innocent people whose only crime was that they had been the last to see the victim before his, or her, disappearance. The Sawney family, secure in their cave, remained unsuspected and undiscovered.

Years went by. The family grew older and bigger and more hungry. The programme of abduction and murder was organized on a more ambitious scale. It was simply a matter of supply and demand—the logistics of a troglodyte operation. Sometimes as many as six men and women would be ambushed and killed at a time by a dozen or more Sawneys. Their bodies were always dragged back to the cave to be prepared by the women for the larder.

It seems strange that nobody ever escaped to provide the slightest clue to the identity or domicile of his attackers, but the Sawneys conducted their ambushes like a military operation, with "guards" concealed by the road at either side of the main centre of attack to cut down any quarry that had the temerity to run for it. This "three-pronged" operation proved effective; there were no survivors. And although mass searches were carried out to locate the perpetrators of these massacres, nobody ever thought of searching the deep cave. It was passed by on many occasions.

Such a situation could not continue indefinitely, however. Inevitably there had to be a mistake—just one clumsy mistake that would deliver the Sawney Beane family to the wrath and vengeance of outraged society. The mistake, when it happened, was simple enough—the surprising thing was that it had not happened many years earlier. For the first time in twenty-five years the Sawneys, through bad judgment and bad timing, allowed themselves to be outnumbered, though even that was not the end of the matter. Retribution when it finally came was in the grand manner, with the King himself taking part in the end game—the pursuit and annihilation of the Sawney Beane tribe.

It happened in this way. One night a pack of the Sawney Beanes attacked a man and his wife who were returning on horse-back from a nearby fair. They seized the woman first, and while they were still struggling to dismount the man had her stripped and disembowelled, ready to be dragged off to the cave. The husband, driven berserk by the swift atrocity and realizing that he was hopelessly outnumbered by utterly

ruthless fiends, fought desperately to escape. In the vicious
engagement some of the Sawneys were trampled underfoot.

But he, too, would have been taken and murdered had not
a group of other riders, some twenty or more, also returning
from the fair, arrived unexpected on the scene. For the first
time the Sawney Beanes found themselves at a disadvantage,
and discovered that courage was not their most prominent
virtue. After a brief and violent skirmish they abandoned the
fight and scurried like rats back to their cave, leaving the
mutilated body of the woman behind. At last the authorities
had found a living survivor, a dead victim, and a score of
witnesses. The incident was to be the Sawneys' first and last
serious error of tactics and policy.

The man, the only one on record known to have escaped
from a Sawney ambush, was taken to the Chief Magistrate of
Glasgow to describe his harrowing experience. This evidence
was the break through for which the magistrate had been
waiting for a long time. The long catalogue of missing people
and pickled human remains seemed to be reaching its final
page and denouement; a gang of men and youths were
involved, and had been involved for years, and they had to be
tracked down. They obviously lived locally, in the Galloway
area, and past discoveries suggested that they were cannibals.
The disembowelled woman proved the point, if proof were
needed.

The matter was so serious that the Chief Magistrate com-
municated directly with King James VI, and the King apparently took an equally serious view, for he went in person to
Galloway with a small army of four hundred armed men and
a host of tracker dogs. The Sawney Beanes were in trouble.

The King, with his officers and retinue, and the assistance
of local volunteers, set out systematically on one of the
biggest manhunts in history. They explored the entire Galloway countryside and coast—and discovered nothing. When
patrolling the shore they would have walked past the partly
waterlogged cave itself had not the dogs, scenting the faint
odour of death and decay, started baying and howling, and
trying to splash their way into the dark interior.

This seemed to be it. The pursuers took no chances. They
knew they were dealing with vicious, ruthless men who had
been in the murder business for a long time. With flaming
torches to provide a flickering light, and swords at the ready,

they advanced cautiously but methodically along the narrow twisting passages of the cave. In due course they reached the charnel house at the end of the mile-deep cave that was the home and operational base of the Sawney Beane cannibals.

A dreadful sight greeted their eyes. Along the damp walls of the cave human limbs and cuts of bodies, male and female, were hung in rows like carcasses of meat in a butcher's cold room. Elsewhere they found bundles of clothing and piles of valuables, including watches, rings and jewellery. In an adjoining cavern there was a heap of bones collected over some twenty-five years.

The entire Sawney Beane family, all forty-eight of them, were in residence; they were lying low, knowing that an army four hundred strong was on their tail. There was a fight, but for the Sawneys there was literally no escape. The exit from the cave was blocked with armed men who meant business. They were trapped and duly arrested. With the King himself still in attendance they were marched to Edinburgh—but not for trial. Cannibals such as the Sawneys did not merit the civilized amenities of judge and jury. The prisoners numbered twenty-seven men and twenty-one women of which all but two, the original parents, had been conceived and brought up as cave-dwellers, raised from childhood on human flesh, and taught that robbery and murder were the normal way of life. For this wretched incestuous horde of cannibals there was to be no mercy, and no pretence of justice—if ever any one of them merited justice.

The Sawney Beanes of both sexes were condemned to death in an arbitrary fashion because their crimes over a generation of years were adjudged to be so infamous and offensive as to preclude the normal process of law, evidence and jurisdiction. They were outcasts of society and had no rights, even the youngest and most innocent of them.

All were executed on the following day, in accordance with the conventions and procedures of the age. The men were dismembered, just as they had dismembered their victims. Their arms and legs were cut off while they were still alive and conscious, and they were left to bleed to death, watched by their women. And then the women themselves were burned like witches in great fires.

At no time did any of them express remorse or repentance. But, on the other hand, it must be remembered that the children and grandchildren of Sawney Beane and his wife had been brought up to accept the cave-dwelling cannibalistic life as normal. They had known no other life, and in a very real sense they had been well and truly "brain-washed", in modern terminology. They were isolated from society, and their moral and ethical standards were those of Sawney Beane himself. He was the father figure and mentor in a small tightly integrated community. They were trained to regard murder and cannibalism as right and normal, and they saw no wrong in it.

It poses the question as to how much of morality is the product of environment and training, and how much is (or should be) due to some instinctive but indefinable inner voice of, perhaps, conscience. Did the younger Sawney Beanes know that what they were doing was wrong?

Whether they knew or not, they paid the supreme penalty just the same.

Chapter 4

THE SAGA OF THE "SANTA MARIA"

NEVER in modern times has a pleasure cruise on a fast luxury liner ended in so sensational a manner as happened aboard the Portuguese ship *Santa Maria* in 1961. The vessel, owned by the Portuguese Colonial Navigation Company, sailed from Lisbon on 9 January on a leisurely winter sunshine cruise, calling at South American ports, the West Indies and Florida. The tour was to end at Port Everglades and the *Santa Maria* was due to return to Lisbon on 6 February. There were some six hundred passengers aboard, many of whom joined the ship at South American ports early in the itinerary, and the crew numbered about three hundred, making a full human complement of nearly a thousand men, women and children who were mainly Portuguese, Spanish, Dutch, Venezuelan and American. In command of this crack liner—which was reputed to be the fastest ship on the Lisbon to South America run, and capable of twenty knots—was Captain Mario Simoes Maia, a ship's master of very great experience. But even Captain Maia's experience could hardly be expected to cope with the dramatic and indeed fantastic events that were about to explode into action on board the peaceful, pleasure-dispensing *Santa Maria*.

Early on the morning of 24 January, when the *Santa Maria* had been at sea for about two weeks, the Portuguese Government put out a startling news announcement which echoed and re-echoed in banner headlines in newspapers throughout the world. The 20,000-ton *Santa Maria* had been seized by armed passengers in an unprecedented act of modern piracy!

Even the staid *Times,* not given to sensationalism or excessive use of headlines, ran four simultaneous headlines on the story, one below the other: 70 *ARMED MEN SEIZE LINER. British frigate in pursuit. "Rebels" scuttle threat.* 600 *passengers on board.*

The early press reports were bald and confused. All that was known about the coup at that stage was that on the morning of Sunday, 22 January, a group of passengers armed with machine-guns and hand-grenades had violently taken over control of the *Santa Maria* when it was off the French island of Martinique. One ship's officer had been killed, and another seriously wounded. The "mutineers" were being led by 65-year-old Captain Henrique Carlos Malta Galvão, an exiled opponent of Dr Salazar's regime in Portugal, who had escaped two years earlier from a Lisbon prison hospital while serving a sixteen-year sentence for subversive activity. While it was obvious to the world's press that Galvão's seizure of the *Santa Maria* was politically motivated, it was difficult to understand precisely how a luxury liner, complete with passengers, in the middle of a pleasure cruise, could usefully serve any attempt at insurrection against the Portuguese Government. The unanswerable question was: having taken over the ship, what did Galvão propose to do with it? What was his destination, and what was to be the fate of the passengers—and, for that matter, the crew? What action did the Portuguese Government propose to take, and the other governments whose citizens were aboard the ship?

The British Government, always a leader in maritime affairs, acted immediately. A Royal Navy frigate, H.M.S. *Rothesay,* which was visiting St Lucia in the West Indies, was sent off in search of the *Santa Maria.* The chase was quickly joined by two United States destroyers. These three warships were briefed to intercept the *Santa Maria* under the international laws governing piracy and insurrection at sea. The question of what action to take when the "kidnapped" liner had been located was a matter for the governments concerned, and would be decided when the time came.

There was no denying the legal charge of piracy, despite the political implications, for by definition from the eight articles of the Geneva Conference of 1958 on the law of the sea piracy is "any illegal acts of violence . . . committed for private ends by crew or passengers of a private ship . . . against a ship or aircraft, persons or property outside the jurisdiction of any state"—on the high seas, for example. And pirates on the high seas are subject to arrest by ships of any nation.

The first official communication from the rebels came later in the day on 24 January—the day when the news had first broken upon a startled world. Captain Galvão issued a statement over the ship's radio. He said that the action had been taken under his personal command as "the first step aimed at overthrowing the dictator Salazar of Portugal". He professed himself willing to put in at the first port that would give firm assurances that the ship would not be seized and impounded, so that passengers who wished to could disembark. Without such assurances, the passengers would be obliged to stay on the ship. Galvão added that "the passengers and crew ask that their families be informed that they are well—and, I add, well and free".

It now became clear that the seizure of the *Santa Maria* was at this stage a *fait accompli*. Captain Maia was being held prisoner in his cabin. The rebels, wearing quasi-military yellow uniforms and blue caps, and always armed, were in command of the situation. The rebels had apparently boarded the ship as legitimate passengers at its previous two ports of call, bringing their guns, hand-grenades and uniforms aboard concealed in suitcases.

The attack, though not entirely bloodless, had been swiftly and efficiently carried out, concentrating principally on the officer-in-charge on the bridge. He had been shot in the back and killed when he had tried to sound an alarm. The captain and the other officers were placed under arrest and forced to sail the *Santa Maria* under Galvão's orders. There had been no panic at all among the passengers, who did not even know what had happened until much later, by which time nothing could be done.

Early on 23 January, the day after the seizure, the *Santa Maria* put into the harbour at Castries, the port of St Lucia in the British Windward Islands. Eight men were hurriedly lowered in a lifeboat and rowed themselves ashore. One of them was the dead officer, and another was the injured purser, who had three bullet wounds and was in a serious condition. The others were members of the crew who had firmly refused to remain on the ship under Galvão. Once the lifeboat had been launched and despatched, the *Santa Maria* quickly put to sea again before the authorities could investigate. The putting ashore of the lifeboat, a considerate gesture on Galvão's part, was a tactical error, as he recognized afterwards, for it broke the secrecy of his operation too soon, and made it impossible for him to carry out his plans.

From 24 January onwards Galvão sent a series of radio messages in which he proceeded to explain and justify his act of piracy. The *Santa Maria* had been seized, he said, "in the name of the international junta presided over by General Humberto Delgado, president elect of the Portuguese Republic, fraudulently deprived of his rights by the Salazar Government". Delgado had been a candidate for the presidency of Portugal in 1958, but was defeated. He was now living in exile in Rio de Janeiro, but remained an active political opponent of the Salazar regime, and a focal point for activities against the State.

Delgado himself sent telegrams to the British and American ambassadors in Rio de Janeiro as soon as the news of the seizure of the *Santa Maria* had been announced. The text read: "I ask you to advise your governments that the case of the *Santa Maria* does not represent mutiny or piracy, but the appropriation of a Portuguese transport by a Portuguese for Portuguese political ends. I insistently ask your governments not to interfere."

And on the same day a Portuguese Government spokesman stated that "the men who attacked the *Santa Maria* are not politicians or ideologists. They are just outlaws."

*   *   *

In order to fill in the background of the *Santa Maria* escapade it is necessary to put Captain Galvão into his proper background context. He was a small, thin and wizened man in

his mid-sixties who had at one time been very active in
Portuguese politics and had held important governmental
posts in the Salazar administration. Originally he had been a
loyal supporter of Dr Salazar, and had done a great deal to
pave the way for his installation as president in 1926.

Galvão was still a faithful Salazar man in 1947, when he
was appointed a government inspector and sent to Portuguese
West Africa to report on economic conditions in Angola. He
was not impressed by what he saw, and he wrote a highly
critical report on conditions in the colony. He was particularly
caustic in his attacks on administrative faults, which dis-
pleased the government to the extent that his report was
suppressed and never published.

This was the point in time when Galvão's loyalty began to
change—first to disaffection, and then defiance. His report on
Angola was a vital and important document, and he was
determined that it should be publicized. Against government
policy he announced the results of his findings to the National
Assembly of which he was a member. This was a dangerous
snub to the rulers of Portugal, for which Galvão was to pay
dearly in due course. No immediate action was taken, however, for Galvão was still an influential public figure, but during
the next few years he was pushed more and more into the
background, and his political career, which once had been so
promising, came to a halt.

It was not until 1951 that Galvão was arrested. Two years
later, after long-drawn-out legal proceedings he was finally
brought to trial and sentenced to three years' imprisonment
for subversion.

But even when he had completed his sentence he was still
held in custody under "preventive detention". Despite the
severe restrictions placed upon his activities he was able to
arrange for the controversial sections of his report on Angola
to be published abroad. At this time Angola was becoming a
burning issue for the Portuguese authorities, who were finding
themselves caught up in the wave of independence that was
sweeping through Africa, and the situation in Angola was
virtually a full-scale war. Galvão's stubborn efforts to
discredit the government on the Angola problem could only
result in more trouble for him. In 1958, while still in detention, he was charged with continued subversion, incitement to
revolt and defamation of the authorities. He was inevitably

convicted and sentenced to sixteen years' imprisonment, which should have silenced him effectively into advanced old age.

However, luck was apparently on Galvão's side. At the beginning of his long term of imprisonment he became ill, and early in 1959 spent five months in a Lisbon hospital under surveillance. Nevertheless, he managed to escape and reach the Argentine embassy, where he sought and was granted political asylum.

Galvão's career lay in ruins because of his stubborn and single-minded integrity, whether based on wrong premises or not. And yet his earlier career as a young man had been distinguished. As an army officer he had served in Africa, and had eventually become the Governor of the province of Huila in Angola. Later he was appointed Senior Inspector of Overseas Territories and was elected to the National Assembly as deputy for Angola. He was regarded as an expert on African affairs—but it was what he saw for himself in Portuguese Africa that changed him from a dedicated supporter of Dr Salazar to a fearless and outspoken critic of Salazar's administration, which he came to regard as a form of tyranny.

On the other hand, he was never an advocate of Portugal's withdrawal from Africa, nor was he in favour of granting independence to Angola in the fashionable "wind of change" of the day. His disapproval was concentrated on the Salazar regime itself. He believed, and still does, apparently, that the first duty of the Portuguese political opposition was to overthrow the Salazar dictatorship which, he claimed, was "stifling Portuguese life and expression".

This, then, was the man who had organized a *coup d'état* on board a cruising luxury liner as the first step in an insurrection against the established Portuguese state. And there is little doubt that the major maritime countries of the world, although required by international law to regard Captain Galvão and his henchmen as pirates, were rather confused as to the real issues involved. American, British and Dutch warships were sent in pursuit of the *Santa Maria,* but with no clear idea as to what they should do when they found her. Portugal also sent frigates to track down the errant ship—but their instructions were undoubtedly more precise. Britain's position was somewhat complex, for Portugal was an old ally, and although certain aspects of the Salazar government had been the subject of criticism, the United Kingdom Government felt obliged by treaty to give full support to official Portuguese government action.

*   *   *

The *Santa Maria* was first sighted by a United States Navy patrol aircraft on the third day after the seizure of the ship. She was about nine hundred miles east of Trinidad, and sailing in an easterly direction across the Atlantic. The American destroyer *Robert L. Wilson,* though some five hundred miles away, was ordered to the area.

In radio messages Captain Galvão stated that he was making for a neutral port where the passengers could be safely put ashore, but to observers it looked as though the ship was heading in the direction of Africa—and Angola in particular. This was Galvão's most logical destination, for because of his political outlook he had many supporters in Angola who were anxious to throw off the Lisbon administration. Galvão warned: "If we are followed by Portuguese or foreign ships we will not surrender nor will we stop. We are not tyrants, but patriots, adversaries of all the forms of totalitarian government, citizens disposed to all sacrifices, including life, for our great cause, but we count on the understanding of our passengers on board."

From South America, General Delgado revealed that the coup had been planned for many months. Again warning off anyone inclined to interfere, he said: "War is war, and this is war on Portuguese territory. It is truly Portuguese business."

On the *Santa Maria* itself life was reasonably normal. According to later reports the rebels consisted mainly of bearded youths, swaggering in their denim-type uniforms, but generally courteous and well-behaved. Their authority lay in their automatic weapons, and they had already demonstrated that they were prepared to use them if necessary. Only six of the "insurgents" were Portuguese; the rest came from Spain and Latin America and were probably hired mercenaries for the most part, or youngsters in it for the kicks. For the passengers life was much the same as before. The only difference was that their destination had changed—was unknown. Food and water were rationed as a precautionary measure, but the rations were adequate. It was known that the *Santa Maria* had enough food on board for twenty days, and carried one and a half thousand tons of fuel oil, enough for five thousand miles of steaming. And the girls swam in the heated swimming pools on the ship as if nothing had happened.

It was clear to Galvão, however, that he could not maintain his unilateral action for much longer. Even if the American and British warships took no positive action, there were Portuguese naval vessels closing in, with fewer reservations as to how to handle the situation. As an earnest of his good intentions, while still steaming towards Angola, Galvão offered by radio to hold talks on board the *Santa Maria* with representatives of any nation other than Portugal and Spain. The Americans accepted this concession. Admiral Robert Dennison, Commander-in-Chief of the U.S. Atlantic Fleet, sent the following signal to Galvão: "Request you proceed any port northern South America you choose to discharge passengers. Please advise port selected and of arrival. Will attempt to arrange conference aboard *Santa Maria* as you request."

Galvão, to make it quite clear that he was not having second thoughts about the adventure, then issued a statement which said: "We consider this ship the first liberated piece of Portuguese territory. We will never surrender or stop, in the face of all the fleets of the world." But this expression of stubborn determination rather overlooked the practical facts of life—that the *Santa Maria* would soon need more food, fresh water and fuel if the first liberated piece of Portuguese territory was to survive for long. And something had to be done very quickly about the six hundred hi-jacked passengers who were making a rapidly growing hole in the available rations.

Meanwhile, in Portugal, the Salazar government was finding the situation rather embarrassing, and generally saying little about it. Nevertheless, the Opposition left-wing newspaper *Republican* was suspended by the government for three days as a penalty for its sympathetic attitude in the handling of the *Santa Maria* news. This ill-considered and totalitarian act of authority merely added some strength to Captain Galvão's so-called "cause".

By 26 January, the British frigate *Rothesay* had dropped out of the chase, presumably for reasons of political expediency. Surveillance of the movements of the *Santa Maria* was left to American long-range aircraft. The ship was continually shadowed, and its course plotted. Very soon, after only five days of "independence", the floating piece of occupied Portuguese territory was observed to reduce speed and alter course southwards, as if abandoning Angola as its destination and making for Brazil instead. One of the reasons for this strategic change of mind was undoubtedly the approach of Portuguese warships, one of which was a frigate, *Pero Escoba,* carrying three-inch guns. Galvão radioed that he would accept escort from the United States Navy—provided they would protect the *Santa Maria* from any action which the Portuguese warships might take. This was the beginning of the end, equivalent of an act of unconditional surrender, but there was still a great deal of argument and drama to be presented on the stage before the fantasy reached its inevitable finale.

In Brazil, at that time, the inauguration of a new president was imminent. Senhor Quadros, who was to be installed as president at midnight on 1 February, sent an encouraging message to Captain Galvão assuring him that the *Santa Maria* would be welcomed at any Brazilian port, once he had assumed power, without any risk of being interned. As a gesture of sympathy and support for Galvão the Brazilian Government had already grounded all U.S. Navy aircraft based at Recife in order to obstruct reconnaissance against the stolen ship—but this restriction was quickly lifted after strong protests from the U.S. Government. This incident in itself was typical of the inept way in which the Brazilian Government handled what was essentially a delicate international political problem.

On 30 January, just one day before the new president took office, Galvão received a positively worded assurance from Brazil of "disembarkation for passengers, political asylum for you and your companions as well as maintenance of your command of the *Santa Maria*"—a declaration that was hardly likely to please the Portuguese Government.

Encouraged by this gesture of support, Galvão decided to take the ship into Recife on the terms stated. He still had some doubts as to whether the Brazilian Government would honour its guarantees under the political pressure which was bound to be exerted by Portugal, and therefore issued a warning that he would scuttle the *Santa Maria* if any attempts were made to seize it, or interfere in any way with his plans. He also announced that the ship had been renamed *Santa Liberdade*, to mark the occasion of the liberation of a small part of Portugal.

When the ship was about thirty-five miles off Recife, the promised conference with the Americans took place. Admiral Allen Smith of the U.S. Navy boarded the *Santa Maria* and spent three hours in conversation with Galvão, discussing policy, politics, and such practical matters as the disembarkation of the passengers. This meeting aroused world-wide press interest. Now that the *Santa Maria* was approaching land and contemplating discharging her passengers, the journalists and photographers who had been frustrated for over a week felt that they would be able to obtain some first-hand eye-witness accounts of what was, after all, one of the most sensational stories of the century.

A tug carrying sixty reporters and cameramen hovered around the *Santa Maria* while Admiral Smith conversed with Galvão, and some were eventually allowed on board. The most original and enterprising of the international pressmen were two French journalists who dropped by parachute from an aircraft and made a wet landing in the sea near the ship. They were rewarded for their pains by being immediately rescued and hauled aboard.

The *Santa Maria* duly steamed into Recife harbour and lay off shore while final negotiations were conducted with the Brazilian authorities. The date was 1 February—ten days after the ship had been seized—and Senhor Quadros was now the new president of Brazil. But the diplomatic cables between Brazil and Portugal had evidently been busy, for Quadros was not nearly so co-operative as he had been before his investiture. Galvão, in his consultations with Brazilian officials, was unable to reach any satisfactory agreement concerning the fate of the *Santa Maria* once it was berthed. The Brazilian Government would no longer give any assurances that the ship would not be impounded, although everything would be done to assist the disembarkation of the passengers.

After a day's delay, the passengers were finally taken off the ship in the harbour and put ashore, while just outside the harbour four U.S. destroyers stood by to assist the disembarkation should any difficulties arise. Three members of the crew, not knowing whether the crew were to be allowed ashore or not, and determined not to remain aboard, jumped into the harbour and swam to a Brazilian ship.

There was a festive air about the occasion. The *Santa Maria* was gaily dressed with flags from bow to stern, while in Recife the carnival was just beginning. The passengers disembarked, looking fit and cheerful after their strange experience. They were segregated and protected by the police from newspaper reporters, photographers and inquisitive onlookers.

The end of Captain Galvão's essay in piracy was near. As soon as all the passengers had been taken off, the *Santa Maria* was boarded by a detachment of eighty-seven armed Brazilian marines, who took up positions all over the ship and assumed control. The rebels made no attempt to resist. Galvão, deprived of his command, called a press conference on the ship at which he explained, with dignity, that the marines had come aboard under an agreement he had made with the Brazilian authorities. But, he insisted, he had brought the first part of his revolutionary campaign against the Salazar regime to a "triumphant finish". He would not disclose his future plans.

The next day President Quadros of Brazil signed a decree handing over the *Santa Maria* to the Portuguese Government. In a simple ceremony, after twenty-four hours of negotiations, Galvão formally surrendered the ship to the Brazilian naval authorities. Then he and his rebels were taken ashore and put under the protection of the Ministry of Security in Recife. Galvão had no alternative but to gratefully accept political asylum after his thirteen days of "independence". He was a slightly pathetic character as he finally returned to exile, looking withered and weary, but he signed autographs for admiring Brazilian journalists.

The *Santa Maria* was officially handed over to the Portuguese Government on 5 February, and it was then returned to the owners, the Portuguese Colonial Navigation Company. But the vessel was in no fit condition to sail, for some members of the crew, acting out of somewhat misguided loyalty, had sabotaged the engines to prevent Galvão from taking the ship from Recife. Repairs were put under way without delay, however, and meanwhile food, water and fuel were taken aboard. Captain Maia resumed his command of the *Santa Maria* and the crew stood by to take the liner back to Portugal as soon as repairs had been completed.

On 7 February the ship finally set sail without passengers for Lisbon, where a cheering crowd of over one hundred thousand people were waiting to welcome her on her arrival. In Lisbon harbour sirens wailed, and liners, tugs and yachts were decked with flags. Dr Salazar went on board the *Santa Maria* in person to embrace Captain Maia. It was a momentous end to an astonishing adventure.

However, it was not quite the end of the story for Captain Galvão. For nine months he remained in quiet obscurity in Brazil, safe from Portuguese charges of piracy, murder and insurrection, since Portugal does not have an extradition treaty with Brazil. Occasionally he came into the news, as when in April he was banned from entering the U.S.A. to attend the African Freedom Day celebration, and later when the British Government refused him a visa to enter the U.K. This decision of the Home Office gave rise to questions in the House of Commons, where it was explained that Galvão had wished to lecture in Britain, and since the theme of his lectures would almost certainly advocate insurrection against the Portuguese Government, his application for a visa had very properly been turned down.

And then, on 10 November, 1961, an airliner on a regular flight from Casablanca to Lisbon was "kidnapped" in the air as it approached Lisbon airport. Six of the passengers, one of whom was a woman, moved casually into the first-class compartment at the front of the aircraft, where they suddenly became active. First they invaded the flight deck and held the aircrew at gunpoint. The pilot, who had been coming in to land, was forced to circle over Lisbon while the gang untied parcels of leaflets and threw them out over Lisbon. Fearing for the safety of his passengers and aircraft, the pilot obeyed instructions, for he realized he was dealing with fanatics. Thousands of revolutionary leaflets descended like huge snowflakes on the city; their printed message urged the people of Portugal to oppose the Government, and to vote against Dr Salazar in a forthcoming election by not voting at all. The leaflets were signed by none other than Captain Henrique Galvão.

The airliner was not allowed to land at Lisbon, but was forced to turn back and fly on to Tangier, where Captain

Galvão was waiting in person to greet and commend his leaflet-dispensing henchmen. They all promptly handed over their weapons to the police and demanded political asylum. After a long interrogation in Tangier, they were eventually guaranteed safe conduct out of the country.

Galvão and his accomplices were sent to Dakar, and then flown to Rio de Janeiro. There a slight hitch occurred, for the police refused to allow Galvão to disembark. They tried to manhandle him back into the airliner, but the captain of the aircraft slammed the door in their faces and refused to have anything more to do with Galvão and his conspirators. Ten days went by while the Brazilian Government reviewed the situation Galvão was clearly becoming an embarrassing liability, and would either have to be deported or, if allowed to stay, severely restrained in his movements and activities. Finally the government decided to extend political asylum to Galvão and the others—but strict conditions were imposed. They were to live at Belo Horizonte, some two hundred miles north of Rio de Janeiro, under continual police surveillance. And Galvão was warned that he would be immediately sent back to Portugal if he engaged in any further political activity or even travelled abroad again.

That did the trick. Captain Galvão, for all his courage and audacity, had no wish to be delivered into the hands of the Portuguese authorities. Since 1961 he has presumably lived in quiet retirement in Belo Horizonte, but he did take the trouble to write a book about the seizure of the *Santa Maria*.

In the book he stated that his intention in taking the ship was to proceed to Angola to "set alight to Portuguese Africa and found a Federation of autonomous Portuguese states". The operation failed right at the start, he considered, because he had been obliged to put ashore eight men at St Lucia and had thereby lost the element of surprise which was essential to success.

In conclusion, summing up rather bitterly, he stated: "I shall probably end as I began; poor, liberal, independent of prefabricated formulas, dependent on my affection for humanity and on my aversion for all forms of tyranny."

Chapter 5

ONE-MAN "COUP D'ETAT"

In this collection of strange crimes throughout history, cases involving insanity have generally been excluded, for there is nothing intrinsically strange in the irrational. Insanity is its own motivation for any kind of act, criminal or not, and one can look in vain for any kind of logical motivation or evidence of reasoning. The law itself takes account of mental unbalance, and it is perhaps significant that since capital punishment came to an end in Great Britain (and it ended in effect some years before the necessary legislation became a reality), murderers are curiously reluctant to make a plea of insanity—for the simple reason that detention under Her Majesty's Pleasure in a criminal lunatic asylum can last a great deal longer than an ordinary sentence of life imprisonment (which is generally specified in the more severe cases as "not less than fifteen years"). It pays to be sane.

Occasionally, however, the odd crime turns up in which the element of fantasy is so pronounced that the facts are virtually incredible. Such an "Alice-in-Wonderland" exploit occurred in Israel in 1952. The events as they happened put one in mind of those early American comic movies of the Keystone Cops era, but happen they did.

In Tel Aviv at that time a young man of impeccable character and quiet disposition held a highly respectable job as a cashier in a bank. His name was Sidney Peters, and so far as is known he was an unassuming individual, law-abiding, and with no particular ambitions—until Saturday, 12 January, 1952.

On the afternoon of that day, when the bank was closed, Peters made a social visit to the home of his boss, the elderly bank manager. He produced a gun, and demanded that the bank manager should give him the key to the bank safe. The bank manager, who was taken aback and thoroughly intimidated by the unexpected truculence of his formerly well-behaved cashier, handed over the key without attempting to put up any opposition.

Oddly enough, the bank manager had no telephone, and so, after Peters had left, he was unable to call the police. He was too afraid to venture out of the house. Quite possibly, realizing that Peters intended to rob the bank, he chose not to thwart him in any way in case of reprisals, taking the practical view that his own life was more important than the bank's money. Whatever the truth, it is clear that the transformed Peters with his gun must have exercised a most forceful effect on his superior.

Peters's next move was predictable. Showing little in the way of caution he went straight to the bank, where he was admitted by the regular watchman who, of course, knew him well as one of the bank's cashiers. It was not unusual for responsible members of the staff to go back to the bank outside of normal working hours to carry out special work or collect documents in connection with some urgent business transaction; consequently, Peters's arrival at the bank did not give rise to any suspicion. It was not until, some time later, when the watchman observed Peters quietly leaving the bank, carrying a big sack, without announcing his departure, that serious doubts began to arise. At this point the watchman decided to call the police—but meanwhile Peters was making good his escape.

The naïve and amateur fashion in which Peters carried out his robbery is illustrated by the fact that, having left the bank, and still carrying his sack of money, he simply hired a taxi and had himself driven to a village about fourteen miles to the north of Tel Aviv. There, to make himself even more easily identifiable, he paid off the driver with a high-denomination bank-note worth many times more than the fare and refused to accept any change. Such an enormous tip from a quiet man carrying a sack merely led the driver to suspect that his passenger was mentally unhinged.

Peters's next move was to hire a car to take him to an immigrants' camp a few miles away from the village—again hardly the least ostentatious way of doing things. By this time the police had started their investigation and were beginning to pick up Peters's fairly obvious trail. They had been to the bank and discovered that a sizeable amount of money was missing, namely, about £26,000 in Israeli notes and some thousands of American dollars.

The police had little difficulty in tracing Peters's initial movements after the robbery. They found the taxi which had taken the suspect to the village fourteen miles away, and at the village they quickly pinned down the car which Peters had hired to take him to the immigrants' camp. So far it had been one fast lead after another, but at the camp itself inquiries ground to a halt. Peters had been and gone. During the brief period he had been at the camp he had visited a number of people, had given them appreciable sums of money, and had asked them to call at a well-known hotel the next day when he would address them on a very important subject. The hotel in question was in a coastal town a few miles away from the camp. The police were now beginning to realize that they were pursuing a very unusual character, for Peters's actions were hardly consistent with those of a bank robber on the run.

A full-scale manhunt was launched in the area, focused particularly on the hotel, its guests, and all new arrivals. But Peters had not been there, nor did he check in at all on the following day. And then, out of the blue, came a message from Nathanya, a town some thirty miles north of Tel Aviv, that a man answering the description of Peters had been arrested after some trouble in a local shop, although he had given his name as Silberman. Detectives went from Tel Aviv to Nathanya to question Silberman, and were immediately able to confirm that he was Peters—at which point Peters freely admitted his identity and confessed to having robbed

the bank. But when he was asked to state where he had
hidden the stolen money he flatly refused to give any information whatever—nor would he explain why he had given
money to the immigrants at the camp and arranged a meeting
at a hotel.

Having got their man, the police were now intent upon
recovering the money. They pursued their interrogation until,
at length, under persistent questioning, Peters suddenly decided to talk. And talk he did—in a most unexpected way. It
was as if something had gone click in his brain. His eyes lit
up, and with excited gestures he declared that he was an
important member of a subversive underground organization
which was planning to overthrow the Israeli Government by a
coup d'état. What was more, the revolution was imminent,
and was to be announced by radio early the following morning after the radio station had been occupied by the rebels.

The police were puzzled by all this, for they were well
informed on underground movements and subversive activities, operating in close liaison with the Israeli secret service
which is considered to be one of the most efficient in the
world. Sidney Peters's particular revolutionary caucus drew a
blank with them. If such an underground movement existed,
it appeared to take the form of a one-man band personified in
Peters himself. Admittedly Peters had confessed to robbing
the bank in order to acquire funds for the revolutionary
movement, and had disbursed sums of money among the
immigrants at the camp to acquire recruits for the movement
—or so he claimed. It seemed to the police that the situation
called for some devious subterfuge, and that the best way of
recovering the money was to go along with Peters and humour
him. It was taking a chance, for the police were not yet able
to decide whether Peters was merely acting, or really believed
his own fantastic story.

During an interval in the interrogation, one of the police
officers approached Peters quietly and confidentially and whispered that he himself was a member of the same revolutionary organization, working as an under-cover agent in the
police. He warned Peters to be careful and not talk too much,
or the whole movement might be exposed and jeopardized.
Peters, reacting suspiciously to this volunteered information
and unsolicited advice, asked the officer for his revolutionary
code-name. The officer identified himself as "Bar-Kochba",

which was the name of a Jewish biblical hero, and Peters in turn confided that his own revolutionary code-name was "Living Fox". Even so, Peters did not seem satisfied with Bar-Kochba's bona-fides; he insisted that he must be identified and guaranteed by the leader of the revolutionary movement.

The police officer, accepting this as a reasonable condition, agreed to telephone the leader in Peters's presence. Before the telephone call was actually made, he arranged for a police colleague to answer the call from another room and pretend to be the leader. And so the call was made, with Peters listening, and then Peters himself spoke to the "leader". He was told that Bar-Kochba was a reliable agent and that he should recruit him as one of the senior officers of the movement. Peters accepted these orders from the leader quite happily, and promptly appointed the police officer as his personal adjutant.

All this took place in the police station, and Peters was under arrest, though he did not seem to realize it. Indeed, it was obvious to everyone except Peters himself that the whole fantastic pretence was just a masquerade. No revolutionary movement existed at all outside of Peters's mind, but having conceived himself in the role of a senior subversive agent, so strong was his obsession that he accepted without further question a fictitious leader and an equally fictitious Bar-Kochba—even though some buried and still rational part of his mind must have known that the police were simply playing up to his fantasy in the hope of finding out where he had concealed the money. But for "Living Fox" his fantasy world was real and, so far as he was concerned, contained no absurdities.

Having appointed Bar-Kochba as his adjutant, Peters insisted on holding a long conference to discuss revolutionary policy and to define their roles in the struggle for power which was to come. Drugged coffee was served to the prisoner during this tedious monologue, in the hope of loosening his tongue even more with reference to the hidden money, but it seemed to have no effect on him at all. He was busily warming up to his theme—explaining how he personally had been delegated by the "leader" to organize the practical details of the *coup d'état,* which was to be proclaimed by radio at three o'clock in the morning (hardly the right hour for a mass audience), and how all the ministers in the existing government were to be executed as soon as the rebels had taken over.

From time to time Bar-Kochba, playing the role of a faithful adjutant, returned to the question of the movement's funds—and in particular the haul from the bank. He pointed out that as the money was vital to the success of the *coup d'état*, the secret of its location could not reasonably be left with one man. Supposing Living Fox were arrested, or even assassinated by reactionary elements? Without the money the revolution would be jeopardized, and what would the leader have to say about that?

Peters, after patient persuasion, saw the logic of this argument and finally consented to share the secret of his hidden funds with his adjutant, and agreed to take Bar-Kochba to the place where part of the money was concealed. The two men drove by car towards the immigrants' camp, but before they reached it Peters stopped the car by a pile of gravel at the side of the road. There, with due ceremony, a bag was dug out from the base of the gravel pile. Inside the bag was some £14,000 in Israeli notes and all of the missing American dollar bills. This contribution to the revolution Peters duly handed over to his adjutant, instructing him that henceforth the police officer (*alias* Bar-Kochba) should call him Commander.

The next scene of the charade began with the arrival of a police car, which stopped close to the gravel pile. Two police officers got out and ominously advanced on Commander Living Fox and his adjutant. Peters, not in the least worried by this apparent threat to the *coup d'état*, ordered Bar-Kochba to arrest the newcomers, which he promptly did. The detectives put up no resistance, and calmly allowed themselves to be arrested, for it was all part of the act. Peters lectured them severely on their indiscretion, and very shortly they acquired a faith in the revolution and asked if they, too, could be allowed to join the subversive movement.

It was necessary, to satisfy protocol as visualized by Peters, that the new recruits should be sponsored by a senior executive of the movement. Bar-Kochba recommended them without hesitation, and they were forthwith accepted and recruited to the movement by Living Fox. The four men stood to attention by the gravel pile and sang the national anthem as part of the swearing-in ceremony. The final idiocy in the

fantasy was the unanimous decision of the four revolutionaries to use the local police station (where Peters was officially
under arrest) as the rebel headquarters.

From the police point of view, there was still a substantial
£12,000 of the missing money to be accounted for. Having
"brain-washed" Peters into handing over £14,000 plus the
American dollars, it seemed not only possible, but probable,
that he could further be persuaded to turn in the remainder
for "safe-keeping" by his adjutant.

The main difficulty about recovering the final £12,000 was
that Peters had earmarked it for his personal use, and to help
his family, but it was put to him that this was a selfish attitude
which was contrary to the spirit of the movement and might
even jeopardize the entire operation. Self-sacrifice was the
order of the day. Reluctantly, but overcome by his mood of
enthusiasm for the revolution, which seemed to be gathering
force, Peters agreed that in all conscience he ought to hand
over the rest of the stolen money to the movement's funds.
But it was buried on the seashore somewhere between Tel
Aviv and Haifa, and the hour was late. It would have to wait
until tomorrow.

The police were not prepared to wait, but Peters was
adamant. It was possible that by the following morning he
might have changed his mind. So, to set his thoughts on a
different tack and eliminate any suspicion that might arise,
they suggested that the movement's funds might be further
augmented by robbing another bank—this time in Haifa. As a
start the money buried on the beach, which was on the way to
Haifa, would be recovered in the morning. To this scheme
Peters agreed.

The project was nearly wrecked overnight when Commander Living Fox was not permitted to make his 3 a.m. radio
broadcast announcing the revolution. Peters was incensed,
outraged and violent—the revolution had been sabotaged. In
order to appease him the two police officers who had joined
the movement the previous afternoon were "arrested" by
Bar-Kochba for having failed to seize and take over the radio
station so that the Commander could make his broadcast
announcing the new regime in Israel. They were suitably
imprisoned in a room at the police station—but were, of
course, released again shortly afterwards when the Commander's attention was elsewhere directed. Meanwhile, as a sop to

the Commander's ego, and to compensate for the sudden depletion of ranks, four more policemen were "recruited" to the movement. The revolution was once more "all systems go".

The next morning Peters and his adjutant and his four newly acquired revolutionaries left the police station by car and made for the coast north of Tel Aviv, where they disembarked. The Commander lined them up in military formation, and then solemnly marched them along the beach for several miles. They eventually came to a smart halt by a large rock. The contingent stood stiffly to attention while Commander Living Fox got down on his knees and dug a hole with his bare hands in the sand under the rock. After several minutes he dragged out a bloodstained coat. In the pockets of the coat was the remainder of the stolen money—about £12,000 in Israeli banknotes. The blood on the coat was Peters's own with which, he explained, he had sacrificially "sanctified" the money in the cause of the revolution (notwithstanding that this was the proportion of the money which he had put aside for himself).

At this point the revolution that never was, and never could have been, came to an abrupt end. Bar-Kochba and his four police colleagues carried out a minor *coup d'état* of their own. Like traitors they overthrew their Commander, and after a fierce struggle overpowered him. They did not technically arrest him, for, in fact, he was already under arrest, and had been for some time.

Peters finished up in the hospital—an insane paranoiac with a "Napoleon complex" who had robbed a bank to start a one-man revolution. But he had been painlessly humoured and tricked by a shrewd and understanding police force who had joined a "revolutionary movement" in order to recover as quickly as possible the stolen money—before Living Fox with his disturbed mind forgot where he had buried it.

Chapter 6

LITTLE BOY LOST

THE charm (if that is the word) of the Dellow kidnapping case in the early nineteenth century lies not in the criminal abduction of a little boy from the streets of London by a woman living in Hampshire, but rather in the motive which drove her in desperation to commit such an act. The story is unusual in the history of crime in that one can hardly avoid feeling sympathy for the pathetic criminal as well as for the distressed parents of the victim.

One Monday morning in November, 1811, a Mrs Dellow went into the city of London to see her doctor in order to obtain treatment for an infection of the eye. She had two young children, a boy and a girl. Baby-sitting problems being much the same then as they are today, she took the children into town with her because there was nobody available to look after them. Even so, she could not take the children into the doctor's surgery, and it was necessary to have them looked after for a short time. There was no difficulty. She arranged to leave them in charge of a woman named Mary Cox who kept a greengrocer's shop in Martin's Lane, Cannon Street. Confident that they were in good hands, Mrs Dellow went off to keep her appointment with the doctor nearby.

People naturally came into the shop from time to time to buy fruit and vegetables, and Mary Cox had other things to attend to apart from keeping an eye on the two children, but in any case there was little danger that they would stray of their own volition from a haven of refuge in which there were lots of things to look at and plenty of nice things to eat. Mary Cox distinctly remembered one customer—a lady of some apparent status, wearing a dark gown, a blue cloak and a black straw hat with a feather—who bought merely two-pennyworth of apples. Immediately afterwards another customer came into the shop, and it was not until after she had left that Mary Cox realized with alarm that the two young children were missing.

She promptly abandoned her shop and rushed out into the street. The little boy's name was Thomas, and the girl's Rebecca. They were nowhere to be seen, so in a state of dreadful apprehension she hurried through neighbouring streets looking for them. In due course she came upon Rebecca, but she was alone and there was no sign of her brother.

Rebecca seemed quite happy. She was holding an apple and eating a bun. Both, she said, had been given to her by the kind lady in the shop who had bought some apples. The kind lady had taken them off to buy some buns at the nearby pastry-cook's, and the lady had then taken her little brother away with her to "find his mother". The little boy, Thomas, was three years old.

Thomas was not taken to his mother, nor was he found after a most thorough and diligent search. It became very clear that he had been abducted by the woman in the blue cloak. A full investigation was set in motion. It was established that a woman in a blue cloak had, on the morning in question, gone into the pastry-cook's shop with two young children, and had bought buns which she had given to the children. Rebecca and Thomas were readily identified as the children in question. A woman answering the same description had also entered a hatter's shop in the area, accompanied by a small boy of about three years of age, and had bought a hat for him. After that there was no further trace of either the woman or the boy, and the trail came to an end.

Enquiries were pursued, however. Within a few days an uncle of the missing boy learned from an acquaintance that a woman had been seen in South London who closely resembled the kidnapper. He was given an address in Southwark. Taking no chances the uncle went to see the woman, accompanied by a police officer and a young woman from the pastry-cook's shop. Her job was to identify the suspect as the woman in the blue cloak who had bought buns for the two children. This she did without hesitation.

The suspect, a Mrs R, was then escorted to the hatter's shop for further identification, but here there was a disconcerting lack of recognition. The hatter agreed that from the official—and superficial—description of the wanted woman, there was a similarity of height and build, but she was sure that Mrs R had never been in her shop. Mrs R for her part denied firmly and indignantly that she had ever visited the hatter or the pastry-cook. A telling point was that a hatter would be far more likely to identify a client by appearance than a pastry-cook because of the focus of attention on the head, face and hair style in relation to the hat worn—a kind of instinctive professional know-how. True, the hat had been bought for the little boy, but the buyer would hardly escape a discerning and even critical inspection.

Nevertheless, the testimony of the pastry-cook's assistant was adjudged sufficient. Mrs R was arrested and her house was searched. The police found no trace whatever of the dark gown, the blue cloak or the black straw hat with a feather which had been worn by the woman who had bought apples and buns—nor was there the slightest indication of the presence of a little boy or the hat she was alleged to have bought for him.

Furthermore, Mrs R claimed emphatically that she had been ill on the day of the kidnapping and had not moved out of her home. She was able to produce two witnesses to prove the point. Other witnesses gave evidence as to her good character. Despite the corroborated alibi and the lack of any reliable identification, the charge was proceeded with. She was tried before a jury, but on such flimsy evidence she was rightly acquitted as a victim of mistaken identity. In the emotional atmosphere of this particular crime the verdict could have swung the other way, and a grave miscarriage of justice would have resulted. After the acquittal the mystery was no nearer solution. Thomas, aged three, was still missing—as was the still unidentified lady in the blue cloak.

At this stage a reward was offered for information leading to the recovery of young Thomas Dellow. Handbills describing him in detail were published and distributed throughout the country, and in the course of time one such handbill reached a man named William Barber, who oddly enough happened to be the keeper of Gosport prison in Hampshire. It so happened that, coincidentally, he had recently been told by a neighbour of a certain Mrs Harriet Magnis who lived in Gosport that she, Mrs Magnis, had suddenly acquired a three-year-old son who had apparently been living with relatives or friends in the country until a few weeks ago.

A description of the Magnis boy who had now "come home" sounded to William Barber remarkably like that of the missing Thomas Dellow in the handbill, and it seemed to him that he ought to make some polite inquiries, even though Mrs Magnis was known to him as a thoroughly respectable and well-to-do woman whose husband was a gunner in the Royal Navy.

Barber, as an officer of the law, kept strictly to the formal and objective protocol. He called on Mrs Magnis and asked her if she had a child. She said she had—a three-year-old boy. Was it her own child? he inquired. Of course, she insisted. What was he implying? Barber demanded to see the boy and talk to him, and Mrs Magnis could hardly refuse without admitting that she had something to hide. The child, at his age not very articulate, nevertheless provided material for further questions, and under the pressure of interrogation Mrs Magnis finally broke down, and in a distressed condition admitted that the little boy was not hers. She said she had "found" him in London, apparently lost, and had brought him home and taken good care of him and had bought him many expensive clothes.

She was arrested and detained. The Dellows in London were notified, and Mr Dellow travelled to Gosport to collect his long-lost son, whom he found fit and healthy and well cared for.

So far the case had followed fairly usual lines. It was a kidnapping—but without the customary demand for ransom. This in itself made the situation more ominous. It meant that an unknown woman had taken a fancy to somebody else's child and had decided to acquire it. There were no mercenary motives. Similar cases occur quite frequently today, particularly among childless women. But the strangeness of this particular case lay in the events which led up to the final act of abduction.

The truth was that Mrs Magnis had abducted the little boy simply "to please her husband". Their marriage had so far been barren and she was only too aware that her husband, Richard Magnis, was very anxious to have a child—preferably a son.

Since Richard was serving in the Royal Navy he spent most of his time at sea, and shore leave at home was infrequent. Naval tours of duty sometimes lasted for years in the days of sailing ships. As time went by her apparent infertility on the occasions when her husband was on leave became a neurotic obsession in her mind until, finally, when he went off on one particular long overseas tour, she was foolishly prompted to write to him to say that she was pregnant and was going to have a baby. She was desperately anxious to please him.

Richard was so delighted with the news that he promptly sent her his savings of some £300 with instructions that it was to be used for the benefit of the child and that he (for he had assumed that it would be a boy) was to want for nothing. And so, what had started as a reckless whimsy became a compulsive obligation. Having thoughtlessly committed herself with a lie to bearing an imaginary baby, and a baby boy at that, the wretched woman felt obliged to continue the deception, even though she had no idea as to how she was to produce a real flesh and blood child for her husband to see and accept as his own when he again came ashore. It did not occur to her to feign a miscarriage. Fortunately, Richard was not due back in England for a year, long after the birth of the non-existent baby, so there was time to build up the deception.

The next letter from wife to husband announced the birth of a son, to be named Richard after his father. In due course, when the "baby" was a few months old, the proud and delighted father arrived home on a brief shore leave to meet his son and heir—only to find that baby Richard had gone away. He had been "put out to nurse" somewhere in the country because of some difficulty in cutting his teeth. The doctor had prescribed a change of air to ease the labour of his teething.

Richard senior's disappointment and frustration were an

equal agony to his deceitful wife, but it was too late to tell the truth and her husband's leave was not long enough, happily, to allow him to visit his son in some hypothetical country place many counties away. It did not occur to him that his son had as much reality as a mirage. He accepted the facts as they were put to him and went off on another long spell of naval duty.

By the time he gained his next home leave his imaginary son was three years old—but again the boy was away from home and staying with "friends in the country". This time Richard was not prepared to be put off. He insisted on seeing his son. More time was available, and if the boy could not be brought to him, then he personally would travel to the country to find the boy.

For Harriet Magnis it was the showdown that she had always feared ever since the deception had started nearly four years earlier. Richard, the son and heir that did not exist, had to be quickly and magically produced like a rabbit out of a hat. She told Richard that she would go off to the country to bring back her son to meet his father, but in fact she travelled to London in search of a three-year-old boy. She chose London because it seemed to her that the terrifying task of abduction would be much easier in London's crowded streets, and there would be a greater selection, for, of course, the chosen boy would need to look something like his "father" and a little bit like herself.

In the event she was right. The kidnapping of Thomas Dellow was simplicity itself—a mere matter of an apple and a bun. True, his sister had to be got rid of, but that presented no problem. After separating young Thomas from his sister, she took him back to Gosport and presented him to his father. Gunner Magnis of the Royal Navy was a proud and happy man—and if the little boy talked oddly at times about people Richard had never heard of, well, they had lived in different worlds for three years, and he had spent so much time in the country with comparative strangers . . .

The sequel to the story is odd, but in a way satisfying. Harriet Magnis was charged with abduction, gaoled and committed for trial at Hampshire Assizes. However, at the trial, after long legal arguments, it was decided by the judiciary that the offence against the law had been committed in

London and not in Hampshire, so that the local Assize Court had no legal authority to try the case. Harriet Magnis was acquitted and discharged, and could not therefore be tried again for the same offence.

Chapter 7

HEART FAILURE

On the morning of 12 October, 1957, the dead body of Dr Lev Rebet was found on the stairs of No. 8 Karlsplatz, Munich, a building housing the publishing offices of the Ukrainian émigré newspaper *Sucasna Ukraina*. Dr Rebet was editor-in-chief of the newspaper, and he was also a noted Ukrainian émigré resistance leader, strongly nationalistic and bitterly opposed to the Soviet regime in his homeland.

At the post-mortem the verdict was heart failure which appeared to have resulted from inflammation and softening of the coronary arteries. There was no suggestion of violence and foul play was not suspected. But, in fact, Dr Rebet had been the victim of a meticulously planned and perfect political murder. Two years later his assassin, a specially trained Soviet agent, was to commit a second near-perfect political murder.

The assassin's name was Bogdan Stashinsky. Today he is in a West German prison serving a sentence of eight years' hard labour.

Stashinsky was born in 1931 in Borshchevitse, a village near Lemberg in western Ukraine. He was the son of a farmer with two sisters older than himself. His upbringing and education were remarkable; when he left school he decided he wanted to become a teacher and attend a training college.

This was the period immediately after the Second World War. During the war the Ukraine had been occupied by the Germans, but in 1944, after the German retreat from Stalingrad, the Russians moved in and took over. The Ukrainian nationalists were unwilling to submit to Soviet rule. An active underground resistance movement evolved which was sympathetically supported by the older members of the Stashinsky family. Against this hazardous political background young Bogdan Stashinsky, who could speak Russian, Polish and German and was considered shrewd and intelligent, committed a trifling misdemeanour which was to alter the pattern of his entire future.

In 1950 (he was then nineteen), while still a student at the teachers' training college in Lemberg, he travelled on a train without a ticket and was caught. He was questioned by the police and later interviewed by a State Security Officer, who made no reference to the matter of the ticket, but amiably informed him that the authorities were well aware that his family were on record as Ukrainian nationalists holding anti-Soviet views and associating with the Ukrainian underground resistance movement. His father had already served a ten-month prison sentence for subversive activity. The Security Officer pointed out that the anti-Soviet Organization of Ukrainian Nationalists (O.U.N.) consisted of traitors, and their leaders were in the pay of the American Central Intelligence Agency.

Stashinsky himself, still a mere youth, was pro-Communist —and possibly the only member of his family who was. But then he was the product of the post-war Soviet education system. This first interview with the State Security Officer, whose name was Sitnikovsky, was not the last. A series of meetings took place during which Sitnikovsky discussed the political situation in the Ukraine, analysing it in simple black-and-white Soviet terms—the "comrades" versus the American-paid traitors. Stashinsky was reminded from time to time that his own family were playing a dangerous game and were vulnerable. Finally, the point having been made in no uncertain manner, it was put to Stashinsky that if he was prepared to work for K.G.B. (the State Security Committee of the

Council of Ministers of the U.S.S.R.) his family would be "safe".

Having no alternative in the face of coercion, and in any case finding himself largely in agreement with the Security Officer's views, Stashinsky accepted. On the basis of a free railway ride he was duly integrated into the Soviet Secret Service machine. His first assignment was a tentative try-out— to join one of the Ukrainian resistance groups as a spy in order to probe the death, some two years earlier, of a pro-Soviet writer who was thought to have been murdered by a member of the Ukrainian underground. Stashinsky was successful in identifying and denouncing the assassin, who was duly arrested and executed.

Having proved his competence and pleased his task-masters, Stashinsky gave up his studies to become a full-time agent, and underwent two years of training in Soviet Intelligence methods. The course was in Kiev and during this period he was not allowed to visit his family. By 1954, having "graduated", he was ready to work professionally for the K.G.B. He was returned to Borshchevitse and permitted to resume contact with his parents and sisters, telling them that he was living in Kiev where he had a good job. His Intelligence activities were, of course, top secret. What Stashinsky did not fully realize at the time was that he had qualified in the Soviet cloak-and-dagger university not as a spy but as an assassin, and Germany was to be his field of operation.

First he had to change his identity. He was to be Josef Lehmann, a German who had lived in Poland up to the war and had managed to obtain a permit to return to East Germany to live and work. He was given forged identity papers and a detailed fictitious personal biography which he had to learn by heart. After exploratory visits to Poland and Germany to familiarize himself with his prefabricated background, he was finally posted, first to Zwickau and then East Berlin. Initially he took a job in a factory to establish his working-class authenticity, but later posed as an interpreter at the Soviet Zone Trade Office in Berlin. At the beginning of the following year, 1956, he started his real intelligence job.

At first he merely acted as a courier, delivering instructions and money to agents in West Berlin and elsewhere and receiving intelligence messages for onwards transmission to the K.G.B. One of his early assignments was to make contact with a Russian agent named Bissaga, actually a Ukrainian exile, who was working as a journalist on the staff of the Ukrainian émigré newspaper of which Dr Lev Rebet, an "earmarked" resistance leader, was editor. Stashinsky's orders from K.G.B. were to enlist Bissaga's co-operation in an attempt to abduct Dr Rebet and smuggle him into the Soviet Zone to be "dealt with" by the K.G.B. Bissaga refused. He said that he was already under suspicion, and to prove the point he was soon afterwards arrested and interrogated by the West German authorities on a charge of espionage. But the charge did not stick, and shortly after his release, with a forged pass supplied by Stashinsky, Bissaga "defected" to the Soviet Zone. This incident made good propaganda for the Soviet authorities—a Ukrainian exile had chosen voluntarily to return to Communism and his homeland.

Stashinsky continued to act as courier, travelling between East and West Germany and carrying sometimes as many as fifty letters concealed in a false bottom in his suitcase. These were posted in the various towns in which he stayed. Among his many duties he was required to note down the registration numbers of all military vehicles which he encountered and to report on convoys and troop movements.

It was not until the beginning of 1957 that Stashinsky was again concerned with Dr Lev Rebet. The K.G.B. took their time, but they were methodical and thorough, and a few years one way or the other did not seem to matter very much so long as the ultimate objective was accomplished. Stashinsky's immediate superior in East Germany—his "case officer", known as Sergey—ordered him to keep a very close watch on Dr Rebet with a view to "clearing him out of the way". Sergey explained that the O.U.N. (Organization of Ukrainian Nationalists) were traitors and criminals who by threats of violence were preventing loyal Ukrainians living in West Germany from returning to their Fatherland. Violence could only be met with violence. It was therefore necessary to eliminate their leaders.

Stashinsky apparently accepted this argument, and seemed to be intrigued with his intelligence work. He admitted during his trial that the word "eliminate" was used so frequently by K.G.B. officials that it ceased to have any real meaning for him. He accepted as logical that those opposed to the Soviet regime should be "eliminated" in the interests of social progress. The repetition of the word produced indifference as to its meaning.

Stashinsky, for the purpose of keeping Dr Rebet under surveillance, changed his identity again, this time to Siegfried Drager. With newly forged identity papers he visited Munich several times for periods of about ten days to observe and record Dr Rebet's movements and pattern of life. In particular it was essential to prepare a timetable of Rebet's travelling and commuting routine in connection with his daily job, and to know when he left home and returned. During these missions Stashinsky would travel with Rebet on the same buses and the same trains, but he was always afraid of being recognized—not as himself, but as a "shadow".

In the summer of 1957 Stashinsky took a much needed holiday to stay with his parents in the Ukraine. He returned to East Berlin and reported to Sergey for the next step in the escalation of the personal war against Dr Rebet. No time was wasted. He was promptly introduced to a K.G.B. officer from Moscow whose sole job was to present him with a special murder weapon and instruct him in its use.

The weapon took the form of a tube about eight inches long and under an inch in diameter. A lever flattened against the side of the tube would, when pressed, explode a charge and shatter a glass ampoule containing cyanide which would be ejected in the form of a spray for a distance of three or four feet. The gas was lethal and could kill a man in a few seconds by contracting the arteries. But shortly after death the arteries would dilate, the cyanide would disperse, and the cause of death would not be ascertained other than by a most detailed and intricate biochemical autopsy, which was unlikely. The most probable inquest verdict on a cyanide inhalation death would be "heart failure". The cylindrical cyanide gun could be conveniently concealed in a roll of newspaper—it was only necessary to point the roll at the victim's face, squeeze the paper and that was that.

Just in case the user of the weapon accidentally inhaled some of the cyanide spray, he was supplied with ampoules of amyl nitrite to crush and inhale. This drug, by dilating the arteries, acted as an antidote to the constricting effect of the cyanide.

The murder weapon was tested on a dog in a wood outside East Berlin. It worked most efficiently, although Stashinsky was rather upset because the dog tried to lick his hand as he drew near and pointed the gun at it. The dog died very quickly and Stashinsky experienced his first genuine feeling of remorse.

The dummy run was over; now Stashinsky had to face the challenge of the real thing. He received a detailed briefing from Sergey, and then, with new identity papers in a different name and about £170 in cash, he went back to Munich to carry out the assassination. The murder weapon was contained in a sealed tin of Frankfürter sausages. At that time he had no particular feelings about the assignment, nor did he question the morality of it. He was aware only of nervous tension.

Installed in a hotel in Munich, Stashinsky removed the cyanide gun and rolled it in a newspaper ready for use, and carried it with him for three days while he kept Dr Rebet under surveillance, checking again the times of arrival at and departure from the newspaper office in Karlsplatz, and always seeking the opportune moment to carry out his murderous mission. He was under considerable psychological strain, although it was not apparent on the surface. Each evening he was able to relax for a few hours when he realized that nothing more could be done that day, but in the morning the tension and strain returned, coupled with an increasing sense of urgency.

On the morning of the fourth day he knew he could delay no longer. He took a tranquillizer, checked the cyanide gun, and made his way to Karlsplatz where he kept watch on No. 8. Rebet was due to arrive at any moment to start his day's work in the editorial offices of *Sucasna Ukraina*. Presently he saw Rebet getting off a street-car some distance away. At this point an unfeeling automatic programme took possession of his mind. He walked confidently into the big building and ascended the stairs to the first landing. There he waited. The place was silent and deserted. Some moments later the street door opened and Rebet entered. He walked up the stairs.

Stashinsky took the rolled newspaper from his pocket and went down the stairs towards the front door. The two men passed each other at the half-way point. Stashinsky raised the newspaper and, pointing at Rebet's face from a range of about two feet, squeezed it. The detonation was hardly audible. As Rebet staggered back and collapsed on to the stairs,

Stashinsky crushed an amyl nitrite ampoule and inhaled the contents, then hurried out of the building. He disposed of the murder weapon by throwing it into the river, returned to his hotel, and by mid-day was on his way to Frankfurt, where he stayed the night. He flew back to Berlin the next day and reported to Sergey that the mission had been successfully accomplished.

Dr Rebet's body was quickly discovered, but he was already dead. At the inquest his death was attributed to heart failure.

Although the murder was accomplished in a methodical cold-blooded fashion, Stashinsky was not without remorse. He was not by nature a vicious or ruthless person. In a dazed state of mind he managed to persuade himself, with a kind of "newthink" logic, that because the weapon was so impersonal and the method of killing so easy—merely squeezing a rolled-up newspaper—he had only committed a murder "in theory". He had performed an academic exercise in practical power politics. Sergey's obvious pleasure at the success of the operation managed to silence his conscience to some extent, but he was not a happy man.

Now came a complication in the attractive shape of a twenty-year-old German girl, Inge Pohl, with whom Stashinsky fell in love. Although she lived in East Berlin, she worked as a hairdresser in West Berlin. They had met in a dance-hall, and all she knew about him was his fictional background as an interpreter with the Ministry of Trade. Inge, however, was bitterly anti-Soviet, and his efforts to convert her to Communism met with no success. Even so, they became engaged in April, 1959, though Stashinsky was well aware that this might create difficulties with his Soviet masters and that, as yet, marriage could hardly be seriously contemplated. For a long time, therefore, he said nothing to Sergey about his betrothal.

Meanwhile he carried out a number of minor intelligence operations for Sergey before the next political murder was lined up for him. The second victim was to be Stefan Bandera, another Ukrainian émigré resistance leader who was living in Munich. The same sinister pattern of operation was followed. Using a new identity—he was now Hans Budeit of Dortmund—Stashinsky was sent to stay in Munich to keep Bandera's house and movements under observation. When he was ready to kill, he reported to Moscow for a final briefing from the K.G.B. They gave him a new and improved cyanide gun with a double barrel (the barrels could be fired separately or simultaneously) and a skeleton key which would open the street door of Bandera's house.

Back in Munich Stashinsky spent a week continuing his surveillance of Bandera, who lived at No. 7 Kreitt-mayrstrasse. Immediately adjacent to the house was a court-yard containing a garage, where Bandera kept his dark blue Opel car. The assassination could be accomplished either in the house or in the garage, depending on the opportunity presented by fate.

The chance came unexpectedly and the circumstances were ideal. Bandera had driven his car into the garage and was standing close to it. The courtyard was deserted. Stashinsky, holding the cyanide weapon, closed in on his unsuspecting victim—and then, inexplicably, changed his mind and hurried away. Immediately he got rid of the cyanide gun as before by throwing it into the river, and then stayed in Munich for another week, analysing his failure and reluctant to go back to Berlin to make a negative report to Sergey.

He had failed to kill Bandera under opportune conditions, he realized, because some humane part of his personality had gained the upper hand at the critical moment. It was slowly becoming apparent to him that something approximating to conscience was beginning to interfere with his sense of politi-cal dedication. He began to wonder whether he was perhaps a schizophrenic.

He was forced to lie to Sergey about the reason for failing to assassinate Bandera. He said that at the crucial moment he had been seen by a third party in the courtyard, and had been obliged to abandon the project and dispose of the cyanide gun. This did not really explain why he had decided to stay another week in Munich. However, Sergey accepted his expla-nation—and supplied him with another cyanide weapon and a further set of skeleton keys.

This time, in a more stubborn mood and rather ashamed of his previous weakness, Stashinsky returned to Munich, and duly murdered Bandera in the entrance hall of his home in what was almost a carbon copy of the first assassination. He made his escape according to plan and disposed of the murder weapon in the usual way.

Bandera was dying when they found him, and dead when he reached hospital. This time foul play was suspected and a careful post-mortem revealed traces of cyanide in his blood. The verdict was suspected cyanide poisoning, but this was never made public, and the case was hushed up. It was referred to as a "mysterious murder".

The truth was that the police suspected that Bandera had been assassinated, probably by a Soviet agent, and the case was referred to security. No progress was made. Apart from the pathological evidence of cyanide in the dead man's body there were no clues and no leads. Stashinsky had done his job well.

By now, however, Stashinsky's conscience was troubling him more and more, particularly when he saw newspaper photographs and newsreel pictures of Stefan Bandera's funeral attended by mourning relatives. For the first time he began to regard himself as a real murderer, and said as much to Sergey. But Sergey took the view that Stashinsky had rendered an outstanding service to his country. He was regarded by K.G.B. as a national hero. Soon afterwards Sergey was able to tell Stashinsky that he had been awarded the Order of the Red Banner for his patriotic exercises in political assassination. There was to be a period of further training for more specialized work that would lead to promotion within the K.G.B.

Feeling himself to be very much in favour with authority, Stashinsky decided that the moment was opportune to tell Sergey of his relationship with Inge Pohl, and that he wished to marry her. He encountered frowning disapproval. Such a marriage would be most unsuitable, Sergey pointed out. Stashinsky insisted, untruthfully, that Inge was steadily coming round to Communist views and attitudes, and eventually received permission to marry from Alexander Shelepin who had succeeded the infamous General Ivan Serov as chairman of the State Security Committee of the Council of Ministers of the U.S.S.R. But a condition was attached, namely, that Stashinsky should bring Inge to Moscow for a few weeks so that she could gain some idea of Soviet life, after which he was to tell her the truth about his work for K.G.B. If she still wished to marry him then no objections would be raised.

At an investiture in Moscow Stashinsky duly received his Order of the Red Banner—and plans were made for his further training in intelligence. He was required to perfect his

German and English with a view to undertaking further
political assassinations in the West.

But by now Stashinsky was losing faith in Communism.
When, during Christmas, 1960, he told Inge some of the truth
about himself—that he was a Russian working for K.G.B.—
but avoiding any mention of the assassinations, she was
greatly shocked. She refused to support him in any way in his
work. They discussed the possibility of defecting to the West,
but he knew that the time was not yet ripe.

He suggested that for the moment it would be wiser to go
to Moscow and take advantage of the eighteen months'
training offered before making such an important decision.
She must appear to be pro-Soviet in her views so that they
could get married. Inge reluctantly agreed, and they went to
Moscow.

The first visit lasted two months and was uneventful, except
that Stashinsky became convinced that he was being kept
under observation by the K.G.B. However, in April he and
Inge were permitted to return to East Berlin and were duly
married in a registry office, followed by a church ceremony to
please his parents. Afterwards they returned to Moscow,
where Stashinsky was to receive special training and political
instruction. His new "case officer" was another Sergey (this
time Sarkisov).

In addition to training, this was also a period of political
indoctrination for both Stashinsky and his wife, but his
disaffection with Communism was steadily increasing. The
feeling that he was being watched became stronger, and his
suspicions were confirmed when he discovered that their
apartment was bugged with microphones behind the skirting
boards. This was the last straw. Escape to the West was now
becoming imperative.

Then an additional complication arose. Inge became pregnant. The K.G.B., when informed, already knew about it,
which to Stashinsky was additional proof that they were being
spied upon, and his disaffection increased. The K.G.B. insisted
that Inge should have an abortion, as this could easily be
arranged in Moscow, but she firmly refused. At one point
Sergey suggested that she should put the child when born into
a State "home" as a donation to the Soviet community. This
was also declined.

When the time for confinement came near the K.G.B.

finally issued their orders. Inge could return to East Berlin to have her baby, but Stashinsky had to stay in Moscow, because of the "political situation". It was put to Stashinsky that his life would be in danger in East Berlin, and that he could not safely go back there for at least five years.

Before the parting, Stashinsky told his wife the whole truth about his involvement with the K.G.B., and his part in the assassinations of Dr Rebet and Bandera. Inge was horrified, but Stashinsky felt as if a great burden had been lifted from his shoulders. They discussed ways and means of defecting to the West in the long term, but in the short term Inge went back to East Berlin while he stayed in Moscow to continue his training under strict surveillance. But at this stage Stashinsky had already made up his mind to give himself up to the Americans and confess when a safe opportunity arose. Stashinsky and the Soviet way of life had parted company.

Inge gave birth to a son. Stashinsky, despite urgent application—indeed, supplication—was not allowed to be present at the event, nor was he allowed to visit his wife when she became ill due to post-natal complications.

The baby was born in March, and by August Inge had made up her mind to return to Moscow with her baby in order to reunite the family. While she was still making the travel arrangements the baby caught pneumonia and died.

Under these circumstances Stashinsky, in desperation, again sought permission to visit East Berlin for a few days to be present at the baby's funeral. The K.G.B. found sufficient humanity in its cold formal protocol to agree. But Stashinsky, who had never seen his son, was more emotionally concerned with the possibility of escape. He was therefore disappointed to learn that he was to be accompanied to Berlin by Alexandrov, a high official of K.G.B.

Alexandrov put it to him that the cause of the baby's death was still to be established. The child could have been killed by the Germans or the Americans as a gambit to force Stashinsky to return to East Berlin, where he would be kidnapped. Alternatively, Inge herself might have murdered her baby to ensure her husband's return. She was known to be sympathetic to the West, and was possibly in their pay. Needless to say, Stashinsky was outraged by these cynical suggestions—but no longer surprised. It was typical Communist thinking, and an excuse to keep him under observation while in East Berlin for his own "safety".

From the moment of his arrival at Spremberg Airport in East Germany Stashinsky found himself under continual surveillance. Having carried out this function himself in the past, he knew what to look for—the recurring anonymous face in the street, the car parked outside the flat, with the driver reading a newspaper and smoking a cigarette, the "changing of the guard" when one car replaced another. . . .

Stashinsky was now quite sure that the K.G.B. did not trust him, because his allegiance was in doubt, and because he knew too much about the assassinations and K.G.B. methods in general. He realized that he himself was likely to be eliminated, just as Rebet and Bandera had been. He discussed the tense situation with Inge and they decided that the only possible solution to their dilemma was to get to West Berlin as quietly as possible, where he would surrender himself to the American authorities and tell the whole sordid story.

And pathetically he and Inge decided that, because the K.G.B. would expect them on sheer emotional grounds to stay in East Berlin for their baby's funeral, the psychological time to make their escape was *before* the funeral—stark but logical thinking.

Although Stashinsky and his wife were kept under close observation by the K.G.B. in the few days preceding the funeral, they finally succeeded in evading the watchers in the streets. Carrying virtually no luggage, they managed to enter West Berlin by taxi and Metro with little difficulty and no identity check. There Stashinsky briefly visited some relatives, and then reported to the police, who handed him over to the Americans. Apparently he told them the truth, the whole truth and nothing but the truth.

At the trial in 1962 Stashinsky's story aroused great scepticism—even the judge seemed unable to accept the incredible facts as cold truth. But in the end Stashinsky's obvious sincerity, his undeniable reversion from Communism and his desire to atone for the two cold-blooded murders he had committed under orders from the Soviet government, convinced everyone—even the cynical press. His confession was detailed, self-incriminating and subject to a wealth of corroboration. He identified and named other agents and Soviet officials. Points of detail proved to be true—for instance, he said that Bandera had unlocked his front door and removed the key with his left hand—and Bandera was, in fact, left-handed. His description of the cyanide pistol was carefully vetted by experts and found to be plausible—and the weapon functional. The efficacy of the antidote, amyl nitrite, was confirmed. Stashinsky proved only too willing to convict himself in a complete about-face of moral conscience.

The judge, summing up, made a true and significant observation. He said: "Yet in the end every political murder is turned against its instigator, just as are all political lies."

The judge also pointed out that Stashinsky had confessed to the murder of Dr Rebet, even though his death had aroused no suspicion whatsoever. "In spite of this he revealed it on his own initiative to the entirely unsuspecting examining authorities so as to make a clean breast of everything."

And finally: "The Soviet principals unscrupulously ordered and had carried out on German Federal Republic territory two political murders, thereby grossly disregarding all international morals and the obligations of international law between two states. The guilt of the highly-placed instigator of the deeds cannot be laid to the charge of the accused. Stashinsky's frank confession has helped to uncover and lay bare the criminal methods of the political struggle."

Stashinsky was sentenced in all to thirteen years' hard labour, but this was later reduced to eight years' hard labour on the combined charges—a reasonable enough sentence for a double assassination, even for one who repented afterwards.

Stashinsky is still in prison, so far as anybody knows, but should soon be a free man. In a final statement he said:

'My wife and I will always live in the fear that one day we shall be overtaken by retribution from the East. Nevertheless, I have decided in favour of the West, because I believe that this step was absolutely necessary for the world at large."

Chapter 8

SKELETON IN THE PIPE

This curious little enigma, which came to light during the Second World War, poses a number of interesting questions but provides no answers—rather like the famous mystery of the *Mary Celeste*. During an air raid on Liverpool in the early years of the war a German bomb demolished a building surrounded by a concrete wall in the Everton district of the city. Civil defence workers, sifting the debris for possible victims, came upon a big steel pipe which had been partly exposed by the bomb crater. The pipe had been buried beneath the wall, and had evidently formed part of the concrete foundations. One end of the pipe had been blown off by the force of the explosion. Inside was a human skeleton.

The pipe itself took the form of a cylinder about two feet in diameter and over seven feet long. It could have been part of a drainage system or an industrial boiler. It had originally been sealed at both ends. It was heavy and cumbersome, and had obviously required considerable manhandling to put in position in the foundations of the wall.

The body inside the pipe, having been reduced by normal decomposition to a skeleton, was clearly not an air-raid victim, and since the pipe had been sealed after the body was already inside, the chance of death by accident or misadventure seemed remote. The discovery was, of course, referred to the police. Some very strange facts were brought to light.

The skeleton was clothed, which was not unusual, but even a cursory examination revealed that the clothing belonged to the previous century. A more detailed examination by experts suggested that the clothes consisted of top-quality Victorian garments of the type worn by the aristocratic dandies of some sixty to seventy years earlier—in the closing decades of the 1800s.

Confirmation of the age of the skeleton was found in the pockets of the clothing: a diary for the year 1885, a railway ticket dated 27 June, 1885, and a postcard dated 3 July, 1885. Everything was consistent, even if faintly incredible. It appeared, on the surface, as if the man in the steel cylinder had met his death more than half a century earlier—and, under the circumstances, it must surely have been a violent death. It was almost certainly murder. The only remaining verification required was a clinical examination of the skeleton by Dr Charles Harrison, the senior pathologist of Liverpool University.

But Dr Harrison's findings failed to verify anything other than that the skeleton was that of a young man aged between twenty-five and thirty, about six feet tall, who had been dead for not more than ten years! This was a startling conclusion, but it was supported by detailed clinical evidence. The Victorian clothes and the ten-year-old skeleton did not belong to each other—but there they were, the one adorning the other in the strange steel pipe.

No further progress was made. It was not possible to identify the skeleton, nor could the origin of the clothes be traced after an interval of half a century or more. The steel cylindrical pipe remained a mystery and nobody really knew where it had come from or what its proper function had been. Many questions were asked, but the only answers consisted of guesswork and speculation. It was just another of the several unsolved mysteries brought to light by wartime bombing raids.

However, if there was no solution there were certainly many theories which were tried on for size. The situation was one which would have delighted a crime novelist. For instance, assuming the pathologist was right and that the skeleton was that of a young man who had met his death not more than ten years previously (there was never any suggestion that this was incorrect), why should the murderer dress his victim in elegant and costly Victorian clothes and provide the props of a diary, a railway ticket and a postcard all dated 1885? Was it a clever subterfuge to make sure that, if the body in the steel pipe were ever discovered, the police would be misled into believing that the murder had taken place in 1885, and would therefore hardly take the trouble to seek a killer who would either be a very old man or already dead and buried?

This was an ingenious but nevertheless reasonable theory, but in turn it raised a new set of awkward questions. Where did the murderer get his Victorian clothes and props from? The clothes were, perhaps, the less difficult proposition. They could have been in the family, carefully preserved as a relic of, say, grandfather's youth. This would imply that the killer was a man of well-established and possibly prosperous background. The props were more difficult to account for. Where could one obtain a diary, postcard and railway ticket all dated 1885? Well, again they could have been in the family—part of a collection of souvenirs and heirlooms—but each additional item of "disguise" merely lengthened the coincidental odds and made the explanation more implausible.

But granted that the murderer had access in his own home to high-quality Victorian clothing, a railway ticket, a diary and a postcard as specified, why the steel pipe, and where did it come from?

The theory had an answer to that, too. The purpose of using the pipe as a coffin, sealed at both ends, was to preserve the clothing and the props, but not the body itself. In this way, after the body had naturally decayed to a skeleton in the course of a few years, the 1885 "deadline" would be established. The clothes would deteriorate too, up to a point, but they would survive for much longer than the corpse. There is no doubt that if buried in ordinary damp soil the clothing and props would have disintegrated long before.

If the theory is correct, then it looks as if the scene had been carefully set with its own built-in "red herrings" to throw inquisitive investigators off the track. If so, it must have called for shrewd thinking and careful long-term planning—the kind of devious thinking that characterized Poe's Montresor in *The Cask of Amontillado*. The only risk the killer ran was that the body might be discovered before it had decayed to a skeleton, but the pipe buried under the concrete wall was unlikely to be discovered until the wall itself was demolished, and that might not be for another half-century.

The killer overlooked two factors, for which he could hardly be blamed. One was that the tomb of his victim might be prematurely uncovered by a German bomb in a war which was still ten years in the future. The other was the progressive accuracy of modern forensic pathology in dating human remains, so that it was ascertainable that between the articles of clothing and the bones of the skeleton was a time lapse of over fifty years. In the event, however, neither error of anticipation put the murderer in any danger of detection.

There are certain obvious lines of investigation which were probably pursued at the time, but not reported. What was the chemical composition of the steel pipe? When was that kind of steel first manufactured, and who made it for what purpose? There were not so many steel companies that a two-foot-diameter steel cylinder would be beyond reasonable identification.

Also, since the pipe was embedded in the foundations of the concrete wall, when was the wall erected, and by whom? Who was living in the house at the time—and were they the kind of people to have had wealthy Victorian ancestors who might have left fine clothing and relics in musty old cupboards and attics?

The mystery of the skeleton in the pipe was never solved, but it is a sombre thought that the person who knows all the answers may still be alive today—an ageing man with secret memories in the darker recesses of his mind.

Chapter 9

THE CHANCELLOR
OF THE EXCHEQUER

THIS, of course, is the dream of many hard-pressed taxpayers, but happily the notion of assassinating the Chancellor of the Exchequer to correct presumed financial injustice seldom if ever emerges from the dream state. But it did on one occasion, at the beginning of the nineteenth century, and it had nothing whatever to do with income tax.

The central character was a tense and rather neurotic man named John Bellingham. There had been some history of insanity in his family, and although he himself was rational enough, he was inclined to have "a chip on his shoulder". He was also, on his record, the kind of man to attract futility and misfortune.

Bellingham was a London businessman who had dealings with Russia. In the early 1800s he spent three years at Archangel working as a clerk to a Russian merchant. He returned to England for a period and in 1804 went back to Russia on mercantile business—to run slap into bad luck, and eventually tragedy.

He was arrested in Russia and imprisoned on charges of

debt which he later insisted were completely false and groundless. He also claimed that during his imprisonment he had
been treated with the utmost severity and brutality to such an
extent that his health had been adversely and permanently
affected.

During this period of imprisonment, which lasted until
1809, Bellingham made repeated requests to the British Embassy at St Petersburg, and in particular to Lord Granville
Gower, the British Ambassador, to intervene and secure
redress from the Russian Government. The Ambassador, after
due investigation and consideration, came to the conclusion
that there was no action that the Embassy could reasonably
take. It appeared that Bellingham was being dealt with in a
proper way under Russian law, and it was no part of the
Embassy's job to attempt to modify the law of a foreign
country.

So Bellingham served his sentence, and on his release
returned to England. His health, he claimed vociferously, had
been impaired by the ill treatment he had endured, and he
was virtually penniless because of the heavy legal expenses
which had been incurred.

Taking account of Bellingham's character and mentality, it
was not surprising that the question of redress and compensation became an obsession which dominated his embittered
mind. He blamed in particular Lord Gower and the Embassy
staff at St Petersburg for failing to protect the rights and
interests of a British subject. Very forcefully and persistently
he put his case to various Ministers of the Crown and
governmental departments, but failed to penetrate the formal
barrier of official indifference. Each time he prodded authority he was informed that his claims were unfounded and could
not be considered—and there was probably much truth in this
reply. At each rebuff, however, Bellingham became more
frustrated and more stubbornly determined to pursue his
cause to the limit.

He was now living in Liverpool, where he had taken up
business as an insurance broker. Consequently, he decided to
approach his local Member of Parliament, General Gascoyne,
with a view to having a petition presented in the House of
Commons. Gascoyne, who was not familiar with the details of
the case, was prepared to back such a petition, which seemed
to him to be justified, but as a matter of formal procedure

Bellingham had first to obtain the approval of the Chancellor of the Exchequer, the Right Hon. Spencer Perceval, whose sanction was absolutely necessary where a petition to Parliament involved a claim for money from public funds.

In May, 1810, therefore, Bellingham wrote to the Chancellor of the Exchequer demanding, in his single-minded way, permission to present a petition to the Commons seeking redress and compensation. No doubt he imagined that with the support of Gascoyne already guaranteed, the Chancellor's approval was a mere formality which could hardly be withheld. He was due for a big disappointment. The reply from the Chancellor of the Exchequer stated briefly that the proposed petition was not considered to be "of a nature for the consideration of Parliament".

Although this was a big setback, Bellingham refused to give up. During the next two years he applied to the Privy Council and to the Regent himself, but with no success. He was informed that his application should properly be addressed to the Chancellor of the Exchequer as it concerned public funds—and so he was caught up in a vicious circle which apparently could not be broken.

Even so, he was not dismayed, even if he was depressed. He was prepared to spend his entire life in pursuit of a lost cause, if necessary—and this, in the event, was what it proved to be.

His next step was to appeal to the judiciary. He wrote in earnest terms to the magistrates at Bow Street Court, giving full details of his case and the subsequent injustice, and threatening to take the law into his own hands if his "reasonable request" continued to be declined. The magistrates evidently did not take this threat very seriously, but they were impressed enough to take the trouble to send Bellingham's letter to the Secretary of State for consideration.

Time went by until Bellingham, impatient for a decision, called in person at the Secretary of State's office to find out what was happening. There he was told, to his great disappointment, that nothing could be done officially, but that he was free to "take such measures as he thought proper". At least, this was what Bellingham later claimed was said to him, and in his obsessive state of mind he regarded it as an open invitation to take the law into his own hands at his own discretion. At this stage it seems clear that Bellingham, who was an educated, literate and in no sense a violent man, was developing a neurosis tantamount to insanity under the stress of the interminable frustration and obstruction.

This was in fact the critical point in time, when one is invited to believe that Bellingham really accepted that he had been given *carte blanche* by the Government to "take such measures as he thought proper". The next step was as dramatic as it was simple. Bellingham analyzed the situation and decided that the one man to blame for the rejection of his claim over the years was the Chancellor of the Exchequer. And he had been told officially to take whatever measures he thought proper.

So, on 11 May, 1812, he went to the House of Commons. In his pockets were two loaded pistols. He took up a position in the lobby near the entrance doors. He was able to wait there unchallenged and probably unnoticed, as his appearance and manner were dignified and poised, and not likely to create suspicion. If Bellingham looked calm, it was because he *was* calm. His attitude was quite objective and impersonal.

Soon after five o'clock Mr Perceval, the Chancellor of the Exchequer, entered the House of Commons. Bellingham immediately drew a pistol from his pocket and, without hesitation, shot him in the chest. Perceval collapsed to the floor, his clothes awash with blood. He was picked up and carried to a room in the House, but died very quickly.

Bellingham, in his characteristic way, having successfully carried out his assassination, made no attempt to escape or even get rid of the murder weapon. He calmly waited for his arrest.

The murder of the Chancellor of the Exchequer created a sensation throughout the country. Huge crowds gathered outside Parliament and in Westminster, and troops were brought in to maintain control and law and order. For a few days it was a national crisis. Meanwhile, the cause of all the trouble, John Bellingham, remained cool, calm and rational, and in no way regretful of what he had done—even though he must have known that it would result in his own death at the hands of the public executioner. He was taken to prison to await trial.

Bellingham's state of mind while he was under interrogation was curiously unconcerned and complacent. After all, he had not killed Mr Perceval, the Chancellor of the Exchequer, from any feeling of personal animosity. He had simply taken upon himself to destroy, in a quite impersonal fashion, the holder of the office of Chancellor, on the grounds that a Minister of the Crown had no right to refuse justice to a person seeking redress. And he was quite sure in his own mind that the Secretary of State's office had given him authority to take whatever action he thought proper—and that amounted to a *carte blanche*. The assassination had been merely a gesture of protest carried out with Government backing. If anything he was impatient at the slowness of the legal proceedings because he was looking forward in an academic way to his trial, which would provide many opportunities for subtle argument. He was, of course, convinced that any question of his apparent guilt would be more than counterbalanced by the only too evident moral justification of his act.

Bellingham was almost cheated of his ambition by an attempt which was made to have the trial postponed on the grounds that the prisoner was of unsound mind. Bellingham himself would certainly have been the first to disagree with such a plea. However, the court decided that the prisoner was fit to plead, and the trial began only four days after the assassination.

At the beginning of the trial, Bellingham pleaded not guilty. He claimed that he was severely handicapped in defending his case and justifying his actions by the absence of various important papers and documents which, he alleged, had been taken from him and not returned. On investigation this proved to be true; anxious to ensure that justice was seen to be done in such a widely publicized trial, the judge ordered the papers to be restored to the prisoner in time for him to prepare his defence.

Meanwhile the trial proceeded, with the prosecution outlining the case for the Crown, the facts of which have already been related. The Chancellor of the Exchequer had been assassinated, and the Attorney-General set out to prove that the manner in which the assassination had been carried out, in a cold-blooded methodical way, precluded any possibility of insanity. To suppose that the prisoner must be insane because the deed was so atrocious would mean that "every act of gross and unusual atrocity would carry its defence along with it".

The only issue at stake in the trial seemed to be that of Bellingham's sanity, for on the facts alone he seemed to have no viable defence. The murder had been well and truly premeditated and coolly executed, with no immediate provocation in any personal sense. When the time came for Bellingham to present his defence, his papers were restored to him. He sorted them out and spent some time inspecting them with perfect composure, and then addressed the court. His manner was polite and respectful.

He began by expressing his gratitude to the judge that the plea of insanity had failed, and seemed anxious to make it clear to the jury that the crime was a gesture of principle, committed from compulsion rather than from any personal hostility to the Chancellor as an individual. He proceeded to offer a justification for the murder which involved a detailed recital of the whole history of his misfortunes in Russia and his subsequent futile attempts to secure redress through the Government. He was, he said, prepared to face death— indeed, five hundred deaths—as a fate more desirable than his sufferings during the previous eight years, but he was convinced that the jury would acquit him of the charge of murder because his action had been more than justified by the immoral refusal of justice which had been accorded him by those appointed to look after the interests of British subjects abroad.

A final attempt to question his sanity and thus save his life was made when two female witnesses were called to give evidence that in recent years they had known the accused to be mentally deranged—and it was pointed out that his father had died of insanity. Bellingham, therefore, could hardly be held responsible for his own actions.

After the judge's summing-up the jury retired for a mere fourteen minutes, and then returned a verdict of guilty—to which the prisoner's reaction was one of surprise. He was condemned to death, and hanged in public three days later— still arguing the justice of his case. Afterwards his body was taken in a cart to St Bartholomew's Hospital for dissection.

On the day before the execution, two days after the trial had ended, Lord Granville Leveson Gower, who had been the British Ambassador in Russia during Bellingham's spell of imprisonment, wrote a letter to the Foreign Secretary explaining the events that had taken place in Russia, and why the British Embassy had been unable to intervene. The Embassy had, at the time, made a full inquiry into the circumstances of Bellingham's committal to prison by the Russian authorities.

Lord Gower's statement ought really to have been presented during the trial, but even so it would have done Bellingham no good, and would probably have made his conviction and execution more certain.

The substance of the Embassy report was that Bellingham, while in Russia, had been involved in a dispute with a Russian business company over money owed to them. On arbitration he had been ordered to pay two thousand roubles to the litigants—but this he had refused to do. He had also been involved in another court case in Archangel of which he was to be acquitted, but before judgment was delivered he foolishly ran away and went into hiding, thus admitting a sense of guilt which had no real justification. He was eventually recaptured by the police, when he even more foolishly resisted arrest, and was consequently jailed—though not for long.

Afterwards he was detained in the College of Commerce until the debt of two thousand roubles had been paid, but it was an imprisonment in name rather than fact. He was not confined in any strict sense and enjoyed considerable personal liberty, going out into the streets and visiting friends under the supervision of a police officer. There was no evidence that he had been cruelly and brutally treated.

The Embassy had no authority whatever to interfere in a perfectly proper legal procedure under Russian law, but they did suggest to the Russians that as Bellingham was unlikely ever to pay his debt they might just as well set him free on condition that he returned immediately to England. However, several years were to elapse before Bellingham was freed, and in the meantime diplomatic relations between Britain and Russia were broken off for political reasons. After this the Embassy had no further information about Bellingham.

On balance, therefore, it looks as though Bellingham's obsessive and neurotic resentment never had any real basis of justification, and that his persistent claims of false and unjust imprisonment were groundless. One may reasonably conclude that Bellingham was insane, but his insanity was a restrained and controlled phenomenon taking the form of a compulsion neurosis—the behaviour pattern of most assassins.

Chapter 10

THE ARTLESS FORGER

THE forgery of banknotes is a serious crime and is generally carried out on a big scale if the risks involved are to be justified by the profits made. It is an industry which calls for skill and a specialized knowledge of photographic engraving and printing techniques. It is seldom a one-man band. The manufacturing side has to be supported by an efficient "marketing" organization employing a number of experienced "couriers" if the business is to be viable. The counterfeit notes have to be unloaded as quickly and inconspicuously as possible. The time factor is vital, for the useful life of even the best forgeries is short, and the gang must aim to reap a handsome profit before detection triggers off police investigation.

For this reason five-pound notes are more likely to be forged than one-shilling postal orders, and half-crowns are a better proposition than sixpences, although there is the real disadvantage that high-denomination notes and coins are far more likely to attract suspicion and scrutiny. Seldom, however, does a forger specialize in small-quantity production of low-value currency for use on a piecemeal basis over a number of years—though there is a case on record of a craftsman who with meticulous precision altered the value of a postal-order just to gain a few shillings, but was caught because he had forgotten to alter the poundage too.

In America the simple dollar bill is seldom the subject of forgery because of its low value (just over seven shillings in sterling), but for a man of modest requirements a slow output of cheaply printed dollar bills over a long period of time might well serve its purpose—which it did for an old man named Edward Mueller who lived in New York. For a whole decade, during the last war and after, he successfully forged and passed crudely printed dollar bills, spending not more than two or three of them a day, until he was accidentally caught by sheer bad luck that had nothing to do with the forgeries at all.

Mueller was a quiet and polite old man, easy-going and considerate, and well liked by everyone who knew him. He lived an uneventful life, working as the superintendent of an apartment block on New York's East Side. In his younger days he had been interested in photography, and had collected an old stand camera and a few odd pieces of equipment which he never much used since he could not afford to pursue seriously what was a rather expensive hobby. He was a gadgeteer with an inventive turn of mind, but had never had any success with his inventions. However, his interest in photographic techniques and processes and his practical mentality were to stand him in good stead in years to come.

In 1937 he retired from his job, and shortly afterwards his wife died. For a while his daughter lived with him and looked after him, but then she married, leaving him alone at the age of sixty-three in a small tenement apartment on 96th Street, with only his dog for company. Even so, Mueller was happy enough—there was little he wanted out of life. He asked for nothing and owed nothing, and continued to rub along on the small amount of money he had managed to save during his working years.

In his own humble way he was a proud and independent character. He refused any kind of help which hinted of charity, and even declined a government pension to which he was perfectly entitled and which would have given him an income of about a thousand dollars a year. Instead, he preferred to set up his own business by buying a small cart and trading as a junk man, but this enterprise proved to be a failure. His money steadily dwindled until his financial position was becoming desperate—and at that point he decided to print his own money, just a small amount to meet his day-to-day needs.

He bought a small and very old printing press and set it up in his apartment. Then he dug out the ancient stand camera which was still preserved among his lumber. More precious money was spent on materials and chemicals, and then he was ready to experiment with his old hobby. He set out to photograph and make printing plates of a one-dollar bill—and eventually succeeded. Then, with quite the wrong kind of paper and even the wrong shades of printing ink, he printed a few bills. They were extremely bad forgeries indeed, but Old Mueller was unconcerned. Crumpled and creased they would pass muster—after all, who ever bothered to look closely at a dollar bill? In any case, he was not out to make a fortune or even a profit. He would spend not more than one bill in any one shop, and buy only the few necessities which would keep himself and his dog alive in happy poverty. And this he proceeded to do.

It was not long before the crude forgeries were detected and referred to the police, who were baffled by certain puzzling features of the crime. For one thing there was the incredibly bad quality of the printing, which made it almost impossible to believe that anyone could be foolish enough to attempt to pass such obvious counterfeits. Another strange factor was the slow and almost tedious one-at-a-time method of disposal of the forgeries in so many different shops, all roughly within one wide area. At the rate the forgeries were being passed it would take years for the forger to make any worth-while profit at all.

The police sent warnings to banks and shop-keepers, but to no avail. Still the forgeries were being issued and accepted and, even worse, as time went by the quality deteriorated as the original printing plates became worn and clogged with dried ink. But Old Mueller happily kept on churning out his dreadful imitations of dollars, just a few at a time, quite oblivious to the ghastly printing and probably regarding them as works of art.

Nearly six hundred forged dollar bills were passed into circulation in the first year—an average of less than two a day. At the end of five years the total was approaching three thousand and after ten years was nearly six thousand—the same steady rate of production and disposal. The police made intensive efforts to track down the audacious and unskilled forger, but in vain. It was obvious to them that they were not hunting an organized gang, but probably an eccentric individual operating in a very small way with primitive equipment and a naïve faith in his luck—which so far had not let him down. This made him the more difficult to trace. If one of Old Mueller's home-made bills was ever challenged to his face in the ten years that he had acted as his own "courier", he had only to claim that he must have unknowingly received it elsewhere, perhaps in change given at another shop. He was too well known and liked for anyone to doubt his honesty, and who anyway would have imagined that a gentle old man like Edward Mueller, an unsuccessful junk trader living alone with his dog, could possibly be the forger? Where could he acquire the necessary technical know-how and specialized equipment for counterfeiting? The idea was ridiculous.

To the police the case became a major irritation and challenge. At one time the head of the New York office of the Secret Service, James Maloney, was assigned to the investigation, but to no avail.

In the end Old Mueller was betrayed by a hazard of unfortunate chance. One day while he was out there was a fire in his apartment. Firemen broke in and attempted to salvage some of his possessions by throwing them out of the window —and among them were printing plates and charred pieces of printed paper which they failed to recognize as dollar bills. Even so, it was not until a boy found some of the partly burnt forgeries and showed them to his father, who passed them on to the police, that the dragnet closed in on Old Mueller. The boy said that he had picked up the bills near the tenement building on 96th Street where there had been a fire—and that was that. The patrol cars went into action. When Mueller returned home to his gutted apartment, the police were waiting for him. The artless forger who had led the police a dance for ten long years was at last arrested. But what really broke Old Mueller's heart was not that the law had finally caught up with him, but that his beloved dog had died in the blaze.

During police questioning Mueller was perfectly open and

honest about his forging activities and was very apologetic for the trouble he had caused. He explained that he had taken great care over the years to ensure that nobody could suffer a serious financial loss from his forgeries; he had made a point of never passing more than one bill at a time to any one person. During his trial, however, he changed his story by introducing a "Mr Reynolds", who had not been previously mentioned. Reynolds, he claimed, had done the actual printing of the forged notes and he, Mueller, had merely passed them. This sounded highly unlikely, particularly as Mr Reynolds could not be traced—in any case, it could make no difference to the outcome of the trial, for the charge was one of "passing counterfeit currency knowing it to be false", and this Mueller readily admitted to having done for many years.

However, there was one factor which, if it could not influence the verdict, certainly mitigated the sentence, and that was the appearance of Mueller's daughter in court to affirm that she was willing to have her father come to live with herself and her husband, when she would be able to look after him. The judge welcomed this gesture, for he was reluctant to send the kindly old man to prison, but forgery was a serious crime and could not be lightly dismissed. In the event, Old Mueller received a sentence of nine months' imprisonment, but this was later reduced to four months—which was lenient indeed.

After he had served his sentence, Old Mueller went to live with his daughter and son-in-law as had been arranged, and presumably spent the remainder of his life in relative peace and comfort. One wonders whether, being the kind of man he was, he would not have preferred to be with his dog in his shabby apartment, printing his dollar bills as a hobby and spending not more than two a day.

The irony of the story is that Mueller, who forged nearly six thousand fake dollars in ten years, would have received almost twice as much in that time if his stubborn pride had not prevented him from accepting a government pension. So, on balance, the State made a profit out of his amateurish but highly successful essay in forgery.

Chapter 11

THE BOGUS
PRINCESS

PRETTY Sarah Wilson, with her dark hair, blue eyes and vivacious personality, may well have been the only nubile young lady in English history to be sentenced to death for stealing a dress from the Queen—not to mention a valuable gold and sapphire ring and a costly miniature portrait of Her Majesty.

That she did not die brutally at the hands of the public executioner was almost certainly due to her natural charm and plausible manner. In those days, the mid-1700s, theft was punishable by death—and theft from Royalty was tantamount to high treason. But Sarah survived to pursue her talent for crime in a much more subtle way, and one which would have pleased the Queen even less had she known about it. Sarah exploited her charm and personality to splendid effect in later years in America, which at that time was still a British colony, by posing as the Queen's sister.

In modern vernacular, Sarah was the female equivalent of a "con man", but her aim in life was gracious living rather than money. For many years she was indeed accepted as the

Queen's sister, and succeeded in living a regal parasitic life in the aristocratic southern states of America just before the War of Independence. Her crime was opportunism rather than fraud, but even that might have carried the death penalty in those days, for they took their monarchs seriously. The war, when it came, changed everything, and even made an honest woman of Sarah.

The daughter of a bailiff, she was born in humble circumstances in a small Staffordshire village towards the middle of the eighteenth century. George III of the German House of Hanover was on the throne of England, with Queen Charlotte by his side. Sarah proved to be an intelligent but restless child. Like many ambitious people she was something of a dreamer, but she also possessed the initiative and a kind of irresponsible single-mindedness to attempt to bring her dreams to reality, although it was only a reality of pretence.

As she grew older she became disenchanted with home life in the village. At the age of sixteen she left her family and travelled to London, which she regarded as the centre of civilization. She was in search of, if not exactly adventure, at least excitement and opportunity.

Sarah had other assets apart from her beauty and personality. She had learned to be a good cook and competent needlewoman. She was polite and well mannered. With such an array of talent she encountered no difficulty in finding herself a superior job as maid to a distinguished woman named Caroline Vernon who happened to be a lady-in-waiting to Queen Charlotte. There seems little doubt that Sarah selected her employer with judicious care, for an entree into Court circles was very much a part of her daydreams.

Sarah, ever a courteous and willing worker, proved to be invaluable to Caroline. She would accompany her mistress to the Queen's House, which predated Buckingham Palace, and there she was able to see Court people, and listen to and absorb Court gossip. She would hear the Queen herself talking to close friends, and very quickly she became familiar with the contemporary topics of Royal chatter, including details of Court scandals.

Fascinated by the luxuriant and sophisticated atmosphere of the Court and its people, Sarah soon developed a royalty addiction. She began to weave fantasies in which she herself was a Court lady, wearing beautiful gowns and fabulous

jewellery, poised, regal and articulate, and admired by noble-
men. From the fantasy to the reality seemed only a short step
in the art of make-believe; it was only necessary to "acquire"
some of the Queen's possessions in order to turn the illusion
into something more resembling fact.

Sarah was familiar with the Queen's private living-room,
known as the Green Closet. She had sat there many times
behind a screen while her mistress talked with the Queen.
From this room one evening, deceiving the Palace guard by
means of a subterfuge, she stole a dress, a ring and a
miniature portrait of Queen Charlotte.

If Sarah had assumed that the Queen owned so many
dresses and rings that the absence of one of each would go
unnoticed then she was seriously mistaken. The Queen was in
the habit of counting her rings and checking her possessions
from time to time, and it was not long before the theft was
discovered. Court officials questioned the staff and investigated the crime without success; it did not seem to occur to
them that the pretty young maid of a lady-in-waiting might
have been the culprit.

All might have been well had not Sarah, encouraged by the
success of her first foraging expedition, decided to repeat it,
not knowing that the servants were now keeping careful
watch on the Queen's room. She was caught red-handed by a
German servant, who passed her over to the Palace guards.
She was tried and convicted by the Lord Steward in a
specially convened Palace court, and duly sentenced to death.
Oddly enough, the stolen possessions were not recovered.
Sarah's brief interlude as a fantasy "princess" appeared, nevertheless, to have come to a sharp and summary end.

But she was not without a friend, even in such a crisis. Her
mistress Caroline Vernon, horrified at the fate of her foolish
maid-servant, implored the Queen to spare her life. The
Queen in turn used her influence on the King. In due course
King George commuted the death sentence to one of deportation for life. And deported she was, to the colony of America.
The year was 1768.

On arrival in America, after an arduous voyage across the
Atlantic in a sailing ship, Sarah was sold as a slave to a Mr
William Devall of Bush Creek. Incredibly, she still had with
her in her bundle of personal effects the Queen's dress,
sapphire ring and miniature portrait. One can only assume

that some kind of chivalrous gallantry among the jailers and officials responsible for carrying out her deportation had restrained them from rifling her possessions. Whatever the reason, she landed in America complete with the stolen articles which had been responsible for her penal transportation. They were to stand her in good stead in the coming years.

Whether the same chivalry and gallantry were extended to her during her period of slavery is not recorded. Her belongings remained untouched, but whether she herself remained untouched in the Devall household is another matter. She was, after all, a convict and a piece of human property bought for cash, but Sarah was generally adaptable and knew how to look after herself.

At all events, slavery did not suit Sarah, and after a few months she decided to escape. There is no reason to suppose that she was badly treated by the Devalls, and she probably enjoyed certain *en famille* privileges, but being a slave had never been a part of her daydreams. She had higher ambitions.

When the opportunity presented itself she packed her belongings and ran away to the South, to the region of gentlemen, aristocracy and plantations. Here was the social climate in which she knew she could flourish, where her experience and memories of Court and royalty could be exploited to good advantage. Here was the chance to realize her old dream—to change her identity and become a princess.

Sarah did not believe in half measures. She knew intuitively that the bigger the lie the more likely it was to be believed. Furthermore, she possessed three valuable "props" stolen from the Queen's house—so what was more natural than that she should become Princess Susanna Carolina Mathilda, the sister of Queen Charlotte of England? What was she doing in America at a time when the colonists of the New World were becoming restive and talking treasonably about breaking away from the British Crown—what would nowadays be called a unilateral declaration of independence? The explanation was simple: she had been exiled because of a quarrel with the Royal Family over an indiscreet amorous escapade in which she had been involved that might have resulted in a Court scandal. Sarah knew that she could put over her story in a completely plausible fashion, and if plausibility were not enough she had the Queen's dress, ring and miniature to lend an air of verisimilitude. How else could she have come to be in possession of them if she were not, in fact, the Queen's sister?

So Sarah became Princess Susanna and launched herself into Southern society. Her anecdotes of Court life, royal personages and aristocratic gossip and scandal bore the ring of truth, mainly because they were, indeed, true, remembered from her days as maid to a lady-in-waiting at the Queen's house. No doubt her stories were embroidered for sensational effect, but Sarah was too shrewd to over-dramatize her audacious impersonation. She chatted with informal expertise and regal authority. Her audiences were quite bemused and considered themselves privileged to enjoy such a guest. They never thought to challenge her authenticity.

In particular she captivated the hearts of the gentlemen of the south by her beauty and charm—and possibly favours. Since the American South was in those days essentially a man's world, their unquestioning acceptance of her for what she claimed to be was sufficient reference to launch her on a long cycle of social engagements and "free-loading".

But, to make absolutely sure that the wives and women of the South were equally convinced of her royal status, Sarah carefully embroidered all her linen with a crown and personal monogram, making full use of her artistic flair and her expertise in needlework. This trick was never mentioned or discussed, of course, but the embroidered insignia was certainly observed and noted by the women who attended to the matter of laundering the "princess's" personal garments, and no doubt they talked among themselves.

As a princess, Sarah became a tremendous social success. In her new career as a professional guest she moved from one grateful and generous host to another in an unending cycle. Even the most influential and aristocratic families vied with each other for the privilege of entertaining the Queen's sister. To have Princess Susanna as a guest was a much sought after status symbol. Sarah was able to live freely and richly in the best households, never lacking invitations, and methodically widening her circle of social contacts among the "best people" in the Southern states of America.

This idyllic form of parasitic existence might have continued indefinitely, for Sarah had discovered a foolproof formula for exploiting the American passion for hospitality, particularly where a guest with snob appeal was concerned—but she became over-ambitious. Her success bred in her a sense of security and with it a feeling of power, and that in turn produced the corruption which power is proverbially alleged to generate spontaneously.

Although exiled and apparently estranged from the Queen and Court circles in England, Sarah claimed to have good friends and considerable influences at Establishment level and particularly with certain Ministers of the Crown. At first this was merely a name-dropping ploy designed to enhance her status, but human nature being what it is she inevitably encountered hosts who were not above attempting to use their royal guest, under the persuasion of lavish hospitality and even cash bribes, to obtain personal benefits. Sarah found herself making promises to secure promotions and obtain commissions by putting her princessly pressures on highly placed Government Ministers and officials in England. For a while she was safe enough. Communication between the colony and England was slow and unreliable, and there was never any guarantee that the Ministers and officials concerned would respond favourably to Princess Susanna's recommendations (no communication was ever made, of course). The men who sought and paid for Princess Susanna's intercession on their behalf did so speculatively, and knew very well that nothing might come of it. Sarah accepted the money, did nothing, sat tight and felt very secure.

Before long she found herself in receipt of a considerable income by way of bribes to secure political or administrative favours. This was plain fraud, but Sarah herself would have been the last to realize the true seriousness of her crime because she had so thoroughly identified herself with the imaginary Princess Susanna that the role had become reality. A modern psychiatrist would probably define her as a schizophrenic—but in the nicest possible way.

The chain reaction of trouble and retribution was steadily building up, however. You can't fool all of the people all of the time. When the promises she had made and had been paid for were not kept, her friends and acquaintances became increasingly suspicious. In the last analysis, money was more important than royal blood, even if one's guest was a princess and one had been technically guilty of bribery and coercion.

One of Sarah's former hosts who had been promised promotion in the Colonial Service, suffering from disappointment and frustration as months went by and nothing happened, took the trouble to do a little personal private detective work and check up on Queen Charlotte's relatives. Some time later he learned that the Queen did indeed have a sister, but she was living in Neu Strelitz, Germany. Furthermore, she was fifteen years older than "Princess Susanna", and her name was Christina Sophia Albertina, and not "Susanna Carolina Mathilda".

Perhaps the most fantastic aspect of this strange story is that even when the deception was exposed and the truth was rapidly spread throughout the important families of the South, no attempt was made to denounce the bogus princess. Whether out of courtesy to a charming and apparently cultured guest, or a feeling that the evidence was inconclusive and unreliable, or even because of the sheer compulsive neurosis of American hospitality, particularly in the South, Sarah continued to be entertained and accepted as the Queen's sister, even though everybody knew now that she was an imposter. But Sarah herself apparently had no idea that she had been exposed, even though requests that she should use her influence to secure promotional favours from the English Government dropped off alarmingly and her income from bribes dwindled to zero.

A possible explanation is that her former hosts were unwilling to admit, even to themselves, let alone to each other, that they had been taken in. It was more dignified to keep up the pretence than to admit gullibility. This is a psychological vulnerability which had been exploited throughout the ages by con men—and women.

Princess Susanna might have continued to survive as an accepted charlatan and impostor had not the spread of rumour reached the ears of her former owner, Mr William Devall of Bush Creek. Without delay he published an announcement throughout the Southern states giving details of his runaway slave as a servant calling herself Susanna Carolina Mathilda, and pretending to be Her Majesty's sister. He described her physical appearance—black hair, blue eyes with a "slight blemish" in the left eye. And, significantly, he added that she marked all her clothing with a crown and a monogram. The notice offered a reward to any person returning the slave to her rightful owner.

For Sarah it was the end of a happy interlude of applied con-manship. Even the families who were still prepared to accept her in order to save face could hardly ignore such an outright statement of fact, and gullibility had to be admitted, however unpleasant it might be. Princess Susanna was duly denounced, arrested, and sent back to Mr Devall to resume her job as servant and her status as slave.

She never arrived. Before restitution could be carried out an incredible thing happened—so incredible that one wonders if Sarah Wilson did not possess a charmed life. By an unlikely coincidence (the odds against it were astronomical, but it happened) another girl named Sarah Wilson had been sent to America for penal servitude as a slave. The "princess" Sarah, learning of this, sought out the girl. With the aid of more than a little bribery and persuasion, she managed to have the second Sarah Wilson substituted for herself, and so regained her liberty.

It could only have been a matter of time before she was once more identified and tracked down, but fate was still on her side. Up in Boston the Americans threw a cargo of tea into the sea, and soon afterwards the War of American Independence broke out. Mr Devall had other things to think about. He enlisted as an officer in the Maryland Militia to fight for the revolution.

The structure of the old American colony was crumbling, and a new society was emerging. King George III sent armed forces across the Atlantic in a futile attempt to put down the revolution, and among them were many young and eligible officers. It was among these that Sarah apparently sought to determine her future against the background of war, exploiting her ability to enchant to good advantage in the search for security and status.

She found both eventually in the person of a Mr Talbot who had served with the Light Dragoons. He was a well-educated young man of good family background. Sarah, older and wiser, no longer aspiring to be a princess, but merely a woman, married him. They lived in New York, and in due course she provided him with a family, and proved to be a good wife and mother.

Chapter 12

THE SEVERED HAND

A CRIME is occasionally "strange" not because of the bizarre nature of the crime itself but because of the odd behaviour of the principals involved. This is certainly true in the case of Arthur Howard, an unremarkable man who worked as a railway engineer in New Zealand in 1885. He lived in Christchurch and, being fond of swimming, would frequently walk to nearby Sumner on the coast where he could indulge in his favourite pastime, even though the coastal waters were, in those days, shark infested.

On one October day in that year Howard walked to Sumner for his final swim. He did not return home. The following morning his clothes and watch were found on the end of the pier, but of Howard himself there was no sign. The obvious inference was that he had drowned, but no body was recovered and the evidence at that stage was merely circumstantial.

Howard's wife, Sarah, after a short interval of grief, wasted no time in claiming insurance under three policies on Howard's life. The total amount involved was around two and a half thousand pounds—a respectable enough sum in the late-nineteenth century. However, Sarah ran into a major snag which had not been foreseen. The insurance companies refused to pay out immediately on the grounds that it had not been established beyond doubt that Howard was, in fact, dead. It was conceded that he was missing, but that in itself was insufficient to substantiate a life insurance claim. In the absence of a body—or at least identifiable human remains—death could not legally be presumed for seven years.

This was a blow to Sarah, who was not willing to wait so long for the law to take its course. She very quickly placed an advertisement in a local newspaper offering a reward of fifty pounds to anyone recovering the body of Arthur Howard, "drowned at Sumner on Saturday last". The same reward would also be paid to anyone producing a recognizable portion of the body. The interval between Howard's presumed death and the publication of the advertisement was only a few days; obviously Sarah's grief was modulated by mercenary overtones.

The advertisement produced no immediate response, and two months went by during which it began to look as if Sarah would indeed have to wait seven years before she could claim her insurance money. Then, a week before Christmas, on 16 December, a strange group of people called at the central police station in Christchurch to deliver a curious package.

The party comprised two brothers named Godfrey, and each was accompanied by a small boy. The package, which they handed over to the duty sergeant, was quite small, and wrapped in newspaper. The sergeant, not knowing what to expect, unwrapped the contents of the package quite carefully to reveal a human hand, white from bloodlessness and wrinkled from immersion in water. The hand had been cut off at the wrist. On the third finger was a gold ring. The sergeant removed the ring and inspected it. On the inside of the band the initials A.H. had been engraved.

The Godfrey brothers then made a statement. The hand clearly and undeniably belonged to the missing Arthur Howard. They had found it that same afternoon on the sands of a lonely bay near Sumner where they had taken their sons for an outing. It was obvious that the hand had been washed in by the tide, and there seemed little doubt that it had been bitten off by a shark.

Then the brothers produced a newspaper clipping of

Sarah's advertisement, now two months old, and made a formal claim for the fifty pounds reward on the grounds that they had discovered a recognizable portion of Arthur Howard's body and had established the fact of his death.

However, it was not quite so simple as that. First there would have to be a coroner's inquest, they were told, and the hand would have to be properly identified. Medical evidence would be presented by a pathologist, and the insurance companies concerned would necessarily be represented. If it was established that the hand was definitely that of Arthur Howard, then the question of the reward could be pursued. For the moment nothing could be done other than to allow the wheels of the law to start turning. Rewardless and disappointed, the Godfrey brothers and their sons withdrew and went home. The police for their part were suspicious enough to keep the Godfreys under observation for some time, believing the hand and ring to be the props in a fraudulent attempt to obtain the fifty-pound reward offered by Arthur Howard's wife.

The next logical step for the police was to take the hand to Mrs Sarah Howard to see if she could positively identify it as belonging to her husband. After her first hysterical shock reaction—it was not a pretty object—she found no difficulty at all in recognizing both the hand and the ring as Arthur's. Poor Arthur had clearly been attacked by a shark which had bitten off his hand. Well, that was for the coroner to decide.

The inquest duly took place, after ten doctors had painstakingly inspected the dead hand. Their statements varied on points of pathological detail, but on certain fundamental matters they were in absolute agreement.

The hand, they stated authoritatively, had not been immersed in sea water for very long, certainly nothing approaching two months, by which time decomposition would have been advanced, with little more than the bones left. Furthermore, the hand had not been bitten off by a shark, but had been cut off by a hacksaw after death. The characteristic grooves of the hacksaw teeth were unmistakably discernible in the sawn bones. And finally, it was not a man's hand at all—it was a woman's hand.

As if that were not enough in the way of damning evidence, an engraver was called as an expert witness to testify that in his opinion the letters A.H. on the inside of the gold ring had simply been scratched into the metal by a non-professional person using a needle or some similar instrument.

The case was now beginning to assume the familiar aspects of fraud and conspiracy centred around the Godfrey brothers. They were closely interrogated by the police, at which point they decided to make a new statement—and here a note of lugubrious fantasy began to enter the so far formal proceedings.

This was the new version of what had actually happened on the day when the hand was discovered. The two Godfrey brothers and their sons had been sitting on the beach near Sumner when a clown of a man wearing blue goggles and a red wig had appeared suddenly from behind a rock to announce, in high excitement, that he had seen a human hand in the sand nearby, and would they come and look at it. Obligingly they had followed the goggled apparition a short distance across the beach where, sure enough, there was a human hand wearing a gold ring on one finger. The weird character in the red wig and blue goggles suggested that it might be the hand of the long-missing Arthur Howard who had disappeared some time ago while swimming in the Sumner area, and then he made off, having apparently lost all interest in the discovery. The Godfrey brothers examined the hand and the ring, and came to the conclusion that it was indeed the hand of Arthur Howard—and worth fifty pounds in reward money. They had wrapped the hand in newspaper and delivered it to the Christchurch police station that same day.

Their statement was written out by a highly sceptical police sergeant, and the Godfreys duly signed it. Routine inquiries were set in motion to find out whether an improbable lunatic in blue goggles and a scarlet wig had been seen in the Sumner beach area on that particular day. The answer was yes—and nobody was more surprised than the police.

There was absolutely no doubt about it. The goggle-wig man had definitely been seen by a large number of people who could have had no personal interest whatever in the Arthur Howard case. Moreover, the man had spoken excitedly to several people to tell them that the Godfrey brothers had found a severed human hand belonging to the missing Arthur Howard. Indeed, it was beginning to look as if the weird goggles-wig man had deliberately made a point of establishing his presence on the beach by his grotesque appearance and his voluntary communiques concerning Howard's hand—almost as if he wanted the Godfrey's story to be corroborated. But why then, on their first visit to the police station, had they not mentioned the man in the red wig? Was it that they had not wished to share the reward money with him?

In the corporate police brain a little red flag went up. It was all too fantastic and ridiculous to be true—but witnesses were witnesses and facts were facts. The goggled man had to be pinned down and reduced to size; he had to be stripped of his gimmicks and his exact place in the pattern of fraud had to be established in minute detail and beyond doubt.

Starting with the Godfrey brothers, the police wanted to know why the goggled man had not been referred to in the original statement. The Godfreys were contrite and penitent— the truth was that the strange man had pleaded with them to remain silent and not mention him, and to claim that they had found the hand themselves. The apparent reason for this display of reticence had nothing to do with the hand at all. It was simply that he had had some previous trouble with the law and wished to remain unknown and anonymous.

On investigation this proved to be true. A man answering the same description, with blue goggles and a red wig, had been arrested some weeks previously for an assault on a woman, but as she had declined to press charges the case had not been proceeded with.

The case made sense and nonsense simultaneously. Faced with this surrealistic pattern of events, there is little doubt that the police were baffled—for a time. But there was enough fact to substantiate the apparent fantasy, and so the police eventually settled down to a methodical and meticulous long-term inquiry. In the course of time certain significant data began to emerge.

In the first place it was learned that the goggled man, who was known by the name of Watt, had first been seen on the night of the alleged drowning of Arthur Howard. He had been on a ferry-boat, travelling north towards the town where he had later been arrested for assault on a woman. Subsequently he had taken several farming jobs. And, significantly, one witness stated that Watt had tried to enlist his aid in opening a grave where there had been a recent burial . . .

Now the pieces of the jig-saw were beginning to click into

place, although the over-all picture was still obscure. The origin of the severed hand was becoming clear. But where and when had the man called Watt finally opened a grave to obtain a hand? And, in the event, had he been aware of his bad luck in opening a coffin containing the corpse of a woman and not a man? In the dark he might not have noticed, but if he had he may have assumed that it was too perilous to start again, and that the hand in itself would be sufficiently decomposed to prevent any kind of proper identification. The "engraved" ring would preclude any deeper investigation. Once the coffin had been opened—contents male or female—his attention would have been desperately concentrated on the hand and the hacksaw.

The long-drawn-out search for the man with the goggles and the wig continued, and of course the police realized that he had probably abandoned or changed his disguise. Watt, however, was evidently not a very imaginative character. In due course the police learned that a man answering the description of Watt, complete with goggles and wig, had been seen in Christchurch from time to time—and more significantly, that he had been meeting Mrs Sarah Howard, who was still waiting for her insurance money, for long walks and talks, although he had never actually visited the Howard home.

Although the police were not able to pin down Watt, they decided that there was enough evidence to convict the Godfrey brothers and Sarah Howard for attempted fraud against the insurance companies. They were duly arrested and charged.

But once again fantasy won the day. Unexpectedly and quite by chance a police officer ran full tilt into an odd character resembling an out-of-work music-hall performer wearing ill-fitting clothes, a red wig and blue goggles. Watt, true to form, was maintaining the disguise which, so he thought, had served him so well. He was arrested, unmasked and identified. Nobody was particularly surprised to discover that he was Arthur Howard, very much alive and complete with both hands.

At the subsequent trial the onus of conspiracy was shifted to Howard himself, although there seems little doubt that his wife had acted in collusion. He was convicted of attempting to obtain insurance money by fraud. Mrs Sarah Howard and the Godfrey brothers were given the benefit of the doubt by a bemused and slightly incredulous jury. They were found not guilty and acquitted.

Although that was the end of the case of the severed hand, a number of questions were left unanswered. Apart from the obvious ones—such as whether there was a carefully contrived conspiracy between the Howards and the Godfreys— there still remains the outstanding question as to why Arthur Howard, after attempting to establish that he had been eaten by a shark, chose to disguise himself in such a flamboyant and readily recognizable fashion—not even bothering to change his apparent identity from time to time. One might suppose that only a fool would make himself so visibly and memorably conspicuous, but there is no reason to suppose that he was a fool. The essentials of his futile scheme were shrewd enough— first, evidence of drowning, and then—with the hand sawn from a dead woman—evidence of death with physical human remains calculated to satisfy the insurance companies. But it all proved to be in vain, mainly because by accident or bad luck he happened to saw off a female hand.

Playing the role of Watt, perhaps Howard imagined that the more clown-like his disguise, the less people would take him seriously and the less suspicion would be aroused. In a sense it was, perhaps, the 1885 version of the "gimmick". On the other hand, when he knew that the case had become one of attempted fraud, and when he was returning to Christchurch to meet his wife in what he imagined were conditions of secrecy, he might reasonably have been expected to leave off the goggles and wig, and alter his appearance to something less readily recognizable.

Finally, the origin of the severed hand itself was never discovered. The police were certain that it had been sawn from a recently interred body after the grave and coffin had been opened, and there was the evidence of Watt's farm acquaintance who had declined to assist him in opening a grave to substantiate this view. But although many new graves in the area were opened and coffins exhumed in an attempt to find a body to match the hand, the mystery was never solved, and Howard himself never volunteered the information.

Chapter 13

THE ART OF
SELF-INVESTIGATION

IT is unusual in the history of crime for a murderer to be a representative of law and order, and to have to initiate the investigation of a murder which he himself has committed. But this happened in South Africa in 1934 when Railway Detective Sergeant J. H. Coetzee, of Pretoria, was called to set in motion the investigation of the death of a young woman whose body was found on a railway embankment a few miles down the line from Pretoria station. She had been brutally assaulted, mutilated and shot through the head.

The body was discovered early in the morning by a ganger, who reported his horrific find to a railway policeman named Fritz, who was on duty at Pretoria station. He in turn reported the incident to Detective Sergeant Coetzee, his superior in the railway police force. An hour or so later both Fritz and Coetzee hurried by motor-cycle to the scene of the crime.

The girl's body was in an ugly condition. She was covered in blood and dirt, and had been terribly disfigured. One ear had been almost torn from her head. A quick examination of the body suggested that an attempt had been made to strangle her, and that when this had failed her assailant had attacked her with an iron bar. Her blood-stained clothing had been torn to shreds. And finally, although it was not revealed until the post-mortem, she had been shot through the head.

A careful inspection of the site disclosed the probable pattern of events. By analysing marks in the soft ground it became apparent that the girl had survived for a short time even after she had been taken for dead. At one point her body had been placed across the railway track, presumably to be run over by a passing train to disguise the fact of murder, but she had managed to crawl a few yards from the track before dying.

The police were called from Pretoria, and they arrived very quickly. Coetzee brought them up to date on the events of the morning. It was obvious, he suggested, that the girl had been hit by a train and thrown clear of the track. The police acknowledged the suggestion but made no comment. They carried out their own methodical and detailed examination of the site, and drew their own conclusions.

They discovered, for instance, that the girl had not been alone. In addition to her own identifiable footprints there were also those of a man, and it was also evident that in approaching the embankment they had climbed a fence running parallel to the railroad. There was no indication of violence or a struggle, which suggested that the girl and the unknown man had been friends or perhaps lovers right up to the moment of the murder.

The body was removed to a mortuary in Pretoria. The post-mortem examination revealed that the girl had been shot in the head with a 0.22 bullet. This had not at first been apparent because of her mutilated condition. The post-mortem also revealed another significant fact—that the girl was pregnant. She carried no identification, or if she had then her killer had removed the papers. For a time it looked as if this was to be another unsolved murder mystery, with evidence so slight that the police had no trails to pursue. However, the case was widely reported in the newspapers, which published a detailed description of the girl, who was fair with short hair.

Detective Sergeant Coetzee himself took a very personal interest in the case. After all, the murder had taken place in his particular railway territory. Coetzee was something of a dedicated career man, and well connected in South African society. For one thing he was engaged to marry the daughter of his immediate superior in the railway police organization, and he was, in fact, living at his fiancee's home; for another, he was a popular and highly skilled Rugby football player—an important game in South Africa—and there was a great deal of talk and press comment that he should be selected to play for the South African team.

Sporting interests aside, Coetzee had been carrying out his own private investigation into the case of the murdered girl, and had managed to discover a railway engine which had traces of blood and fragments of flesh adhering to its front. But, unfortunately, a pathological examination of the remains established beyond doubt that they were from a sheep which had been struck by the engine, and were not human at all.

When it seemed as if the case was about to fade into obscurity, unsolved and unsolvable, the press publicity paid off. A letter was received from a farmer living more than one hundred miles from Pretoria. He thought it possible that he might be able to identify the dead girl. The police brought him to the town to view the body, and he recognized the girl as a young woman named Miss Opperman, who had been his domestic help.

He also handed to the police a letter which had arrived for Miss Opperman after she had left the farm for her rendezvous with death at the end of January. It was a letter confirming arrangements for a meeting with a man in Pretoria, and it was signed by J. H. Coetzee.

The farmer was additionally able to confirm that the Coetzee who had signed the letter was without doubt Railway Detective Sergeant Coetzee. He knew quite a lot about Coetzee's clandestine relationship with the girl. He was able to tell the police that Miss Opperman had first met Coetzee at a dance six months earlier, and that they had met on several occasions since then, and had once been found in bed together.

Challenged by the police, Coetzee was baffled. The farmer's evidence was completely false. Either he had wrongly identified the body (which in view of its mutilated condition was difficult to identify, anyway) or by sheer coincidence he had managed to turn up another man named Coetzee who had gone off with Miss Opperman. As for himself, he had never even heard of Miss Opperman, let alone go to bed with her.

How could anyone suppose that he, a well-known public sportsman, could be cynical enough to investigate with dogged persistence a brutal murder which he himself was alleged to have committed? The farmer's story was ridiculous.

Nevertheless, the farmer's story could not be easily dismissed. The evidence was still circumstantial, but on the strength of it Coetzee was arrested and charged with murder.

The trial took place six weeks later, but meanwhile the police were able to dig out prosecution evidence which proved to be damning. In the course of intensive investigations they discovered that Coetzee, on the date in question, had sent a native railway constable to Pretoria station to meet Miss Opperman on her arrival, he was to give her a message that she should wait there until he (Coetzee) joined her.

The message had duly been delivered, and Miss Opperman had been seen waiting at the station. Later she had been observed leaving the station in the company of a man in a brown suit, and there was a witness to swear that he had seen Coetzee arrive at the station at about that time wearing such a brown suit.

Finally, the police in a search of Coetzee's home found a supply of 0.22 revolver ammunition, but no trace of a gun which might be the murder weapon, even though it was known that Coetzee was normally armed with a 0.22 revolver in the course of his duty.

At the trial the prosecution suggested that the motive for murder was clearly that Miss Opperman's pregnancy, with Coetzee undeniably the father of her gestating child, represented a serious threat both to Coetzee's career in the railway police and his pending marriage to the daughter of his superior officer. Under pressure from Miss Opperman, at a time when she was six months pregnant and probably demanding either marriage or financial support, he had arranged for her to travel to Pretoria to meet him in order to discuss the situation.

In the prosecution's view they had been unable to reach any kind of agreement. The railway embankment seemed an odd place for an intimate and possibly recriminative discussion, but at least it offered privacy and isolation—the conditions Coetzee would have been seeking if he had had murder in mind. At some point, in fear or anger, he had attempted to strangle her; when she was unconscious he had dragged her body on to the railway track and had savagely beaten her with an iron bar to make it appear as if she had been struck by a train and killed. Finally, just in case she was not properly dead and a train might not arrive in time, he had shot her through the head with his official 0.22 police revolver.

The prosecution's case was admittedly strong, and there was only a feeble defence, concentrating on points of alleged-ly inconsistent detail. Defending counsel put it to the jury that Coetzee could not have been the father of Miss Opperman's unborn child if one examined carefully the dates on which they had met, when intimacy might be presumed to have taken place, and related that time-table to the pathological estimate of the age from conception of the foetus. This particular exercise in correlation was not taken seriously in court. An attempt was made to prove that the male footprints on the embankment were not those of Coetzee's, and that, in any case, according to entries in his diary he had been elsewhere on certain occasions when he was supposed to have been with Miss Opperman (the prosecution claimed that these diary entries had been written in after the murder).

It was also put forward by the defence that although Coetzee went to Pretoria station on the night of 31 January to meet Miss Opperman, she had not turned up (on the other hand, the native constable had testified that he had in fact met her and acted as escort for a short period). But it was impossible for the defence to counter the prosecution's strong-est point, namely, why had Coetzee denied all knowledge of Miss Opperman when first challenged by the police, when the farmer had produced the letter to Miss Opperman bearing Coetzee's own signature?

Virtually the only demonstrable fact in the accused's favour was that, despite the incredibly violent mutilation of the girl, no traces of blood were ever found on Coetzee's clothes. The prosecution suggested that while committing the murder he had worn a raincoat which he had later destroyed. Presum-ably he had also destroyed his shoes and trousers.

Under the circumstances, however, with the evidence heav-ily weighted against him, it was not surprising that Coetzee was found guilty. A man who had started with the advantage of being assigned to investigate a murder committed by himself had failed to get away with the crime. But other extraneous factors were to intervene surprisingly to save his life.

Although found guilty and therefore liable to the death penalty, Coetzee benefited by a new South African law passed just a few days before his trial. This law gave a judge power to pass a lesser sentence than death upon a convicted murderer—provided there was a recommendation of mercy from the jury.

Since Coetzee was a well-known sporting figure in South African circles, and therefore vulnerable to malicious rumour and publicity, the jury decided that the charge of paternity made by the dead Miss Opperman might well have been false. There was no denying the fact of her pregnancy, but this did not necessarily prove that Coetzee was the father of the child. Such a charge, if false, would constitute a severe provocation to a man whose career and future marriage were at stake. In any case, it seemed obvious that the crime had not been coldly premeditated but had been committed on impulse, perhaps in an instant of uncontrollable anger and resentment. The jury therefore added a rider to their verdict recommending mercy.

The judge therefore sentenced Coetzee to life imprisonment with hard labour, but he made it clear that he was unhappy at having to pass such a severe sentence on a reputable citizen who had acquitted himself in a manly fashion on the sporting fields and who had shown such a "heroic demeanour throughout this terrible fortnight of trial".

Coetzee went to prison instead of the gallows by a fortuitous change in the South African penal law at a timely moment. He was probably the only brutal murderer in history to receive the compliments and commiseration of the judge and jury because of his prowess in Rugger.

Chapter 14

THE DOLL LADY

IMAGINE receiving one day a returned letter in the post marked "Address Unknown". On examining it you find that it is addressed to someone you have never heard of in Argentina, a country with which you have had no contact whatever. But in the top left-hand corner of the envelope is typed your own name and address for return in case of non-delivery.

On opening the envelope you find a typewritten letter signed by yourself and mentioning certain matters which only you could know about—but the phrasing, grammar and spelling of the letter are only semi-literate and it could not have been written by you, not even in a moment of aberration.

Such was the experience of a Miss Mary Wallace of Springfield, Ohio, in the United States of America, in June, 1942. There was no mistaking her own name and address in the top left-hand corner of the envelope—nor the rubber-stamped impression which announced "Address Unknown" in both English and Spanish.

The envelope was addressed to a Señora Inez Lopez de Molinali, 2563 O'Higgins, Buenos Aires, Argentina, but Miss Wallace knew nobody in Buenos Aires, let alone a Señora Lopez de Molinali.

The letter itself was even more disturbing, for though it was typewritten it had been signed with a pen in a passable forgery of her own handwriting. And that in itself was perhaps the most disturbing thing of all.

As to the contents of the letter—well, it consisted of domestic and rather vague chit-chat, giving recent news but saying nothing very much. There were references to personal domestic events which were perfectly true, however: the fact that a nephew of Miss Wallace had been very ill with a brain tumour, a brief reference to Miss Wallace's collection of costumed dolls, and the fact that she had recently given a talk to an arts club on the subject of dolls—all as if actually written by herself, but not in the way that she would, in fact, have written it.

Certain other statements in the letter were quite meaningless—that she had acquired "three lovely Irish dolls", one of which was an old fisherman with a net over his back, another an old woman with wood on her back, and the third a little boy. There was also an obscure reference to an unknown Mr Shaw who "has destroyed your letter", and whose car had been damaged but was now being repaired. Finally, an enigmatic postscript which announced: "Mother wanted to go on to Louville but due to our worry the Louville plan out our minds now". It was hardly the kind of grammar and syntax that Miss Wallace would have written, whether the message had been meaningless or not.

Needless to say, Miss Wallace felt most uneasy about this strange letter which purportedly had been written and signed by herself, and posted to an address in Buenos Aires which did not exist. She did the sensible and logical thing—she handed it over to the postal authorities for investigation. And so she set in motion a complex investigation which was to involve the U.S. Federal Bureau of Investigation in two years of painstaking work to solve the mystery. Miss Wallace, without realizing it, had hit a very sinister jackpot that had to do with dolls and Japanese in the months following Pearl Harbour.

So far as the American Post Office was concerned the letter had been handled in the usual way. It had been posted in New York, and as it had been addressed to a neutral country in time of war it had been censored before transmission, and that was as much as they could say. That none of the contents of the letter had in fact been censored merely revealed that it apparently contained no information infringing on security. However, to be on the safe side, the Post Office decided to pass the letter on to the Federal Bureau of Investigation, and the F.B.I., who were at that time more bemused by the war against Japan than by chatty letters about Irish dolls, tended to regard it as some kind of unintelligible hoax. There was no such address as 2563 O'Higgins in Buenos Aires. It could have been that an error had been made in the address on this one occasion. It could also be that if previous letters had been sent to the same fictitious address that they too had been returned to the sender, stamped "Address Unknown"—not necessarily to Mary Wallace. It was a kinky line of investigation and would almost certainly prove to be a waste of time, but the F.B.I. in its methodical way decided to play out the permutations and combinations of chance and circumstance. It was probably flogging a dead horse, but every dead horse was not necessarily irrevocably dead, and it might kick.

As a matter of routine the F.B.I. checked dead-letter offices throughout the United States on the grounds that some of the senders' addresses might have been fictitious. On the other hand, the writer of the original "doll" letter must have known Mary Wallace quite well in order to be able to mention certain personal domestic matters—and must have had a specimen of her signature in order to make a reasonable forgery of it. This proved to be an unrewarding line of investigation, for Mary Wallace was very well known throughout the state for her collection of accurately costumed dolls representing different countries and different periods of history. She was regarded as an expert on the subject. She had lectured extensively and had been featured in newspapers and magazines, and her circle of friends and acquaintances was very wide. Much of her life was therefore public domain. She conducted an extensive correspondence with strangers on the subject of dolls, so that her signature was available to many people. Her nephew's illness had been a topic of local conversation for a long time and could hardly be regarded as a secret. The number of people who could, therefore, have written the letter and forged the signature was too large and too diffuse to permit of serious investigation. A parallel line of attack was required, but meanwhile the routine check on dead-letter offices throughout the country went on.

Some weeks later the F.B.I. and the Post Office managed to turn up four dead letters, in different parts of the country, all addressed to Señora Inex Lopez de Molinali at the same O'Higgins address in Buenos Aires. All had been stamped "Address Unknown", but had never been returned to the sender because the return addresses had also proved to be non-existent. The letters had been mailed from places as far apart as Seattle, San Francisco, Oakland and Portland in Oregon. When opened, all the letters were found to refer to dolls and doll collections—but not one of them was signed by Mary Wallace.

At this point the F.B.I. began to sit up and take notice. The coincidental odds were beginning to mount up, if not add up. Even if Señora Inez Lopez de Molinali existed in real life, her address certainly did not. At least five letters had been posted to her from different parts of the U.S.A., four of them from fictitious addresses and the fifth from the real address of Mary Wallace, although she claimed that the letter was a forgery. All the letters referred to dolls. The over-all pattern of this strange and apparently futile operation seemed rather sinister.

This was the year following the Japanese attack on Pearl Harbour, and America was well and truly in the war. Already there had been numerous investigations by the F.B.I. of alleged espionage, and the exposure and arrest of German and Japanese sympathizers. Although on the surface there was nothing to suggest that the doll letters were in any way connected with espionage or subversive activity, the F.B.I. could not afford to take any chances.

The letters were handed over to the Bureau's code and cypher department, where they were given the full treatment. Little emerged. It was vaguely suggested that the references to dolls and figurines might be a type of cryptogram containing information on the condition and disposition of U.S. naval vessels. The mention of "Mr Shaw" in the first letter—the one supposedly signed by Mary Wallace—was thought to be a possible reference to a U.S. destroyer named "Shaw" which had been bombed at Pearl Harbour, and, at the time the letter was written, had been under repair at Honolulu. But even so, the cryptographic analysis of the letters was too nebulous to justify jumping to conclusions.

The F.B.I. agents switched to a different tack, and began to concentrate on the idea of dolls—the one factor common to the contents of all the letters. This brought them back to Mary Wallace, the point of origin of the whole mysterious case, and her famous collection of specialized dolls. They asked questions which she answered quite openly, and they asked permission to examine the various letters, papers and documents in her files relating to the acquisition and disposal of dolls.

A detailed study of the typewriter faces used in all the letters produced a positive result. The F.B.I. discovered that the five letters to Señora Inex of Buenos Aires had been typed by the same machine that had typed some of the business letters. And, most important discovery of all, the letter which had been returned to Mary Wallace had been typed by the same machine that had typed a business letter from a doll shop on Madison Avenue, in New York. At last there was a lead to follow up.

This particular doll shop was well known to Mary Wallace, and indeed to all connoisseurs of the doll-collecting world. It was a small shop which specialized in "sophisticated" dolls for those who took their hobby seriously, in the same way as a stamp shop caters exclusively for dedicated philatelists. The shop was run by a tiny middle-aged woman of slight build (five feet tall and weighing only seven stone) named Mrs Velvalee Dickenson, who was acknowledged to be an expert on dolls of all kinds. At the time Mrs Dickenson and her shop came into the focus of the F.B.I.'s bleak eye she was in mourning, for her husband had died three months earlier.

Mrs Velvalee Dickenson was a disappointing suspect. She was the most unlikely candidate for espionage activity imaginable. She was frail and gentle and devoid of cunning. She was highly regarded by collectors of dolls for her integrity and experience. Nevertheless, the F.B.I. systematically checked her background. It was routine—maybe a waste of time—but it had to be done to complete the basic paper-work.

They discovered that before opening her doll shop she had worked in the doll department of a big store, and this seemed to indicate that dolls were a product which had always interested and fascinated her. They were as much a hobby as a job. The shop had been successful enough, but the war had produced a big slump in the special doll and figurine business. Nevertheless, she seemed to enjoy continued prosperity. It was also learned that up to the time of Pearl Harbour she had been a regular visitor at the Japanese Club in New York, and at the Japanese Institute. This was not particularly significant, for many Americans had maintained social relations with the Japanese in America prior to the war, and their loyalty was not in doubt.

However, the F.B.I. decided that Velvalee's financial background merited more careful investigation. They pursued the subject methodically and unobtrusively. The first thing that became apparent was that Mr and Mrs Dickenson had started with very little capital. From 1937, when they had first come to New York from California, until 1941, the year of Pearl Harbour, they had largely survived on loans and bank over-drafts. Then, unaccountably, in 1941 they had suddenly ac-quired a substantial sum of money—enough to enable them to open the doll shop on Madison Avenue. The explanation was that Mr Dickenson had been repaid a large outstanding debt from friends on the West Coast, but as he was now dead that was difficult to check.

The F.B.I. also discovered that Velvalee Dickenson had visited the West Coast on several occasions during the year following Pearl Harbour—the period when the Buenos Aires letters had been mailed and duly "returned to sender".

Things were beginning to crystallize, but not into any recognizable shape, and so far there was no firm evidence to justify action of any kind. More spadework was required to get down to the roots of the matter. The San Francisco office of the F.B.I. was asked to investigate the Dickensons' back-ground before they moved to New York. This was a long and arduous task. But eventually the San Francisco office reported back that Velvalee had been born and educated in California, and after leaving school had married and worked in her husband's brokerage business—handling Japanese accounts. Furthermore, she had been well connected, both socially and in business, with members of the Japanese Consulate. The brokerage business had gone into liquidation in 1935 after the depression, and from then until 1941 the Dickensons had been in financial difficulties.

The evidence was accumulating. It was beginning to look as if frail, gentle Velvalee was a Japanese agent, unlikely though it seemed. On the other hand, it could have been her husband, who was now dead and beyond interrogation. The letters to Buenos Aires now began to fit into the jig-saw—they might have been code messages to other Japanese agents in neutral Argentina. It was possible that the letters had actually been typed by her husband, who had been alive at the relevant time, but different typewriters had been involved, and the letters had been posted from different West Coast towns. It was Velvalee herself who had occasionally travelled and toured in the West.

The next step in the long investigation was a detailed and meticulous check on hotels at which Mrs Velvalee Dickenson had stayed during her visits to the West Coast—plus a methodical search for typewriters which could have produced the Buenos Aires letters posted from Seattle, San Francisco, Portland and Oakland on the dates concerned. It says much for the unremitting patience of the F.B.I. that in due course all the hotels in question were identified and the actual typewriters located.

So far so good—but the evidence still did not add up to a viable prosecution case in law. It was not illegal to send letters to a fictitious address from another fictitious address; it was not illegal to write about dolls; and it was not subversive to have been friendly with Japanese before the war. There was no positive proof of espionage. The F.B.I. at this stage were sure that they had pinned down a spy, but there was not a shred of solid evidence that would guarantee a conviction in a court of law. Intuition is not fact.

Taking another deep breath, the F.B.I. agents went back to the accounts of the doll shop on Madison Avenue. After a careful study of bank statements and balance sheets they came to the conclusion that the revenue from turnover was hardly sufficient to meet expenses, and that Mrs Velvalee Dickenson was, in fact, spending more in cash than she was withdrawing from her account at the bank. Where, then, was the extra money coming from?

Further painstaking enquiries revealed that Velvalee frequently paid many of her bills in high-denomination banknotes of one hundred dollars or more. From the moment America entered the war, records of the numbers of such notes were kept by banks as a protection against black market activities. But, more significantly, a similar check had been made on American currency issued to Japanese embassies and consulates in the U.S.A. for some six months prior to the

Pearl Harbour attack, when Japanese assets had been frozen and trade restrictions imposed.

It was therefore possible, if you liked doing things the hard way, to compare the numbers of the high-denomination notes paid by Velvalee Dickenson in personal transactions with those issued to the Japanese embassies. After a long and wearying number-by-number audit—computers had not then been devised for commercial purposes—four 100-dollar bills used by Mrs Dickenson were identified as money supplied to the Japanese for embassy budgeting. The case was closing in.

At this point the F.B.I. were keeping frail little Velvalee under continual surveillance, although she was not aware of it. They had incriminating evidence, but still not evidence enough. Four hundred dollars paid out in Japanese allocated currency did not amount to a watertight case for the prosecution. It was possible to argue that the money had been passed on to her by customers in her doll shop, and that she had received it and used it in all innocence. Something more definite was needed.

Finally, in 1944, Velvalee was followed by F.B.I. agents into a bank where she asked for the key of a safe-deposit box. The agents, with the co-operation of the bank manager, intervened just as the little woman was opening her box. They took possession of it and checked the contents. Inside they found nearly eighteen thousand dollars, of which eight thousand dollars were later identified as high-denomination currency issued to the Japanese by the U.S. Treasury before Pearl Harbour.

Velvalee was indicted on four counts: espionage, conspiracy to commit espionage, secret service as an agent of the enemy, and violation of the censorship laws.

In defence she claimed that she knew nothing of what had been going on, and that the entire operation, if it was espionage, had been carried on by her dead husband. The false address, "O'Higgins" in Buenos Aires, had presumably been an unfortunate error of misreading the street or mishearing instructions. She had not taken any part in it other than to use the money which she had inherited. Even the Buenos Aires letters, she claimed, had been written by her husband—although she admitted to having copy-typed them and posted them, but the contents had been meaningless to her, except in so far as they had been concerned with dolls.

The case may have looked clear-cut to the F.B.I., but Velvalee had a point, and the dead husband could not be called to give evidence—nor could the Japanese embassy officials who had made use of his or her services. The available evidence was circumstantial; admittedly Velvalee had been using Japanese-allocated currency, but it could not be shown that she personally had passed on information about the U.S. Navy to the enemy. Because of this, three counts of the indictment failed, and she was only convicted on one count—the lesser one of violation of the censorship laws. She received the maximum sentence of ten years' imprisonment plus a ten thousand dollar fine.

Perhaps the most curious incident in this strange and still debatable case was the letter to Buenos Aires which was returned to Mary Wallace. The four previous letters to Señora Inez had been from fictitious names and addresses, but for the fifth the real name and address of one of her customers who was an expert on dolls and something of a local celebrity had been used. It was this one foolish and inexplicable slip which set the F.B.I. on the trail of what was probably one of the oddest and most futile espionage operations of the century.

Chapter 15

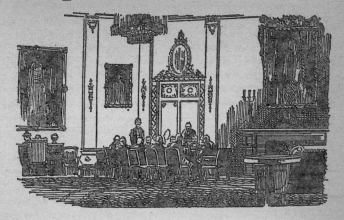

THE CHEAT

HONOUR has always been taken very seriously by the English, and at one time a question of honour could frequently be a matter of life and death. In the Victorian era, to be accused of cheating at cards was a very serious charge indeed, particularly among the upper strata of society. Such a charge could ruin a man's career, and kill him stone dead in social terms. And to put oneself in the position of being accused of cheating a member of the Royal Family was seldom if ever done. But to defend such a charge by bringing an action for slander and calling the Prince of Wales as a witness was guaranteed to create a scandal that would reverberate in the press for a long time after the event, and gave rise to a spate of hypocritical moralizing and pontificating—a pastime at which the English tend to excel.

Sir William Gordon-Cumming did all this and more in 1890, and so unleashed a tidal wave of criticism which was directed at, not Sir William himself, but "Bertie", the Prince of Wales, whose only offence was that he had joined in a game of baccarat at a house-party.

Aged forty-two, Sir William was, if not exactly wealthy, at

least a man of adequate means. He was a lieutenant-colonel in
the Scots Guards, and had served as a regular officer for
twenty-three years. He was well connected in aristocratic
circles and had, in fact, been a personal friend of the Prince
of Wales (Prince Edward Albert, popularly known as Bertie)
for many years. He was regarded in society as a blue chip,
and this was a very good reason why he was invited to join an
important house-party organized by a Mr Arthur Wilson, who
was a well-known ship-owner, during St Leger Week in
September, 1890. The guest of honour was the Prince of
Wales.

After dinner on the first day of the party, a game of
baccarat was played, with the Prince of Wales accorded the
privilege of being "banker". In the game the players are
divided into two teams on either side of the banker, who acts
in partnership with the croupier. Cards are dealt, and the
object of the game is for a player to obtain an eight or a nine,
the dealer offering further cards for this purpose. Each side is
represented by one player, and the other members of the side
in placing their bets have to rely upon the luck or judgment of
their representatives. Coloured counters are used for stakes.
On this particular occasion the stakes were not high, and the
game was being played for amusement rather than profit.

The guests sitting at the long table on either side of the
Prince of Wales included, apart from Sir William Gordon-
Cumming, distinguished people such as the Earl and Countess
of Coventry, the Earl of Craven, Lady Bingham, General and
Mrs Owen Williams, Mr Christopher Sykes, and, of course,
their hosts, Mr and Mrs Arthur Wilson, and their son, twenty
two-year-old Stanley Wilson. Stanley was sitting next to Sir
William, and it was he who first instigated the accusation of
cheating which was to cause so much trouble.

Stanley himself was what today might be described as a
wealthy idle layabout. He had spent one year at Magdalene
College, Cambridge, but had left because he considered his
studies a waste of time. After that he had spent a few weeks
in his father's shipping business, but didn't fancy it. For some
two years he had not worked at all, though he claimed to be
an expert baccarat player. Certainly, he followed the game
that evening with close interest, and before long was surprised
to observe a certain irregularity.

According to Stanley, Sir William was adding counters to

his original stake as the game progressed favourably for his own side. On one occasion, he claimed, a single red five-pound counter was mysteriously multiplied to three red counters worth fifteen pounds when Sir William's side won the game, so that he was paid out three times as much by the bank.

It was done this way, Stanley explained. During the game Sir William had a habit of keeping his hands loosely clasped over the table in front of him—and Stanley had seen something red—a five-pound counter—concealed in those clasped hands. Worse, Stanley had actually witnessed Sir William's hands opening to allow three red counters to fall on to his original five-pound stake, thus winning twenty pounds. And Stanley also accused Sir William of quietly withdrawing counters when the game was running against him—and all in the presence of the Prince of Wales.

Stanley, hardly able to credit the evidence of his own eyes, told one of the guests. He happened to be an officer named Levett who was serving in the same regiment as Sir William. Naturally Levett was sceptical, but he undertook to keep a watchful eye on Sir William's style of play. To his astonishment, he saw his brother officer add two red counters to his stake during the progress of the game. The counters had been dropped from Sir William's clasped hands, just as Stanley had said.

However, Stanley was circumspect enough to say nothing to the others that evening. Levett quietly asked him to take no action for the sake of the regimental honour. Later that night Stanley decided to mention the matter to his mother, and also his brother-in-law, Lycett Green. Both were incredulous and appalled, but most anxious to hush the whole thing up to avoid any scandal in the presence of the Prince.

The next day followed the same pattern, and after dinner baccarat was again played. But this time Sir William was playing under unsuspected surveillance by four people, three of whom no doubt were fervently hoping that the whole sordid business had been an hallucination of Stanley's. Before long, however, Lycett Green saw to his horror that Sir William was indeed adding to his stake when the cards were running favourably, and so increasing his winnings in an unbelievably brash and naïve fashion.

It was a tricky and dangerous situation, but Green did the right thing. Resisting an urge to denounce Sir William there and then, he left the table and went to his room. There he wrote a terse note to his mother describing what he had observed, and had it delivered to her by the butler. Mrs Wilson, an experienced hostess, did nothing immediately, but merely kept a closer watch on the game, and Sir William in particular. Then she too noticed that during one coup Sir William's original five-pound stake increased mysteriously to fifteen pounds as the game was won by his side. She took no action, but spent a great deal of time pondering the delicate situation.

On the following day the entire party went to see the St Leger, and, this entertainment having been successfully accomplished, Mrs Wilson and Lycett Green decided that the moment had come to expose Sir William's unethical behaviour. Green asked the Prince of Wales and a few of the principal guests to attend a private meeting. He told them bluntly that he and others had seen Sir William cheating at baccarat, and a question of honour was involved. After some discussion it was decided that the best way of dealing with the situation would be to ask Sir William to sign a declaration that he would never again play cards, against a solemn guarantee that those who had witnessed the actual cheating would undertake never to mention the matter again. In this way it was felt that an unpleasant scandal which might involve the Prince could be avoided.

The Prince having given his assent to this procedure, the deputation left him and sought out Sir William himself, to put to him this considerate and humane solution to the problem which his peccadillo had created. To their surprise, Sir William not only declined to do as they suggested, but angrily denied their accusation of cheating and insisted on seeing the Prince himself.

Although Sir William was an old friend of some ten years' standing, the Prince quite correctly maintained an objective and impartial attitude. He pointed out that an impressive number of eye-witnesses claimed to have seen for themselves the alleged cheating. It was not for the Prince to act as judge or take sides; the parties involved would have to negotiate their own settlement by agreement.

The matter was referred back in a democratic way to the deputation of principal guests. Sir William demanded the right to refer the matter to the Duke of Cambridge, his Commander-in-Chief, since regimental honour was involved. General Owen Williams, however, thought that the Commander-in-Chief might take an even more serious view of the situation, whatever the rights or the wrongs of the matter, since it involved the Prince of Wales. In the cut and thrust of argument, Sir William suddenly surrendered and agreed to sign the proposed document in which he would undertake never again to play cards. The document was a clear confession of guilt, but taking advice from two friends, though still protesting his innocence, Sir William signed. The incident was apparently over.

The document was duly witnessed by the Prince of Wales himself, and six other guests. It was then handed over to the Prince's private secretary for safe keeping. The actual wording of the statement which Sir William signed was:

"In consideration of the promise made by the gentlemen whose names are subscribed to preserve silence with reference to an accusation which has been made in regard to my conduct at baccarat on the nights of Monday and Tuesday, 8th and 9th of September 1890 at Tranby Croft, I will on my part solemnly undertake never to play cards again as long as I live."

The matter might honourably have ended at this point if Sir William had not had second thoughts about the matter. Suddenly, bitterness and resentment took possession of his mind. He became obsessed by a single-minded determination to vindicate his reputation among his small circle of accusers. He started legal proceedings for slander, claiming that he had been obliged to sign the damaging undertaking, fully realizing that it was an admission of guilt, in the belief that it was the only possible way of avoiding a public scandal involving the Prince of Wales—whether the facts were true or not. Subsequent events demonstrated that the question of cheating was of minor importance compared with the Prince's involvement in a game of baccarat.

On Sir William's side, one might well consider it unlikely that a high-ranking officer of a prestige regiment, a man of private income who had been a personal friend of the Prince of Wales for over a decade, should cheat at cards for relatively low stakes in full view of the Prince, his hosts, colleagues and friends—cheat in a fashion that could hardly escape detection by any player studying the pattern of stakes in consecutive games. But why should he cheat when he did not need the money, and could ill afford to run the risk of jeopardizing his honour and integrity—not to mention his long-standing friendship with the Prince? He had everything to lose and nothing to gain, apart from a comparatively trivial sum of money.

On the other hand, his accusers had not acted from any malicious motives—on the contrary, they were only too anxious to hush up the whole sordid business. The written and signed confession was probably a tactical error, but they were not trying to ruin him, for they too had promised to make no further reference to the incident. They were merely trying to restrain him from what they regarded as any further dishonesty which might provoke a scandal. The thing could have died a natural death, but it was Sir William himself who initiated the slander action and thus exposed the indelicate matter to the critical and unsympathetic gaze of the public. This was not an error of tactics, it was an error of strategy.

At the trial the emphasis was placed squarely on Sir William's utter denial of the accusation of cheating that had been laid against him. It was hoped that the defendants would withdraw and settle out of court. But the situation was complicated by the undeniable fact that Sir William, the plaintiff, had signed the compromising document—which amounted to an admission of guilt. Would an innocent man have thus smeared his reputation in the presence of the Prince of Wales, who was also an old friend, knowing that he intended to pursue the fight to the bitter end? On the other hand, might not the fact that the Prince of Wales would almost certainly be involved in any subsequent scandal have exerted a moral pressure on Sir William to take the easy way out through a strong sense of loyalty—to accept the role of scapegoat for a while, until he had had time to reflect and build up indignation and resentment against his accusers? The issues involved were complex and confusing, and the aftermath which materialized in print in the newspapers was equally so. The case evoked an eruption of British po-faced moralizing almost without equal in the long history of English hypocrisy.

At the trial, democracy came to the fore. One of the points which was underlined was that Sir William had been accused and condemned in the presence of the Prince without a proper hearing, and certainly without any acceptable investigation. He had been denounced and sentenced in an arbitrary manner; it had been all prosecution and pressure, with virtually no defence. The incriminating document which he had signed on the advice of his old friends Lord Coventry and General Owen Williams had been not so much a confession as a gesture of self-sacrifice—and yet neither Lord Coventry nor the General had personally witnessed any evidence of cheating, nor had the Prince. All three of them knew Sir William as an officer and gentleman of undeniable integrity. The issue had clearly been prejudged, and indeed prejudiced, by the Wilsons, because as hosts they had been particularly sensitive as to conduct and protocol in the presence of His Royal Highness.

Sir William's counsel made a brilliant closing speech which many people thought had swung the sympathy of the jury towards the plaintiff. But the Lord Chief Justice in his summing-up seemed to favour the defendants. The jury took only thirteen minutes to reach a verdict: they found for the defendants. The inevitable implications of this decision was that Sir William had been cheating, after all.

So much for unfortunate Sir William Gordon-Cumming, whose career was shattered from that moment. He was discharged from the Army and went into an embittered retirement. Shortly after the end of the trial he married, despite the profound disapproval of his bride's parents. He died in May, 1930, at his home in Scotland. The obituary notice in *The Times* referred back to the scandal and the trial, but the terms were more gentle and sympathetic than those used at the time of the event. Whether Sir William ever played cards again during his retirement is not on record; having signed the undertaking not to do so, and being a man of honour, it is likely that he did not.

However, the end of the trial was by no means the end of the matter. The battle continued in the newspapers of the day, but the target of criticism now was not Sir William but the Prince of Wales. The fact that Sir William had cheated was of no great moment; what aroused the ire of the critics and hypocrites was that the heir to the English throne had been playing baccarat.

The Prince of Wales was very popular, and he was generally and affectionately known as Bertie. But for some years there had been an atmosphere of antipathy towards the royal family because of Queen Victoria's long seclusion following the death of Albert, the Prince Consort. She had been criticized in the press and in Parliament, and there were even advocates of setting up a British republic.

Bertie was very active and made many public appearances. Although he was well liked, however, certain factions noted his inclination towards pleasure-seeking and gambling. Victorian England was a great hunting ground for puritanical killjoys, who self-righteously ordained that the Monarchy should set a correct moral tone for the nation to emulate. The baccarat slander case was, therefore, a wonderful opportunity for the pontificators to express their hot-gospelling ideas in print.

The Times claimed that the nation was shocked to learn that the Prince of Wales had been associating with gamblers at the baccarat table—and added that it was a pity that the Prince had not also been obliged to sign a declaration that he would never play cards again.

The case and subsequent commentaries were widely reported throughout the Continent, and gave some European commentators plenty of scope to sneer at the English mask of hollow virtue—not to mention the smug complacency of press sermonizing. In France and America, however, the papers took a more sympathetic view, and could see no reason why the Prince should not be entitled to seek relaxation from his onerous duties in an occasional game of chance. While there was no sympathy for Sir William, the cheat (he had virtually been forgotten), American and French opinion tended towards the view that the Prince, whose involvement in the unsavoury affair had been merely coincidental, was being unfairly pilloried for what was hardly even an indiscretion.

The Church, too, had to have its say. It greatly deplored the Prince's support of the evil vice of gambling, and suggested that the Prince would be much better employed in setting an example by refusing in future to acknowledge gambling in any form at all. One ecclesiastic stated uncompromisingly that the Prince "had been convicted of being concerned in an infamous abomination". Condemnation came from pulpits all over the country, and most of it was grossly unfair. The Prince, unable to reply, had to suffer in silence.

The situation was precisely what Sir William's signature on the confession document had been calculated to prevent.

Even the Archbishop of Canterbury intervened to deplore the deluge of ill-considered utterances from so many religious organizations and denominations. He felt constrained to explain that His Royal Highness was very much opposed to gambling as such, but playing cards for stakes which all the players could well afford could hardly be considered as gambling. But what he apparently did not realize is that any slight and apparent misdemeanour by a Royal personage becomes an inevitable target for cant and spleen from busybodies who are more concerned with publicizing their narrow views than reforming social evils and injustices. Even today the Royal Family is a welcome target for attacks by the would-be do-gooders, Sunday observers, and other self-appointed upholders of archaic and stifling conventions.

What should have been a storm in a teacup was lashed up into a veritable typhoon, and it was all centred on the Prince of Wales who was not even a principal in the affair.

And as for Sir William Gordon-Cumming himself—had he really cheated or not? Had the court action gone against him because of the involvement of the Prince? It must be remembered that to defend one's honour by bringing an action for libel or slander is one of the most dangerous ways of seeking vindication in the courts, for if the case is lost it is tantamount to a conviction against the plaintiff.

One wonders if the case would have been lost if the Prince of Wales had not been involved—indeed, one even wonders whether there would have been a case at all.

Chapter 16

THE LOST-PROPERTY OFFICE

JONATHAN WILD was born in Wolverhampton, Staffordshire, in 1682 and hanged in London in 1725, having earned during his relatively short career of crime the title "the prince of robbers". His particular niche in the hall of fame is merited by his original approach to the big business of theft. He established a "lost-property office" through which he sold back to his victims valuable possessions which had been stolen from them, and to all intents and purposes the trade was legitimate, above-board and if anything a service to society.

Wild's early life was undistinguished. He married in his mid-twenties and his wife bore him a son. Soon afterwards he deserted his family and left Wolverhampton for ever, travelling alone to London. With no proper skills or means of supporting himself, and little inclination to work honestly for a living, he soon ran into debt and was sent to jail for more than four years. This was to prove a useful apprenticeship in the subtler business of crime. While in jail he made of point of cultivating the friendship of his fellow prisoners, and learning from them their criminal exploits and techniques in order to further his anti-social education.

By the time he was released from prison, Wild had established a useful circle of contacts among professional thieves and robbers, and he was already beginning to formulate in his mind the kind of profitable business which he could run successfully with the minimum of personal effort and involvement. As a first step he went to live with a prostitute named Mary Milliner who herself was well connected in the underworld; in this way he was able to extend his circle of acquaintances in the world of crime. He became a receiver of stolen goods, which at that time was not illegal (although very soon an Act of Parliament was to be introduced to make receiving an offence punishable by transportation for fourteen years).

When he had acquired sufficient money from his thriving business, he opened a public-house in Cripplegate, London, as a base for operations. The legislation against receiving, when it finally received the authority of Parliament, seriously inconvenienced the professional activities of Wild and his ring of thieves. But he was not a man to be defeated or outwitted by a trivial point of law. With characteristic cunning he devised a system by which he could continue receiving quite legally and at the same time "render a service" to the unfortunate victims of robbery.

It worked in this way. Stolen property was deposited with Wild. He did not run the risk of having it on his own premises, but stored it in a small warehouse which he had acquired for the purpose. Each stolen article was carefully identified, as far as was possible, with the person from whom it had been taken. Wild would then get in touch with the owner, explaining that an honest friend of his had apprehended the thief and had recovered the stolen property. The friend, finding the thief to be a wretched fellow more to be pitied than punished, had humanely decided not to put him in the hands of the authorities, for he would certainly have been hanged. The property was safe and would be returned to its owner—but, of course, the honest friend would need to be rewarded for his trouble and integrity. Most of the robbed victims were only too pleased to regain their possessions, and some willingly paid as much as half of the value of the stolen goods as a reward to the "honest friend".

Business boomed to such an extent that Wild was soon able to open an office which he ran quite openly as a kind of official lost property office. His reputation for being able successfully to recover stolen property spread so rapidly that he found it no longer necessary to communicate with his victims—they came to him. Indeed, people applied to him for the recovery of stolen articles even when he and his gang of thieves had not actually stolen them.

The cynical trade was carried on in a businesslike fashion which impressed Wild's gullible clients. A ledger was kept to record full details of claimants and their missing valuables, and the reward they were offering. Clients would be invited to call back in a few days, by which time Wild would probably, he thought, have some news of their property for them. If the reward offered was not high enough, he would say on their return visit that the thief had told his contact that he could get more money from a pawnbroker, and that the only way of making sure that their property was safely returned was to increase the reward—and this they invariably did. The "honest friend" had disappeared from Wild's negotiations; his business now operated on "confidential information" received from his extensive network of contacts who were in close touch with the underworld.

On the other side of the coin, Wild's dominion and authority over his small army of thieves and robbers increased with every new crime committed, for he knew so much about their activities that he had virtually a blackmail hold over them. In a society where theft was punishable by hanging, he was in a position to send any one of them to the gallows. He was therefore able to command their loyalty and obedience—they had little alternative.

As Wild became more prosperous and influential, so he sought to improve his social standing. He cultivated the friendship of a man named Charles Hitchin, a city marshal who operated a profitable protection racket. Wild eagerly joined in the game, which consisted of seeking out brothels and other disorderly places and demanding money as an alternative to imprisonment on trumped-up charges. Although Wild's collaboration with Hitchin did not last very long, the fact that he had associated with a city marshal conferred respectability and did much to attach a cachet of apparent official approval to his "lost-property" enterprise, which was becoming more and more lucrative. He acquired status and vanity; he dressed in expensive elegant clothes trimmed with lace, and even wore a sword—with which, one day, he cut off one of Mary Milliner's ears. Understandably they parted company soon after this incident, which was probably what Wild had intended, for it was no longer becoming of him to live with a well-known prostitute who was too openly connected with the underworld, and his own underground criminal empire was now well established and autonomous. Mary, who had helped to bring about his material success, was now an embarrassment and a liability—so she went.

It might be wondered how Wild was able to conduct this superficially legitimate business without being accused of collusion and conspiracy with the thieves concerned. His argument was plausible enough. His extensive contacts with "informers" in the underworld were such that he was able to operate an efficient intelligence service. When he received details of a robbery from a client, he was able to leave messages at certain places where the suspected thieves were likely to call and so negotiate for the goods to be returned and the reward paid—but, he insisted, at no time did he ever come into personal contact with the thieves, nor were the stolen goods ever in his personal possession.

The Wild "intelligence service" was no myth. He was only too well informed on the who and what of robbery and criminal activities generally, and for this reason he was able to exert a severe discipline over his criminal contacts. He was a good friend to those who obeyed his directives and a dangerous enemy to those who sought to break away from his domination. When, as occasionally happened, thieves whom he regarded as loyal friends were arrested and brought to trial, Wild was invariably able to secure an acquittal by arranging for essential witnesses to be bribed, or to disappear, and he would also brief the prisoners with a plausible "hard luck" story that would gain the sympathy of a judge or jury. Wild was more than just a racketeer—he was a mentor and protector of those who were faithful to his precepts. He was now justifiably known in the underworld as "the prince of robbers", not because he himself had ever stolen a thing in the accepted sense, but because he had established his own autocratic leadership and was in a position to exercise a telling summary jurisdiction which commanded the allegiance of his

subjects. Above all, Wild was no fool, nor would he suffer
fools gladly.

As part of his over-all business operation, Wild acted in
effect, and at times with utmost vigour, as a kind of one-man
police force. He was responsible for bringing many criminals
to book in the days when there was no such thing as a police
force as we know it now.

For example, in March, 1716, a young man named Knap
and his mother were attacked by a gang of five thugs at Grays
Inn in London. The young man was knocked down and
robbed, and the mother, who screamed for help, was promptly
murdered. The gang escaped, and a large reward was offered
to anyone who could provide information leading to their
arrest. Wild, using his "intelligence" service, very soon as-
sessed the identity of the five criminals. They were rounded
up at his instigation, and three of them were subsequently
hanged for murder and robbery. The large reward went to
Wild, of course, but it is doubtful whether his motives were
simply mercenary. It seems more likely that he was anxious
to use such opportunities to establish his image as a guardian
of law and order to gain official recognition as to the respectability of his lost-property office, and, generally, as a cover for
his illegal operations.

The halo of respectability was all-important, for Wild's
curious business activity was beginning to attract the attention
of the authorities. It was slowly being appreciated in official
quarters that Wild was making use of loopholes in the law to
line his own pocket without risk of imprisonment. It was also
realized that if Wild was operating within the law, and was
therefore invulnerable, then the law had to be changed. So, in
1718 a new Act of Parliament was introduced which specifi-
cally penalized Wild's "lost-property" trade. The Act laid
down that anybody recovering and returning stolen property
for reward without taking steps to prosecute the thief was
guilty of an offence punishable by imprisonment. But the new
Act did not deter Wild, whose cunning was equal to the
situation.

His policy now was to refuse to accept money at all from
clients in search of stolen property, although he agreed to
investigate their claims. When he had succeeded in "tracing"
the missing possessions, he would simply state that on information received they should deliver a certain sum of money

to a specified place on a certain day, when the stolen property would be restored. Thus, Wild was never suspected to be in direct contact with the thief, but only with the injured party, and he apparently received no reward for his intelligence operation—although, in fact, the reward money ended up in his own pocket. But since it was necessary to demonstrate to authority that his lost-property business produced some kind of income, however nominal (after all, why run a business which is not making a profit?), he pointed out to his clients that while he asked for no fee whatever for his services, if they cared to make him a gratuitous gift of money out of sheer kindness of heart, then he would not offend them by refusing it. Most of the clients were intelligent enough to realize that they were taking part in a complicated legal "fiddle", but they preferred to pay up and get their possessions back. Thus Wild obtained his reward money and gratuities too.

The new restrictions made no difference. Business continued to boom. Wild opened another "lost property" office in London and appointed a man named Abraham as manager. Abraham proved to be loyal, trustworthy and highly efficient. On one occasion a woman was robbed of £7,000, and Abraham was successful in tracking down the thieves and recovering the money in full. This was returned to the woman, who paid to Abraham a reward of £400 which he, with due honesty, handed over in full to Wild. The thieves were allowed to go free.

One wonders why Wild simply did not pocket the recovered money in a case of this kind (of which there were many). Although he was a criminal, he observed his own meticulous code of honour, and he was convinced that he was performing a useful service to society. It never occurred to him that he was exploiting society for his own personal gain. There is reason to believe that when Thief X stole silver and plate from Sir YZ, probably with Wild's knowledge and connivance, he regarded his role in returning the property for a reward as a laudable enterprise—otherwise the silver might have been pawned or melted down and never recovered. Wild, in his perverted way, thought of himself as an upholder of the law—or, at the worst, as a man of basic integrity who made a well-merited living out of restoring stolen goods to their owners, even though he had been indirectly concerned in the stealing of them.

The secret of his success was that he never became too greedy; he performed the service, accepted the risk and took his profit. He was merely an agent, but operating on rather more than a ten-per-cent basis, and even today agents balance risk against profit, but without openly flouting the law.

His policeman-like attitude was demonstrated on one occasion when Wild was approached by two women who put to him a scheme for the robbery of a wealthy old woman living in a house near Bishopsgate. They claimed she had thousands of pounds on the premises. But Wild—perhaps suspicious that the scheme was a trap—took the two women into custody and they were convicted and jailed for six months.

On another occasion when a thief named John Butler had cheated him of the proceeds of a robbery at Newington Green, Wild, in a furious rage, pursued Butler to a house in Bishopsgate where he found him hiding in a coal cellar. He threatened to have Butler hanged unless he paid up his dues on the proceeds of the robbery—and this Butler did. Even so, Butler was soon arrested and charged. He would certainly have been sentenced to death had not Wild, obeying his own strange code of honour, intervened by bribing and influencing witnesses, so that Butler was sentenced to transportation and not hanged.

One of the big problems which Wild had to solve from time to time was how to dispose of stolen property which was not claimed by its owners. To resolve this situation he bought a ship which he put in command of a man named Roger Johnson, who was an experienced thief. Wild then went into the "export" business, shipping stolen property to the Continent and trading it for other commodities such as wine, brandy, lace, etc., which were invariably smuggled into the country. So vast was the scale of this operation that Wild's overseas trade was substantial enough to operate profitably for two years. But for Wild it was the beginning of the end, and perhaps it would have been better for him had he continued to concentrate on the home market and left exports to take care of themselves.

Inevitably there was a quarrel between Wild and Johnson over the relatively trivial matter of some missing lace which Wild suspected Johnson had stolen. In the ensuing recriminations Johnson laid information with the authorities against Wild, and during the investigation which followed large quantities of stolen property were found in Wild's private warehouses, Wild's self-assurance deserted him. He went into hiding and employed numerous subterfuges to transfer blame and liability to others, but in the end he was arrested and taken into custody.

Wild was charged and indicted on eleven counts, among which the more important were:

. . . that he had been a confederate of thieves, and had directed an organization of thieves behind a cover of detecting and prosecuting offenders against the law—but in practice had prosecuted only those who had cheated him on his share of the booty.

. . . that he had established gangs of thieves and robbers for town and country districts to account to him on a business-like basis, with a view to organizing robbery as a profitable industry.

. . . that the persons employed by him were mainly ex-convicts who had returned from transportation; because they were ex-convicts they could not give evidence against him, and he had clothed, sheltered and protected them.

. . . that he had been a receiver of stolen goods for over fifteen years and had been actively engaged in robbery, owned warehouses for storing stolen goods, and had acquired a ship to export stolen property to Holland and Europe generally, where he had appointed an ex-convict as his agent.

. . . that he had employed experts to alter valuables such as watches, rings and jewellery to destroy recognition, and had used blackmail to procure false evidence to protect himself or secure protection for his criminal employees, in many cases perverting the course of justice.

The indictment was very serious, and Wild knew only too well that his life was at stake. He attempted to delay his trial by claiming that two important witnesses could not be located, but this move was not successful. In May, 1725, he was formally charged with just one typical transaction of his successful "lost property" business—stealing a quantity of lace and selling it back to the owner without apprehending and prosecuting the actual thief.

Wild was not slow in publicizing his own defence. He had pamphlets printed and distributed listing the many thieves he had "discovered, apprehended and convicted". The list included thirty-two highway robbers, twenty-two housebreakers and ten convicts who had illegally returned from transportation. Wild implied that the present charges laid against him were the result of a conspiracy of other felons who had escaped justice but were afraid that they might be tracked down and handed over to the authorities by himself. Wild, he emphasized, was a public-spirited man who had devoted his life to the fight against crime and the restoration of stolen property.

The case of the stolen lace proceeded. Wild had not actually stolen it himself, and this was admitted by the prosecution. But, it was alleged, he had been an accessory before the fact, and had received the property knowing it to be stolen. Although the evidence should have been sufficient to secure a conviction, it was narrowly based on the one instance of the stolen lace. Wild's luck held. He was given the benefit of a certain element of doubt and was adjudged not guilty.

Wild was then prosecuted on a second charge, for an offence committed while imprisoned at Newgate. This was again concerned with the stolen lace, and had to do with the restoration of the stolen property against a payment of ten guineas. After long legal arguments the judge decided, though apparently with some reluctance, that Wild was guilty in that he had maintained a secret correspondence with felons and had received money for restoring stolen goods to the owners, the money being divided between himself and the felons.

Jonathan Wild was therefore sentenced to death. Frantically he protested that he had always been a law-abiding citizen and had served the public well in returning stolen property. He pointed out that he had apprehended many felons, most of whom had been hanged. Furthermore, he had been injured and wounded by criminals during his courageous services to society, and had twice sustained a fracture of the skull and had once had his throat cut by a felon. But his eloquent pleading was all in vain. The State demanded Wild's life, and the price had to be paid in full.

Just before the time came for his execution, Wild attempted to poison himself by taking a quantity of laudanum, but it was not strong enough and merely made him sick and sleepy. While still in a semi-conscious state he was put into the cart which was to convey him to the gallows. It is reported that he was badly treated by the people in the streets, who pelted him with stones and dirt—but a public hanging was always an occasion for the release of a little harmless viciousness and brutality to which the law turned a blind eye. It was an entertainment with a Bank Holiday atmosphere.

As Wild was still in a state of confused torpor due to the laudanum, the public hangman chose not to execute him immediately, but allowed him some time to recover so that he could fully appreciate what was about to happen to him. However, this "humane" concession so angered the watching crowd that they threatened to kill the hangman himself unless he proceeded instantly with the entertainment.

So Jonathan Wild, the prince of robbers, was duly hanged for his sins against property, although he himself had never stolen anything at all. He was buried in St Pancras Churchyard, but even then he was not allowed to rest, for a few days later his corpse was stolen by body-snatchers and presumably sold for anatomical dissection. It was an ironic twist of fate which might well have amused him, had he been in a position to know about it.

Chapter 17

THE TRAIN-WRECKER

In 1931 a series of cleverly planned attempts to derail and wreck passenger trains in Eastern Europe attracted the attention of the police. Two of the attempts had been successful, resulting in great damage and loss of life, but the other two had failed and there had been no casualties. Although there was no obvious inter-connecting link, the four incidents had occurred within a period of nine months, between December, 1930, and September, 1931, within a fairly circumscribed area overlapping Austria and Hungary. The police took the view that all four derailment attempts were the work of a single agency, and an intensive but fruitless investigation was set in motion. That the wrecker was eventually caught was due to his own foolishness and lack of judgment.

The first two incidents occurred in Austria, near Anzbach. On 31 December, 1930, somebody removed a section of rail from the track in advance of the arrival of an express train. Fortunately the sabotage was discovered in good time, and no derailment took place.

A month later, on 30 January, 1931, a steel bar was fixed across the railway track in such a way as to lift the wheels from the rails. This time the train was derailed, but the driver was able to bring it to a rapid halt with minimal damage and no injuries to passengers. Since these two attempts at derailment happened within a few weeks, the Austrian police thought it possible that they had been carried out by the same individual, although the method used had been different.

Nothing happened for many months, and then a serious train crash occurred at Jueterbog, some forty miles west of Berlin. At about 9.45 p.m. on 8 August, 1931, something exploded beneath the wheels of the Basle-Berlin express. The entire train, which included seven coaches and a dining car, plunged over a thirty-foot embankment, but miraculously nobody was killed, although more than one hundred passengers were injured. This time dynamite had been used. The police located the concealed spot where the train-wrecker had detonated the explosive charge. It was about two hundred yards from the scene of the derailment, but nothing had been left behind which could possibly lead to identification of the criminal. There was no reason to link this sabotage attempt with the two which had happened in Austria some nine months earlier, but the police did not overlook the possibility. However, their investigations made no progress.

Then, just over a month later, came the final and most serious train crash in the series. It happened at half-past eleven on Saturday night, 13 September, 1931. The Budapest-Vienna Express was crossing the viaduct at Bia Torbagy, about sixteen miles west of Budapest, when a violent explosion on the track sent the train hurtling over the viaduct to the bottom of the ravine below. The engine and six coaches fell seventy-five feet. The death roll was high, and included British tourists; the casualty list was even higher. Local villagers helped to drag the dead and dying from the wreckage.

Police and railway experts carefully examined the site of the accident on the viaduct. They discovered traces of a bomb which, reconstructed, appeared to have been made up of sixteen sticks of dynamite packed into iron tubes, and they also found the electric cable used to detonate the charge.

Now the police of three countries—Austria, Germany and Hungary—were looking for train-wreckers, but with a fairly strong suspicion that they were all seeking the same man, although there was still nothing definite to connect the first two unsuccessful attempts with the second two successful ones. One factor they all had in common, however, and that was that they had all taken place either on Saturdays or on days preceding public holidays. But police enquiries seemed to lead nowhere.

In all railway crashes involving damage to property and injury to persons the railway authority inevitably receives claims for compensation, and the Bia Torbagy tragedy was no exception. Among the claims received by the Budapest Ministry of Transport responsible for railways was one from a man named Sylvester Matuska, who asked for compensation for facial injuries and loss of luggage. He had been one of the luckier passengers. But on closer inspection the authorities discovered something odd about Matuska's claim. He stated that he had been seated in the second coach on the train—but it was known for a fact that the second coach had been totally wrecked and that all the passengers in that coach had been killed outright.

The railway authorities, suspecting that Matuska was making a false claim and had never even travelled on the ill-fated train, referred the matter to the police. Checking up, the police learned that Matuska was a Hungarian who had been living for some time in Vienna. He was a thick-set middle-aged man with heavy glasses and a beard—the kind of untrained beard that had been recently grown, perhaps as a disguise. He had a wife and a twelve-year-old daughter, and was making a good living in a property business. There was no reason why he should make a false claim for what was only moderate compensation, unless for some reason he wished to establish that he had actually been on the train at the time of the crash and not elsewhere. It was in a way as if he were trying to set up an alibi of some kind. But if so, why . . . ?

The police began to dig deeper. They discovered that Matuska travelled around quite a bit, particularly at weekends. Coincidentally, he had been in Berlin at the time of the Jueterbog train derailment some forty miles to the west of the city—and he had been away from home on the two previous significant occasions when attempts had been made unsuccessfully to derail trains in Austria. Things were beginning to add up, but there was still no firm evidence. The police kept up a probing interrogation for ten days until, in the end, Matuska confessed. Yes, he admitted, it was he who had sabotaged all four trains. When his primitive efforts to tamper with the rails in Austria had failed, he had devised the dynamite charges, even going to the extreme of buying a small stone quarry in Austria where he could experiment and perfect the efficiency of his home-made bombs.

As for a motive—there was no sign whatever, except in that he claimed at one point that he had planned the derailments in order to draw public attention to a safety device which he had invented which would remove all hazards from rail travel! And, oddly enough, he himself was present at the Bia Torbagy catastrophe and helped to rescue people from the wreckage. He was identified retrospectively by a policeman as a bearded and bespectacled man whom he had seen frantically shouting for his missing luggage—and then suddenly he had tried to tear a shattered coach apart with his bare hands in order to rescue a trapped child.

Here then was a cold-blooded motiveless saboteur and murderer who took the trouble to rescue his victims, and yet was foolish enough to deliver himself into the hands of the police by making a false compensation claim in an attempt, presumably, to establish a precautionary alibi. And yet there was nothing in his history to account for this quite sudden and inexplicable aberration. He was born in 1892 in Cantavir, a village on the Hungarian-Yugoslav border. His father was a cobbler. He became a teacher, and during the First World War served as an officer and was decorated for bravery. After the war he abandoned teaching and started a new career as a corn merchant in Budapest. This brought in a great deal of money, but it was not what Matuska wanted from life. Eventually he went to Vienna to live, and made even more money in real estate business. By 1930, before the urge to destroy trains came upon him, he was a prosperous, happily married man with a daughter almost in her teens.

Matuska was tried twice, on different counts. The first trial took place in Austria for the two unsuccessful attempts to derail trains near Anzbach. He was found guilty and sentenced to six years' imprisonment. The second trial was in Budapest in connection with the Bia Torbagy train disaster. Again he was found guilty and this time sentenced to death. He could also have been tried in Germany for the Jueterbog crash, but there was apparently no point in pursuing the matter further after the death sentence had been pronounced in Hungary.

His only defence put forward during the trials was that he had been possessed by a spirit which had ordered him to commit the crimes for the glory of God and to combat atheism in the world. The spirit had told him to derail five trains just as Trotsky, the Bolshevist leader, had done. The reasoning was very *non-sequitur*, and it is possible that Matuska was playing for a verdict of insanity in order to avoid the inevitable sentence of death.

However, both the Austrian and Hungarian courts discounted any suggestion of insanity—but Matuska's luck held. He served his prison sentence in Austria first, and was then transferred to Hungary—to find that the death sentence could not be carried out. Under Hungarian law an execution had to be effected within a certain time limit after sentence, so he was committed to jail for life instead.

Matuska's luck had not yet run out, however. The war came, and he remained safely in prison. Then, in 1945, when the Russians were pursuing the retreating Germans and fighting their way through Hungary into Austria, he managed to escape from jail, along with many other prisoners who were able to take advantage of decaying security at that critical time. His trail was lost; the Austrian authorities had far more important things to think about.

Sylvester Matuska appears to have finished up in the hands of the Russians, where he seems to have not only survived but made good in his own peculiar way. His next appearance was during the Korean war, when he was captured by the Americans. He had been working with a group of North Korean partisans who were attempting to sabotage a railway line near Pusan. Whether or not his "spirit" was still ordering him to derail trains in the tradition of Trotsky is not known—nor has the world heard of him since. At least, not so far!

Chapter 18

ARSENIC GALORE

MURDER by poisoning is by no means a strange crime. If anything it is far too commonplace, though it is less fashionable today than it used to be, mainly because forensic methods have improved enormously during the present century, and detection is virtually guaranteed. But from the point of view of strangeness, a great deal depends on who poisons whom. When a young, attractive woman poisons all her children (six by her first marriage, and others) plus a trio of husbands, then the word strange is if anything an understatement. And when the poisonings are carried out for reasons of kindly compassion, according to the poisoner, then the case definitely falls into the odd category.

The young woman in question was named Lydia Danbury, and at the age of seventeen she married a policeman named Edward Struck and lived in New York on 125th Street. Lydia was born in New Jersey in 1829, and by the time she married in 1846 she was a tall, dark and very attractive girl. The marriage seemed to go well enough. In the first seven years Lydia produced six children, which must have resulted in conditions of drudgery for her on a policeman's pay. Her husband was a plodding, conscientious man who always seemed to miss promotion, perhaps because he was too honest.

The first serious trouble hit the family when Edward Struck was dismissed from the police force for arriving too late after being called to a gunfight in a saloon bar. The gunman escaped, and Edward was accused of having deliberately held back, from motives of cowardice, until it was safe to enter the premises. In view of his undeniable integrity, this was an unjust accusation, but nevertheless he lost his job. There is reason to believe that the affray in question was connected in some way with local graft and corruption in political-police circles, and that Struck had to be sacrificed because of his basic honesty in case he had found out too much.

Edward Struck never recovered from the sense of injustice caused by his summary dismissal. He became bitter and withdrawn, and hostile even to former friends in the police, whom he refused to see. Lydia grew more and more worried by her husband's changed manner. She eventually sought the advice of Edward's former superior officer in the police precinct. He suggested that her husband was losing his sanity because of his obsessive resentment over his dismissal from the police force—he had developed a persecution complex which was unhinging his mind, and the best place for him was in a lunatic asylum. It may have been that this opinion was given to discredit any critical remarks that Edward may have made about police morality.

The pattern of behaviour of Edward Struck deteriorated steadily. On one occasion he became so truculent and bad-tempered that Lydia was obliged to call in a police sergeant who lived in the same apartment block in order to calm him down and restore the peace. Afterwards the sergeant said to Lydia in confidence that in his view Edward ought to be "put out of the way" for his own good—meaning no doubt that he should be sent to an asylum, a suggestion which had been made before.

Lydia evidently misconstrued his words. "Put out of the way" to her held a much more decisive and permanent connotation, and perhaps she could at that stage have been pardoned for thinking in such a vein because life with Edward, plus six children to look after, must have been extremely difficult. However, she was nothing if not practical, and she promptly went out and bought some arsenic and put it in her husband's food on a May evening in 1864. The next morning he was dead. The doctor who was called in failed to diagnose the proper cause of death. He apparently did not suspect poison because the death certificate merely stated that he had died of "consumption".

Lydia thus became a widow—and a young, attractive widow at that—with six children. She was obliged to go out to work to support her family and keep a roof over their heads. Edward had left virtually nothing in the way of an estate, and Lydia had not foreseen the disadvantages of being a widow with a family of six to care for. For, although she was young enough and pretty enough to attract the interest of men, her need was for a husband rather than a lover, on sheer econom- ic grounds. But even the most eligible and infatuated bache- lor, however much he approved of Lydia herself and was willing to give her a new home, baulked at the idea of taking on her six children too.

Consequently Lydia, in order to earn a living, was forced to spend two depressing years of her young life working in a sewing-machine factory in a drab quarter of New York. It was an intolerable experience, and she hated every minute of it. But during those two years a curious thing happened. All six of her children died one after the other, and at the end of that time the main obstacle to her re-marriage had completely disappeared.

In a statement made much later, Lydia explained how this came about. At first, just a few months after the death of her husband, she had come to the conclusion that her two youn- gest children, a boy of four and a little girl, had no future without a father, and with a widowed mother forced to go out to work. They were virtually orphans, and she reluctantly decided that they would be better off if they were "put out of the way". Very soon, in what she described as a mood of compassion, she put arsenic in their food. They died very quickly, and once again there was no suspicion of poisoning. The cause of death, according to the doctor, was fever in one case and bronchitis in the other.

Then, in March, 1866, her twelve-year-old daughter Anna became ill from a perfectly genuine disease. The doctor was called in, and he prescribed medicine. Lydia, distressed to see her daughter in bad health when she was such a happy child, and wishing to see her at peace, put arsenic in her medicine. The death certificate said she had died from typhoid fever.

One can only conclude that the doctors of the day who were concerned in these various deaths were guilty of some degree of negligence, for one post-mortem would have quickly revealed the truth. But there were no post-mortems, and it may be that the doctors fell to some extent under the influence of Lydia's good looks and charming manner—and also the psychological block which makes even professional men believe that a mother could not deliberately poison her own children.

The next arsenic victim was the eighteen-year-old daughter, and during 1866 the remainder were disposed of—always without suspicion. During this period she met a Mr Hurlburt, a middle-aged man who owned property and had a bank credit of some ten thousand dollars. His health was not very good, but from Lydia's point of view that was an asset. He probably desired Lydia's youth and beauty as much as she desired his wealth. It was a strictly mercenary match, and Lydia and Hurlburt were duly married in November, 1868, about two years after the last of her six children had been murdered and buried.

To the outside observer the marriage no doubt seemed happy enough. Hurlburt was evidently well satisfied for he made a will leaving everything to his wife. Lydia, for her part, made a point of telling friends and neighbours that she was worried about Hurlburt's health; apparently he suffered from unpredictable dizzy spells.

Early in 1870, after just over one year of marriage, Hurlburt had an acute attack of "fever", with head pains and stomach cramps and a strong sensation of "burning". The local village doctor was called in, only to be baffled by the symptoms, and he decided to summon specialists to advise on treatment (a stomach pump would have been the best treatment, had they but known). Before they could agree on a diagnosis, however, Hurlburt died—and while the cause of death was still being argued, Hurlburt was buried. Once again poisoning was not suspected, and Hurlburt was certified as having died from natural causes.

Lydia was now in the happy position of being a young and attractive widow once more, but this time with plenty of money and no liability in the shape of a family. She could now afford to enjoy life and perhaps eventually marry by choice rather than necessity, financial security being no longer important. And, as might be expected, she chose an irresponsible young man with a great thirst for alcohol. His name was Nelson Sherman.

One of the ironies of this third match was that Sherman was a widower with four children, and it surely must have occurred to Lydia at some point that she had murdered her own family of six children, not to mention her husband, in search of the freedom that would enable her to marry a devil-may-care layabout with four children. Sherman was a mechanic, but a fairly successful mechanic, and he was attracted to Lydia by her looks rather than her money.

They were married in September, 1870, just a few months after Hurlburt's funeral, and one might reasonably have supposed that at this stage, with no money problems, Lydia would attempt to settle down to live a quiet semi-affluent life with a personable though semi-alcoholic husband. But not a bit of it. Habits are more easily acquired than discarded.

Within two months of the marriage Sherman's seven-month-old baby son suddenly became seriously ill and promptly died. In December of the same year Sherman's fourteen-year-old daughter mysteriously contracted "typhoid fever". She also died. And still there was no suspicion of foul play, fantastic though it may seem.

After these two bereavements the state of happy matrimony between Mr and Mrs Sherman began to decay. He took to sleeping with his four-year-old son, as if he subconsciously sensed that the boy was in danger, while Lydia was obliged to sleep in another room. This withdrawal of conjugal relations did not please Lydia at all, for she had been attracted to Nelson Sherman in the first place by his boyish, irresponsible and amoral personality. But Nelson had become less boyish and irresponsible, and could be described as celibate rather than amoral.

In May, 1871, Sherman left home for a week, ostensibly to attend a party in New Haven. When he did not return home, his seventeen-year-old son went off in search of him. The money for the trip was provided by Lydia who, possibly for the first time in her life, felt that she was losing control of the situation. Nelson Junior eventually tracked down his father, to find him in a state of extreme alcoholic hangover. He managed to bring him back home, but he was not in a fit state to return to work for several days. It was during this period that Lydia and Sherman had a particularly vicious row which was basically concerned with their non-existent sex life, and Sherman, not realizing the danger he was placing himself in, told Lydia that he knew too much about her and that there was trouble coming up between them. There is no doubt that he was implying that he suspected her of having murdered his two children, and perhaps her own as well—all he lacked was proof. Lydia took no offence; she soon made up to him and became affectionately all sweetness and light—for a few days.

One evening, later in May, Sherman drank some brandy offered by his wife, and presently developed the familiar symptoms of headache, stomach cramp and intense fever. He was attended by two doctors, but died nevertheless. For the first time a death certificate was not readily available. Looking back on the recent history of the Sherman family, and bearing in mind that Sherman himself, though a drunk, was in good health, the doctors decided that there was sufficient justification for a post-mortem.

Part of Nelson Sherman's liver was sent to a pathologist for analysis, and a few weeks later the pathologist reported that there was enough arsenic in the liver to kill at least three men. A warrant was issued for the arrest of Lydia Sherman, but it was held in abeyance, for the fact that Nelson Sherman had died of arsenical poisoning was not of itself proof that Lydia had administered the poison. More evidence was required. The bodies of Sherman's dead children were exhumed and examined by a pathologist. In each case there was unmistakable evidence of arsenical poisoning.

Meanwhile Lydia, realizing that the law was finally on her track, decided to leave town, She went to New Brunswick to live, quite unaware that the police were following her movements with great interest while evidence was being collected. When the police finally succeeded in identifying the pharmacy at which Lydia had bought her supplies of arsenic, the Deputy Sheriff decided to put the arrest warrant into effect. Lydia was picked up and taken to New Haven, where she was formally charged with the murder of Nelson Sherman. She was imprisoned pending trial.

Hurlburt's body was then exhumed, and found to contain a lethal dose of arsenic. A second warrant was issued, so that if she were acquitted of Sherman's murder she could be immediately arrested and charged with the murder of Hurlburt. This step was considered necessary because the police were not convinced that they could make the Sherman murder charge stick; after all Sherman had had no money and no estate to provide a mercenary motive, and they knew nothing of the breakdown of sex relations between Lydia and Sherman. Hurlburt was a stronger case, for he had been a fairly wealthy man and had made a will in favour of Lydia. That was a valid motive and more likely to produce a conviction. And as a third line of attack, there was the rapid series of deaths of Edward Struck and the six children of Lydia's first marriage, which were now arousing great suspicion, although no exhumations had yet been ordered. All things considered, Lydia had manoeuvred herself into a tough spot.

She became known in the newspapers as "the modern Borgia". It was an apt enough label. The trial began in New Haven on 16 April, 1872, under the presidency of Judge Sanford. Lydia's demure appearance was to her advantage; she was poised and pretty, soberly attired in a black dress with a white hat, thus striking the right note of elegance and mourning. She pleaded not guilty, and there must have been many in the court-room who, looking at her, were inclined to believe her.

The first prosecution witness was Dr Beardsley, who had been called in by Lydia when Nelson Sherman had been first taken ill. Lydia had given the impression that Nelson was sick from alcoholic excess, and as this was by no means an unreasonable diagnosis, the doctor had prescribed appropriate treatment—but the patient had got worse. Beardsley stated that even before Nelson died he had detected symptoms of arsenical poisoning, and it was his opinion that between his visits to the dying man further arsenic had been administered by Lydia.

The defence did not attempt to deny the presence of arsenic, but tried to show that arsenical poisoning could have resulted from a great variety of causes. It was a fact known to pathologists that significant traces of arsenic had been found in the bodies of people when there was no question of poisoning whatever. Nelson Sherman was admittedly an alcoholic, and he had been warned by Dr Beardsley that any further drunken bouts could kill him—whether there happened to be arsenic in his body or not. This was a reasonable statement of the clinical condition of Sherman before his death.

The prosecution's case against Lydia was, on the whole, rather shaky, and permitted an element of doubt. But the judge admitted in evidence the pathological findings in previous deaths, particularly the discovery of arsenic in Hurlburt's body.

A pharmacist gave evidence that he had sold Mrs Sherman a quantity of arsenical rat poison in the spring of 1871. Further medical evidence followed, this time giving details of the pathological examination of Sherman's liver, which had been found to contain five grains of arsenic.

Nelson's brother, George Sherman, was called as a witness to lift the lid off the domestic matrimonial cold war that had been going on in the Sherman household. He had visited their home on a number of occasions, and it had soon become apparent to him that all was not well and that they were not living happily together. Lydia had complained to him that she would never have married Sherman at all if it had not been that she had lent him a considerable sum of money. She accepted marriage as a form of security, so far as recovering her money was concerned. She had also told George that Nelson would not speak to her at all unless it was absolutely essential, and that he preferred to sleep with his young son rather than his wife. It wasn't really a marriage at all.

The defence based their case largely on Nelson's alcoholism. He had been drinking heavily on the day before he died, and had arrived home in a state of "extreme intoxication". All the evidence pointed to death from acute alcoholism. As for the arsenic in his stomach—well, it was impossible to say how it got there, and for all one knew he might have committed suicide in a fit of depression because of the failure of the marriage.

Defence witnesses also testified that Lydia's conduct had at all times been kindly and "becoming"—with no hint of antipathy or hostility as one might expect in a woman who was alleged to have poisoned her husband. This, however, was something of a *non sequitur*, and made little impression on the jury.

Summing up, the defence case was largely based on a conjecture of accident or suicide supported by dubious evidence of Lydia's virtues as a wife in the face of her husband's alcoholic and dissolute indifference to her devotion to him. As an argument it possessed a certain unlikely charm.

The prosecution summed up by observing that the only thing on which either side seemed to agree was that Nelson Sherman was dead. But while the defence had suggested accident or suicide without any substantiating evidence, and leaned heavily on Lydia's innocent demeanour, the State's medical testimony was irrefutable. Whether Nelson Sherman had been drunk or not on the night before his death, his body contained more than a lethal dose of arsenic. On all the evidence, and taking into account previous arsenical poisonings which were outside the charge but inside the evidence, there could be no doubt whatever of her guilt.

And no doubt was there. The jury returned a verdict of guilty after being out for less than one hour. While awaiting sentence, Lydia made a confession in which she admitted to poisoning Sherman's young baby, and had made up her mind to kill her third husband when she discovered that he had been stealing her small reserve of "medicinal" brandy.

Her reason for killing the baby was "humane"; Nelson himself had told her that he wished the baby would die so that his mother-in-law would no longer have an excuse to stay in the house. She had taken him at his word, with the best of intentions—and plenty of previous experience and practice. With equal humanitarian motives she had put arsenic in his brandy in the hope that it would put him against drinking liquor. It did. She had not really meant to poison him at all. Her other children she had killed because she could not stand to see them sick.

The truth was probably that Lydia was a psychopath who chose murder by poison as a means of resolving any situation which frustrated her. She was essentially egocentric and loved nobody and nothing other than herself. Where people were an obstacle, whether adult or child, they had to be "put out of the way". There is also reason to believe that she was highly susceptible to suggestion from others, and that the mere hint that someone should be eliminated "for his own good" was a complete justification for murder.

Lydia was sentenced on 11 January, 1873, to life imprisonment in the state penitentiary at Wethersfield.

Chapter 19

THE CASTRO
IMPERSONATION

THE longest and perhaps most unusual trial in legal history took place in 1873. It lasted 188 days. The prosecution's final speech took ten days, that of the defence twenty-three days, and the judge took twenty-two days for his summing-up. After all that, the jury reached its verdict in half an hour. The charge was simply one of perjury.

This long and complex judicial process began in May, 1871, when a man who claimed to be Sir Roger Charles Doughty Tichborne applied through the English courts to have the existing holder of the title evicted and to seek official recognition of himself as the eleventh baron and heir to the valuable Tichborne estates.

The story really started some years earlier when, in 1854, Roger Tichborne, at the age of twenty-five, sailed from South America to Australia in a three-masted sailing ship named *La Bella*. The ship foundered in a storm near the Virgin Islands and there were no survivors. Fourteen months went by before Tichborne was legally presumed dead, at which point the insurance company paid up, and the family estate and title were inherited by a younger son. He, in the event, turned out to be something of an irresponsible black sheep of the family, and ultimately ended up in bankruptcy.

Roger Tichborne himself had been born in Paris in 1829. Although, as the eldest son, he was heir to the estate, in his early twenties he became involved in an intense and secret love affair which, when disclosed, aroused considerable family opposition. The emotional clash was so bitter that, in a stubborn and singleminded mood, he left home and went to South America to live. Apparently the environment did not suit him very well, and subsequently he sailed to Australia— and so lost his life.

Although Roger may have been presumed dead in law, there was one person who never doubted for a moment that he had survived the shipwreck and was still alive—and that was his mother, the Dowager Lady Tichborne. She refused to accept the fact of her son's death. Indeed, she had been positively told by a clairvoyant that she would one day see her son again, and privately she believed that somehow he had managed to reach Australia where he was maintaining his proud silent independence and preserving the family feud over his illicit and frowned-upon romance.

Convinced that there must have been some survivors from *La Bella*, Lady Tichborne advertised in various newspapers offering a reward to anyone who could give information, but also—perhaps ill-advisedly—mentioning that Roger was heir to the estate of the late Sir James Tichborne. The scene had been set, and it was the first act of a strange play which today would seem "far-out" on any stage.

The second act began in the small town of Wagga Wagga in New South Wales, Australia. A butcher named Castro saw one of Lady Tichborne's advertisements in a newspaper and duly consulted his solicitor. On the strength of the legal advice received he presently set sail for England. His story was simply that he had survived a shipwreck in the Pacific Ocean, and was the true Roger Tichborne, and therefore heir to his father's title and estate.

Castro arrived in London on Christmas Eve, 1866, some twelve years after the reported death of Roger Tichborne. He was accompanied by a negro servant named Bogle who had coincidentally at one time been a servant to the real Roger

Tichborne's uncle. Bogle had finally settled in Australia, but when the newspapers reported that the missing heir, Roger, had apparently turned up as Castro, the butcher of Wagga Wagga, he very quickly sought him out and very quickly convinced himself that Castro was indeed the true Roger Tichborne. From that point on he devoted himself to Roger's service, perhaps from a sense of family loyalty, but no doubt with one eye on the main financial chance.

In fact, Castro's real name was William Orton. He was the son of a butcher in the Wapping dockside area of London and, although described as coarse and gross, he was shrewd and intelligent, with the personable manner which is the main stock-in-trade of the "con man". Whether Castro was in truth a con man in pursuit of a fortune, or whether he honestly believed his claim to be genuine, has never satisfactorily been decided. All that remains in legal terms is the verdict of the jury.

One of the first things Castro did on arriving in England was to go to Paris to meet Lady Tichborne. It was a strange meeting. Lady Tichborne, calling at Castro's apartment, found a fat man (he weighed twenty-five stone) lying flat on his bed, fully clothed. She kissed him and commented that he looked like his father, but his ears were more like his uncle's. At all events she recognized him without hesitation, even after an interval of twelve years. For Castro the confrontation was a triumph, particularly as Lady Tichborne immediately gave him an allowance of a thousand pounds a year. Thus encouraged, Castro wasted no time before hotly pursuing his inheritance through the courts, since, naturally, other members of the Tichborne family regarded him as a brazen impostor. Legal proceedings were initiated to establish formal proof of his claim. It was not so easy as Castro had perhaps imagined, even given the whole-hearted support of Lady Tichborne herself, and the battle in court went on for the best part of five years, with Castro never losing heart or self-assurance.

The judge, Mr Justice Bovill, made it quite clear even before the trial started that he was prejudiced against Castro— that he believed him to be a charlatan and a fraud. In this attitude he was strongly supported by the press of the day.

Against Castro's claim that he was Roger Tichborne, rightful heir to the Tichborne estate, the defence sought to prove that Castro was, in fact, William Orton, a butcher from

Wapping, who had emigrated to Australia and was now fraudulently seeking claim to title and wealth in the guise of a dead man. It is not difficult to see which argument offered the more sensational story from the point of view of the press and scandalmongers. Castro had to fight public opinion as well as the judge and defending counsel, not to mention the generally hostile Tichborne family. Unless he actually *was* Roger Tichborne, it must very soon have become apparent to him that he had bitten off more than he could chew.

The long trial lasted one hundred and two days. The claimant produced eighty-five witnesses, including a baronet, six magistrates, one general, three colonels, one major, two captains, thirty-two sergeants and corporals and other ranks, and four clergymen. The defendants put up only seventeen witnesses.

During the trial certain unexpected facts came to light—for example, defence witnesses were called to give evidence that the real Sir Roger had tattoo marks on his body, which Castro clearly did not possess. On the other hand, counsel for the claimant was able to produce witnesses who positively affirmed that William Orton, the butcher, had red hair, while Castro, as could be observed, had dark hair. If this evidence were not enough to destroy the myth that Castro and Orton were the same man (after all, Castro could have dyed his hair black), evidence was presented of a more detailed anatomical nature. It was put to the jury that Castro and Sir Roger shared an identical and unusual defect of the genitals, which Orton did not have. Lady Tichborne herself submitted an affidavit on this matter which ought to have demonstrated beyond doubt that Castro could not have been Orton. Well, even if Castro was not Orton, the real point at issue was simply: was Castro Roger? The defence were attempting to demolish Castro's claim by attempting to prove that he was Orton, but even if they failed, and Castro remained just Castro, it did not constitute proof that Castro must therefore be Roger Tichborne.

This was apparently the view taken by the jury, for after 102 days of examination and cross-examination in the Chancery Court, they stopped the trial and found for the defendants. Castro had lost his action in law. The judge considered that the jury had made a sensible and right decision—but he went further than that. He stated that in his view the claimant, Castro, had been guilty of perjury, and he committed him to jail to await trial.

While awaiting trial, which was to be delayed by a year, Castro was released on bail. During this period he toured the country addressing public meetings to gain support for his cause—a state of affairs which could hardly happen today. Public interest in the affair was now immense, and he was widely reported in the press. Because it was thought that the attempt to identify Castro as William Orton had failed— indeed, had been little more than an unfair defence trick—his supporters who believed that he was in truth Sir Roger Tichborne were by now about as numerous as his opponents who considered him to be a fortune-hunting impostor. The balance of pros and cons seemed to be fairly equal.

In due course the trial of Castro on the charge of perjury began. It was to cost £50,000 and was to last for most of a year. A total of 212 witnesses was to be called for the prosecution and 256 for the defence. Although the charge was now perjury, it was in effect a trial of Castro's original claim for recognition as Sir Roger Tichborne.

Of the 468 witnesses who gave evidence, some swore that the claimant was Roger Tichborne and some that he was not; some that he was William Orton, the butcher, and others that he was not. The evidence came in all shapes and sizes and shades of significance. Witnesses blithely contradicted each other to confuse the issue—and the jury.

There is little doubt, however, that members of the Tichborne family who had known the real Roger before his disappearance to South America made a considerable impression on the jury when they affirmed positively that the Roger they had known could not possibly have turned into the rather uncouth and uncultured Castro who was still pursuing his claim in court.

The evidence became more detailed, more conflicting and more damaging to Castro's case. In statements he had made to his Australian solicitor in Wagga Wagga, Castro had said that he had been born in Dorset, whereas it was known that Roger Tichborne had been born in Paris. Castro had said that he had been educated at a High School in Southampton, whereas Roger had been educated at Stonyhurst. Castro claimed to have served as a private in the 66th Regiment, but Roger had held a commission in the Carabineers.

Other witnesses, including Lord Bellow, an old school-friend of Roger Tichborne, described in detail the tattoo marks on Roger's arm—a crossed heart and anchor with the initials R.C.T. There were certainly no such marks on Castro's arm, and this seemed to be one of the most damning and conclusive pieces of evidence.

Some of the witnesses who claimed to have known Roger during his service as an Army officer testified that he spoke English with a notable French accent. This was logical enough, as Roger had been born in Paris and had spent the first sixteen years of his life in France. It was said that his French was better than his English. Castro, on the other hand, had virtually no knowledge of French at all. It seemed highly improbable that a man who had spoken a foreign language fluently could have forgotten it all, even in a period of twenty years.

The prosecution persisted in the attempt to prove that Castro was really William Orton, the butcher. Among the witnesses who were prepared to swear that Castro was Orton was a young woman who claimed to have been his girl friend at one time. She duly identified him as Orton. The defence countered this serious challenge by producing in court an equal number of witnesses who had also known Orton and were absolutely sure that Castro was not the same man. On this issue the argument resulted in a stalemate, as before.

Castro's defending counsel was Dr Kenealey, who was genuinely convinced that his client was the true Sir Roger Tichborne, and that the Tichborne family, with the exception of Lady Tichborne, his mother, were engaged in a vicious conspiracy to deprive him of his rightful inheritance. Kenealey conducted a spirited defence, and met what he considered to be viciousness with an equal display of viciousness, even to the extent of criticizing the judge and law officers—for which he was subsequently disbarred. His brash and occasionally arrogant conduct of the case won a great deal of public admiration and sympathy, and he was cheered by the waiting crowds as he entered and left the court each day.

In his treatment of witnesses, Dr Kenealey was frequently abusive and insulting. He would call a witness a liar with no adequate justification. Lord Bellow, one of the more important prosecution witnesses, was subjected to offensive questioning on details of his private life which had nothing whatever to do with the case. During his opening speech for the defence, Kenealey dismissed the tattoo evidence as "an after-thought"—but failed to destroy the jury's awareness of its vital importance. He also made a number of virtually slander-ous statements about the Tichborne family as a whole. Roger Tichborne himself he described as a weakheaded, depraved and badly brought-up boy, so was it really surprising that he had grown up to be a coarse and uncultured adult? Precisely what Kenealey was hoping to achieve by such a display of ill-mannered and unethical behaviour is not clear. He may have entertained the public and provided the press with some first-rate sensational "copy", but he must also have antagon-ized the jury and lost a great deal of their sympathy.

Dr Kenealey's opening address lasted for a whole month, and later in his closing speech he was to talk for another month. He then began to call his 256 witnesses.

The first and perhaps most important defence witness was Andrew Bogle, the elderly negro servant who had known Roger as a boy and had sought out Castro in Australia on reading newspaper reports of the claim to the Tichborne title. Bogle positively identified Castro as Roger Tichborne, grown older and fatter. It was suggested by the prosecution that Bogle was Castro's partner in crime; with his background of service in the Tichborne family he was a key member of the conspiracy contrived by Castro to pursue his fraudulent claim. This accusation did not explain away the fact that Bogle had only made contact with Castro after the latter had put forward his claim and achieved newspaper publicity. The chances were that otherwise they would never have met at all. It seems more likely that the elderly negro was simply mistaken, that though his conviction that Castro was Roger was genuine enough, his memory was defective. It is possible that he was influenced to some extent by Lady Tichborne's unshakable belief that her son was still alive, and he deceived himself in his anxiety to make her dream come true.

As with the prosecution witnesses, so with the defence, again came a parade of confusing and contradictory testimo-ny. In the main, Dr Kenealey's line was to prove beyond doubt that Castro could not be Orton, and if it was established that he was not Orton, then he could well be Roger Tich-borne. Castro apparently knew Paris fairly well, and it was known that Orton had never even visited Paris. Furthermore,

Castro, despite his apparent "coarseness", possessed a wide knowledge of music and was a skilled chess player—accomplishments which Orton had never acquired. But evidence of this kind—highly circumstantial and tenuous—must have made little impression on a jury which had been sitting for many months and was weary of the complex and long-drawn-out legal marathon.

Towards the end of the trial Kenealey called as a witness a man named Jean Luie, who claimed to have been mate on an American sailing ship, the *Osprey*, which had been bound for Australia at the time the ill-fated *La Bella* had sunk in a storm. According to Luie's story, the *Osprey* had come upon an open boat with six men in it; they had been taken aboard and found to be survivors from *La Bella*. One of the six men was Castro, whom Luie identified in court. He had been in a weak and delirious condition, and had given the name of Payne. Luie admitted that during the examination of "Payne" by the ship's doctor, and during subsequent treatment, no sign of tattoo marks had been observed.

Such positive evidence might well have swayed the jury in favour of Castro had not the prosecution demonstrated that Luie's story was completely false and fabricated. At the time when he claimed to have been mate on the *Osprey* it was proved that he was living in Hull. Furthermore, Luie's record did not inspire confidence—he had been frequently in and out of prison. After the trial he was duly charged with perjury, convicted and sentenced to seven years' penal servitude. It may well have been Luie's bogus evidence which lost the case for Castro, for up to this point it was very much in the balance.

Although the trial was now practically over so far as the parade of witnesses was concerned, the jury still had to sit through 55 days of prosecution and defence closing speeches and the judge's summing up. At the end of that time they retired to consider their verdict. It took just half an hour. They found the prisoner guilty of perjury, and sentenced him to fourteen years' penal servitude.

This should have been the end of the matter, but it was not to be so. Dr Kenealey demonstrated his dedicated devotion to the Castro cause by carrying on a vigorous campaign on behalf of the prisoner for many years, writing in the papers and giving lectures throughout the country. His theme was that there had been a gross miscarriage of justice. Even after he had been disbarred he continued his efforts to secure the release and recognition of Castro. Eventually he became a Member of Parliament with a keen interest in law reform.

Castro was set free at the termination of his sentence in 1884, an ageing and embittered man—and still he continued to press for recognition as Sir Roger Tichborne, and campaigned around the country. One can only speculate that by this time he had convinced himself by some kind of introspective brainwashing while in prison that he really was Sir Roger, or that alternatively that he *was*, in fact, the other man. His chance of establishing his right to the Tichborne title and estate at that late hour was nil. He had been discredited, and few people took him seriously any longer. Over the years of his imprisonment public interest in the case had faded.

In the end Castro—or was he really Orton?—died destitute and in ill-health in 1899 at the age of seventy. He was buried in Paddington cemetery and—strangest thing of all—the Tichborne family gave permission for the words "Sir Roger Charles Doughty Tichborne" to be inscribed on his coffin. Could it have been that they had known all along that Castro was indeed the rightful heir, or were they simply making a final generous, or perhaps cynical, gesture to a determined impostor who had devoted his life, liberty and fortune (such as he had) to the pursuit of a tantalizing crock of gold at the end of an elusive and ever-receding rainbow?

Concerning the trial itself, Lord Maugham commented that the verdict was gained by the combination of an able prosecuting counsel, a sadly mismanaged defence, and a strong and distinguished presiding judge . . . plus the fact that the prisoner was "as guilty as Hell".

The last had not yet been heard of the case, however, for it transpired that Castro—or Orton, as he had been adjudged by the court—had a daughter who after his death continued to call herself Theresa Mary Doughty Tichborne. In 1924 she was jailed for libel, and while in jail made a remarkable statement. She said that her father had told her, on his release from prison after having served his sentence, that he really was the genuine Roger Tichborne. While in Australia he had known William Orton, but during a fierce quarrel had shot him dead. He had never mentioned this at the trial for obvious reasons, and he asked his daughter to keep his secret until after his death.

This statement by itself carries little weight, but it is supported to some extent by another statement made by an Australian who claimed to have known both Tichborne and Orton, who with two other men had run a butcher's business. Their supply of cattle was mainly stolen. But this particular informant alleged that it was Orton who murdered Tichborne during an argument.

The two conflicting stories have at least one thing in common—that both Tichborne and Orton existed in Australia and knew each other, and one killed the other. Whether the survivor was Tichborne or Orton, if the above is true, will never be known.

Another theory which was advanced, with apparently some substantiation, was that the claimant, Castro, was the illegitimate son of Roger Tichborne's father, Sir James Tichborne, who in his younger days had had an affair with—of all people—Mrs Orton, wife of the butcher Orton of Wapping, and mother of Castro. Mrs Orton had at one time, when she too was in her younger and more attractive phase of life, been employed as housekeeper in a large house which had been frequented by Sir James. The supposition was that one of the several Orton children was a child of that illicit union, and that Arthur Orton, later to be known as Castro, was in that sense a Tichborne and of noble birth—but, of course, he could hardly be the illegitimate son of Sir James and the legitimate Roger at one and the same time.

Of the several theories put forward in an attempt to elucidate this strange enigma, all are interesting and to a greater or lesser extent plausible, but none will stand up on its own as a proper explanation capable of satisfying all points of detail and answering all the inevitable questions. All that is left today is the verdict of the court, and the tombstone in Paddington cemetery. The rest is a matter of opinion.

Chapter 20

HE GOT AWAY WITH MURDER

One would imagine that a man who had committed murder, had been tried at the Old Bailey (in the days of hanging) and had escaped with a modest sentence of twelve years' imprisonment on a lesser conviction of "accessory after the fact", would tend to be rather circumspect on his release from jail and try to arrange his future with a view to staying on the right side of the law. In the ordinary way he would hardly be likely to confess to the murder after having served his sentence, even though he knew he could not be tried twice for the same crime. He would be even less likely to seek the maximum possible publicity by selling his confession to a popular Sunday newspaper, although the money might be useful. He might reasonably be expected to lie low, keep his dark secret to himself, and attempt to "go straight".

But some criminals have a psychopathic drive which strips them of all principles and makes them professional enemies of society. Often they are intelligent and personable men of imagination and action, capable of holding down a good executive-type job if their determination and ingenuity were properly applied. But such civilized behaviour is alien to their minds; for them the law-abiding qualities of integrity, honesty and decency symbolize unconditional surrender to a despised authority. They use their sharp brains to outwit society. They believe the world owes them a living.

Such a man was Brian Donald Hume. In January, 1950, he was sentenced at the Old Bailey to twelve years' hard labour on conviction as accessory after the fact to the murder of Stanley Setty, a car dealer. His function as an accessory, it had been held, was to dispose of the dismembered body of Setty by dropping parcels containing Setty's dissected remains into the Thames estuary from a small private aeroplane which he flew himself. Hume had been a learner pilot in the Royal Air Force.

Many months went by before parts of the body were discovered. A careful pathological examination of the remains suggested that they had been dropped from a considerable height into the sea. The trail led inevitably to aeroplanes and airfields and ultimately to Hume himself.

When arrested and charged with murder, he pleaded ignorance. He had merely been commissioned and paid by three unknown men to dump some parcels into the sea from a hired aircraft. He had had no idea what the parcels contained, nor did he know who the three men were.

The jury, clearly influenced by his smooth and plausible manner, and perhaps by his undeniable personal charm, acquitted him of the murder charge. He pleaded guilty to the subsidiary charge of being an accessory and was jailed.

Good conduct during his stay in Dartmoor secured his release some eight years later. The first thing that Hume needed to rehabilitate himself was money, preferably in large quantities. Having been acquitted of the murder of Setty he could now afford to tell the truth without fear of legal reprisal. He very quickly sold his "confession" to a Sunday newspaper for two thousand pounds. The story amounted to a full admission that he himself had murdered Setty by stabbing him to death—and that he himself had cut up the body in his own flat, parcelled up the pieces, and had hired a small aircraft from Southend Airport to drop the parcels into the sea at the Thames estuary.

Hume was quite safe in making this admission. He had already been acquitted of the murder of Setty and had served his sentence as an admitted "accessory". He could not be charged and tried again. No further action could be taken against him.

There seems to be little doubt that Hume enjoyed the publicity in an egocentric fashion. It was not sufficient for him to know secretly in his own mind that he had murdered Setty and got away with it—he also needed an audience. He was proud to have cheated the hangman and considered himself a smart operator. But, of course, he needed the money, and that was the most important consideration of all. The morality of the Sunday newspaper in paying £2,000 to a self-confessed murderer and thereby unwittingly furthering his subsequent career in crime is something which society never took beyond the stage of mild protest. Circulation sometimes outweighs ethics.

After the "sensational" confession in the newspaper, Hume lay low for a while, coasting along on his press handout and making plans for the future. He had resolved to go abroad where he was not known to the police, and to change his name to avoid identification. He acquired a passport in the name of Stephen Bird and took to wearing glasses to change his appearance. Eventually he went to Zurich in Switzerland— not the cheapest country in the world in which to live. However, he had enough ready money to survive in reasonable comfort for some time, and he was fortunate in meeting an attractive Swiss girl named Trudy Sommer to whom he became engaged.

Here was the chance, if he had been willing to take it, to break with the past, find himself a job and go straight, but Hume was incapable of controlling his own egocentric and fantasy-loving mind. For instance, he told Trudy that he was a Canadian test pilot, and she believed him. He possessed much of the smooth amiable personality of the professional con man.

A few days after they became engaged, Hume told Trudy that he had to go to Canada, hinting that he was engaged on some secret mission. In the Walter Mittyish depths of his mind he had no doubt hoped she would think of him as a secret agent involved in some mysterious kind of intelligence or espionage operation.

Canada was not a success, however. He spent only one week in Montreal, and it proved to be far more dreary than he had anticipated. In search of the glamour which his particular personality demanded (he was an illegitimate child and had spent the early years of his life in various children's homes) he went to California and for a time hovered like a moth around the bright fascinating flame of Hollywood, where he lived a lazy layabout life, spending his limited capital, and wondering how he could install himself permanently in the tough cynical dazzle of the motion-picture suburb of Los Angeles.

At one time, it was alleged, he planned a pay-roll hold-up to replenish his funds, which were dwindling rapidly, but decided against it at the last minute. Hume was never happy when trying to organize crime in strange surroundings and it is significant that in his later ventures into bank robbery he returned to old familiar London.

Finally, Hollywood was "all wore out", as was his bank balance. There was no future in the place, and money was too hard to come by, even dishonestly. He returned somewhat apprehensively to Switzerland and his fiancée, Trudy.

Playing the part of a wealthy Canadian test pilot cum secret agent was now becoming more difficult for the simple reason that money was in short supply. The two thousand pounds from the Sunday newspaper had been consumed in high living at high speed. It never occurred to Hume that he might get himself a job, although he had more than enough intelligence and ability to establish himself in commerce or industry. Taking a job would have destroyed the image of easy affluence with which he associated himself and which he had been cultivating—it made a nice change from Dartmoor. He came to the conclusion that the easiest way to restore his waning fortune was to rob a bank. What could be more logical?

From his apartment in Zurich, the banking centre of Europe, he made up his mind to go back to London in order to carry out his crime. Possibly (and as it turned out, quite rightly) he felt that his knowledge of London and British banking procedures would provide some degree of advantage in carrying out the robbery and making a clean getaway afterwards.

So Hume, fingers crossed and supremely confident, pushing his luck as far as it would go, went back to London under the assumed name of Donald Brown. He installed himself, settled down for a short time and carried out some reconnaissance.

Then, one Saturday morning, just before closing time, he entered a branch of the Midland Bank at Brentford, Middlesex, and successfully carried out a single-handed hold-up. He shot the cashier in the stomach and took all the money he could find. In all it amounted to not more than £1,500, which was disappointing, but nevertheless it was enough to sustain him and preserve his affluent image until the next armed robbery became necessary.

The getaway after the robbery was clean and swift. Hume had organized his time-table efficiently. On the following day he was back in Zurich with Trudy, unsuspected and once more able to maintain himself in the manner to which he was becoming accustomed.

The new supply of money lasted only three months, which meant that Hume was spending at the rate of more than one hundred pounds per week. Well, easy come, easy go. More money was needed, so another bank robbery would have to be arranged. Where better than London, and even the same bank that had been raided last time? What had worked once would work again. Practice makes perfect—and all that. So Hume went back to London with the Midland Bank at Brentford as his target once more. No need for much in the way of reconnaissance—the joint had already been well and truly cased on the first occasion. All that was needed was a carbon copy of the first successful enterprise, and with careful timing supported by experience gained previously little could go wrong.

But what Hume had overlooked was that the staff of the Midland Bank at Brentford had also gained in experience. The opposition was tougher and quicker. On this occasion they raised the alarm the instant Hume entered the bank. He was carrying two guns, and the attempt was a complete failure. True, he managed to shoot one cashier and scuffle with the staff, but he gathered no currency and made off very rapidly when he realized that he could not afford to delay as the police had already been alerted.

Even so, his luck held. He was able to escape by air under his Canadian guise of Stephen Bird, with corroborating passport, and returned to Zurich.

The police, presented with two identical bank raids, were now in a position to make some progress. They were now looking for a man named Donald Brown who, they thought, could "help them in their enquiries". They knew now that the same man had been responsible for both lone-wolf raids—and one chief inspector had a pretty shrewd idea of the true identity of Brown. It was suspected that Brown was operating from somewhere in Europe, so Interpol was notified. A photograph of the wanted man, Brown alias Hume alias Bird, was published and a reward of £6,000 was offered for his capture.

Hume, somewhat disconcerted by the pace of the pursuit, took time off to plan his future. He realized that he was now on the run, that Interpol was involved, and that unless he acted quickly he would be relentlessly screwed into the ground. He decided that the safest bet, from the point of view of maintaining his personal liberty, not to mention his life, was to go back to Canada. He told Trudy that he had been offered a very important job there, and he planned to 'eave very soon. At this point even Trudy must have begun to lose faith in her fiancée.

There was only one thing that prevented an immediate flight to Canada, and that was the important question of money. He needed capital—enough capital to get him to Canada and sustain him for a few months until he could organize some kind of reliable income. Once again the only solution to the problem seemed to be another bank robbery, but he was only too aware that he could no longer return to London where he felt more secure in his criminal raids. Time was in short supply. The job obviously had to be done on the spot, in Zurich.

So Hume, under stress and on his own personal count-down, planned his final bank robbery. It was to take place on 30 January, 1959. His activities on that day were a departure from his normal cool and self-assured self. During the morning he had a shave in a barber's shop, and then for a while he walked through the streets of Zurich, not exactly finalizing his plan, for any direct over-the-counter bank robbery must by its very nature depend on luck, but probably taking a deep breath and building up his determination and courage. Escape was so near, and yet so very far away. His successes in London did not guarantee success in Zurich.

Then he did something unusual and rather out of character. From a rubbish heap he took a small cardboard box. When unobserved he put a loaded gun into the box, which he arranged in such a way that he could easily put his right hand in the box to fire the gun when necessary. The fact that on this third robbery he chose to camouflage the gun, which he had used openly in London, is perhaps an indication of his waning self-confidence nerve. Hume was a man under desperate tension.

Towards noon on that day he decided that the moment had arrived for action. He went into the Gewerbank in Ramistrasse, approached a teller, raised the cardboard box and shot him in the stomach. He then jumped over the counter to seize all the money he could lay his hands on while the staff were still paralyzed by shock. Unfortunately, they were not paralyzed enough, and almost immediately he found himself struggling in a hand-to-hand fight with the bank personnel. Using the reversed gun as a club, he managed to hold off the opposition long enough to snatch some money, and tried to break open a drawer near the cashier's desk—but time was slipping by and the alarm had been raised.

The drawer refused to yield, and the bank staff were on the offensive again. Hume abandoned the attempted raid with the demoralizing realization that things had gone awry and that he had failed. Canada suddenly became remote, and the police were much closer. He fled from the bank and ran through the side streets of the town.

He was followed by a young bank clerk, who unknowingly risked his life because Hume was still holding the gun and was prepared to use it. Others joined in the chase after the bank robber and the pursuit became hot. A passing taxi-driver, observing the commotion and making his own interpretation of what was happening, overtook him and tried to intercept the prey. Hume shot him dead at close range. He had murdered for the second time, but on this occasion there was no question of being an accessory after the fact.

The chase continued, but by now Hume's chances of getting clear were remote. There were too many people on his track. Soon he was at bay, surrounded by his pursuers. He did not shoot again, and presently he was seized and overcome. The police arrived and he was arrested.

The Hume saga was over at last, but he still tried to push his luck in the hope that it had not finally deserted him. He made a fantastic statement to the police, in which he claimed that he was John Stanislav, the son of a naturalized American

Pole. He had left his job in Germany and had come to Switzerland to escape from embarrassing involvements with possessive women. Unfortunately he had arrived in Zurich with very little money. In desperation he had decided to rob a bank. He had not been in his normal state of mind, for he had taken a large quantity of "pep pills" to give him courage. In fact, when the police searched him they found pep pills and a razor blade hidden in a thin bandage round his foot.

The Swiss police, however, were not nearly so gullible as Hume had hoped. They sent full details of their prisoner to Interpol headquarters in Paris, and very quickly received a positive identification. John Stanislav was none other than Donald Brown, wanted for two bank robberies in London, and was formerly known as Brian Donald Hume, who had served a prison sentence in connection with the Setty murder. He was the man who had cheated the hangman—but finally failed to cheat the bank.

For Hume it was goodbye to Canada and goodbye to Trudy. He was tried and convicted in Switzerland for robbery and murder and was sentenced to life imprisonment—and to be banished from the country on his release from jail, whenever that may be.

Chapter 21

THE CIGARETTE
VENDETTA

ONE of the strangest tales of modern piracy on the high seas began in Shoreham-on-Sea, Sussex, in 1952. Shoreham is a small seaside town close to Brighton, and among those who frequent its public houses is always a sprinkling of men who know about boats, from merchant seamen to amateur yachtsmen. And it was in one of Shoreham's public houses that Captain Edward Erckmann, a Belgian seafaring man, signed on a four-man British crew for an ex-naval launch named *Esmé* which he had just bought for an unnamed client.

The launch was a fast motor-boat of about 120 tons, and the job held the promise of a certain amount of glamour. The destination was Tangier, the international free port, where the *Esmé* would undertake charter work in the Mediterranean area. The British crew would be paid ten pounds a week, plus a bonus of £ 50 on arrival at Tangier, the base of operations. To the Britishers it sounded like pleasure rather than business —almost as if they were being paid to enjoy themselves on an extended sunny Mediterranean cruise. The launch had been painted white, and looked trim and attractive. There was no hint of danger.

With Erckmann as captain the *Esmé* reached Tangier without incident. Almost immediately the first assignment came up—to salvage a ship reported to be in distress near the coast of Spain for a fee of three thousand pounds. To the British crew it seemed that fortunes could be made in this kind of casual charter work.

But there was one snag. Just before the *Esmé* sailed on her errand of mercy six men came aboard as extra crew members. They had been taken on, it was explained, to help transfer the valuable cargo of cigarettes aboard the distressed ship. All except one of the new crew members were French. The odd-man-out was an American known as "the Yank". They kept to themselves, and the original British crew were not particularly pleased to be thus invaded, even on a salvage operation.

They had even less reason to be pleased when the *Esmé* left Tangier in search of the distressed cargo boat. No sooner had the mainland fallen back to the horizon than the Yank and his colleagues broke open some barrels aboard the launch and took out six revolvers and six automatic carbines, or "tommy-guns". And forthwith they deposed Captain Erckmann and took over the launch. Against such a formidable array of armament the captain and his British crew could do nothing but obey orders.

*　　　*　　　*

The *Combinatie* was a 250-ton Dutch cargo boat which had been chartered by a Señor Pastorino, an Argentine businessman, to carry a cargo of 2,700 cases of American cigarettes from Tangier to Malta. The skipper of the boat was Captain Van Delft of Rotterdam, a tough and seasoned officer who had spent most of his life at sea. This particular job was one of the easiest he had undertaken. The Mediterranean was calm, and Malta was not very far away.

While on the bridge early in the morning of 4 October, 1952, when the *Combinatie* was about one hundred and twenty miles north-east of Tangier and some sixteen miles from the Spanish coast, Van Delft saw what appeared to be a big white motor-boat approaching rapidly on the port side. As it neared the cargo boat the white launch slowed down. When it was almost alongside the *Combinatie* a metallic voice called over a loud-hailer and ordered the captain to stop the ship's engines. To underline the command there was a sudden burst of gunfire from an automatic weapon in the launch. Bullets hissed over the bridge.

Van Delft, uncertain as to what was happening, but only too well aware that the white launch could outclass the *Combinatie* in speed, manoeuvrability and armament, signalled the engine-room to stop. It seemed to him in the darkness that the white motor launch was manned by six figures, all armed, with their heads covered by strange hoods.

"Wno are you and what do you want?" Van Delft demanded, although by this time he had a pretty good idea of what they wanted, even if he did not know who they were.

The voice ignored the question and curtly announced that they were coming aboard, and that there would be gunplay at the slightest sign of resistance. By now the small crew of the *Combinatie* were all on deck, having been awakened by the firing and the shouting. As the cargo boat slowed and drifted, they were astonished to see the white launch with its masked crew move alongside and tie up. In a few moments five of the men, carrying tommy-guns, had climbed aboard. They were wearing green hoods which completely covered their heads, so that they looked almost like members of the Ku Klux Klan.

At gun-point the captain and crew of the *Combinatie* were escorted to the largest cabin below deck, where they were locked in. And there they stayed for nearly two weeks while the hi-jackers took over the cargo boat. When morning came they discovered that the portholes of the cabin had been painted over from the outside so that they would see nothing. But the ship's engines had started again and they were proceeding to some unknown destination.

During this long period of enforced imprisonment the only members of the crew allowed out of the cabin to carry out normal duties were the two engineers and the cook, but they were kept under strict supervision and locked up again each night. Nevertheless, they were able to glean a few items of information not known to the others—that a member of the raiding gang was called "the Yank", that the white launch was a former British naval vessel named *Esmé*, and that cases of cigarettes were being transferred from the *Combinatie* to the launch. The cook, who had sailed in the Mediterranean for many years, recognized the coastline of the south of France, and when the boat eventually dropped anchor he was able to identify the spot as near Marseilles.

A small boat came out from the mainland to take the Yank ashore, but he returned about an hour later. The *Combinatie*, followed by the white launch, then went on to Corsica, where they anchored near Ajaccio. This was the destination for the cargo. The cases of cigarettes were unloaded from both the cargo of cigarettes. Van Delft wasted no time in telling the waiting lorries and driven away. The act of piracy had been successfully completed. The *Combinatie* and her crew had served their purpose and were no longer required. With the wheel lashed and the crew still locked in the cabin, the cargo boat was allowed to drift out to sea. Five of the raiders were taken ashore to stay in Corsica, while the Yank ordered the *Esmé* to proceed to Sardinia, where he himself went ashore. And that was the end of that. Their mission accomplished, the pirates had dispersed.

When Captain Van Delft in the *Combinatie* heard the launch start its engines and then slowly fade away into the night, he broke open the door of the cabin and, followed by his crew, went up on deck. Nothing could be seen in the darkness except a navigation light far away. Van Delft's first impulse was to use the boat's radio to report the theft of the cargo, but the radio equipment had been thoroughly smashed. The raiders had overlooked nothing in their carefully planned operation.

With the arrival of dawn, Van Delft was able to recognize the distant coastline of Sardinia, and thus fix his position. He decided to return to Tangier to give a full report to the police. The *Combinatie* sailed into Tangier on 4 November, exactly one month after her departure, but minus a £35,000 carge of cigarettes. Van Delft wasted no time in telling the Tangier police the incredible story of piracy in the calm Mediterranean, and they in turn reported the case to Interpol in Paris.

Interpol set the wheels of investigation in motion, and the hunt was on to find the motor-launch *Esmé* and its crew of hi-jackers, for it was not known to Van Delft or the police at that time that the *Esmé* herself, with her original crew, had been "stolen" by the hi-jackers as part of the over-all master plan. The search for the white launch had been in progress for only one day when, to the immense surprise of Interpol and the Tangier police, *Esmé* calmly sailed into Tangier and the crew went straight to the police and told them their own astonishing story.

* * *

Captain Erckmann and his four British seamen from the *Esmé* were able to corroborate in virtually every detail the statement made to the police by Captain Van Delft. At the time when the *Combinatie* had been boarded and taken over, the *Esmé* crew were locked in a cabin, and were only set free when the cargo boat had been captured. They were ordered to carry on with their normal jobs, to do as they were told, and ask no questions. Erckmann was only too aware that they had become involved in top-level international crime, and that the *Esmé* herself may have been acquired and manned as part of the plot. He was dealing, therefore, with ruthless men hired by big operators, and it paid to be circumspect and play the game carefully by ear. The raiders were well armed, and he did not doubt that they would use their weapons in the event of resistance or provocation.

Soon after the seizure of the *Combinatie*, cases of cigarettes were off-loaded on to the launch to the limit of available storage capacity. The reason for this, Erckmann suggested, was that in the event of police interception before the two vessels reached their destination in Corsica, the *Esmé*, with its speed and armament, stood a reasonable chance of getting clear away with a worthwhile proportion of the loot.

The account of the rest of the journey to Marseilles, Corsica and then Sardinia followed that already given by Captain Van Delft. After the Yank had been taken off the launch at Sardinia, the *Esmé*, now with its original captain and crew, sailed to Spain for some repairs. There, discussing the situation, it had occurred to them that they might be taken for the original pirates—and, indeed, this was probably the intention of the hi-jackers. Erckmann decided that the best thing to do was to go back to Tangier and tell the whole story to the police.

The Interpol investigation, under Marcel Sicot, continued, and in due course some of the pirates were identified. One was arrested in Tangier, and another in Marseilles. The Yank, it was thought, was a man named Sydney Varney, otherwise known as "Nylon Syd" because of his proficiency as a smuggler of nylon stockings.

Further Interpol enquiries were directed at the receiving end of the piracy operation in Corsica, where plans had obviously been laid with equal care and efficiency. The receiver-in-chief, whose task it was to buy the cigarettes and sell them at a high profit, was identified as a man named Antoine Pasqualini of Ajaccio. But while he was still negotiating the sale of the stolen cigarettes he learned that Interpol had been quicker off the mark than was expected and some of the pirates had already been arrested. The news that Interpol were now turning their attention to Corsica gave him cold feet, so he postponed the negotiations and arranged through a friend for the cargo of cigarettes to be stored in a safe hide-out until the Interpol investigation had cooled off.

Pasqualini's fears were justified, for shortly afterwards he was arrested and imprisoned, but at least the booty was safe—or so he thought. Unfortunately the friend also ran into trouble with the police on a small matter of violent assault, and decided to disappear. Before he went into hiding, and just in case he should be arrested and join Pasqualini in jail, he told a Monsieur Cavanna, who was the mayor of a small Corsican town, where the cigarettes had been hidden. M. Cavanna, he imagined, was a man to be trusted and not likely to fall under police suspicion.

The scene was now all set for a cloak-and-dagger intrigue of violence and murder reminiscent of a Mafia feud. Nothing happened for a time, as many of the key actors in the drama were still in prison. In 1954 Antoine Pasqualini was released on parole. So far as he was aware the stolen cigarettes were still in Corsica, and M. Cavanna knew the location of the cache. The time had come for Pasqualini to recover what he regarded as his property and to arrange for it to be marketed via his underworld connections.

Accordingly Pasqualini called on M. Cavanna to talk business, but Cavanna proved very reluctant to talk at all, and made it clear that the secret of where the cigarettes were hidden was going to remain a secret. He trusted Pasqualini about as much as Pasqualini trusted him. Diplomatic relations between the two men were broken off. There was a brief uneasy lull before the outbreak of hostilities as both sides planned their campaigns.

The first casualty was Cavanna himself, who was ambushed by three men outside a small hotel in Ajaccio. They shot him six times and then escaped in a waiting car. Miraculously he survived the attack, but lost his legs—both had to be amputated in hospital. Cavanna swore revenge.

A few weeks later Pasqualini was shot while driving a car in a deserted street, but he was lucky enough to get away with only a minor wound. After this opening gambit both sides withdrew for a while to consolidate and plan ahead. So far Pasqualini was winning—by two legs.

Nothing happened until March of the following year when a friend of Pasqualini's was ambushed in his car a few miles from Ajaccio. Two months later, with Cavanna's men now putting the pressure on, another ally of Pasqualini's was murdered. The time was due for a reprisal, and it came shortly afterwards when Pasqualini's gang ambushed and killed the younger brother of Cavanna.

But the end was approaching. In November of the same year Pasqualini was found dead in the docks area of Marseilles —he had been shot through the head. It was one up for Cavanna, but by no means a victory or even an armistice, for there were still members of Pasqualini's gang out for blood.

Several more assassinations followed, with the police apparently powerless to intervene. Then, finally, Cavanna himself was murdered by tommy-gun fire in Marseilles. The vendetta had reached its climax—and so far nobody had benefited from the stolen cigarettes.

With the deaths of the principals, the feud died out, but by way of an anti-climax the police succeeded in tracing and arrested Sydney Varney, the "Yank", in a small village in the south of France. He was duly convicted for his part in the piracy and sentenced to three years' imprisonment, but the sentence was later changed to three years on probation.

What happened to the cigarettes, the cause of all the trouble, is not recorded. They were apparently never recovered, and were presumably disposed of in the course of time through the usual underworld channels.

Chapter 22

MURDER WITHOUT MOTIVE

At about six o'clock in the morning on 4 August, 1952, a motor-cyclist driving along a winding road near the village of Lurs in the Provence region of southern France was waved down to a halt by a man standing at the side of the road. This was wild open country in a mountainous area, pock-marked with jagged outcrops of granite and scarred by deep ravines. It was off the beaten track of tourists, though travellers would camp in the area from time to time. At this particular moment the place was desolate and deserted in the early-morning sunshine, apart from the man at the side of the road, who was stocky and rugged in appearance and appeared to be a member of the local farming community. He was a young-ish man in his early thirties.

The motor-cyclist stopped. The man, in a sullen disinterested fashion, asked him if he would go to the police station at the small town of Forcalquier, about twelve kilometres away, to report that there had been a murder near a farm called La Grande Terre, near Lurs. He would wait at the roadside until the police arrived.

It was an odd early-morning request, but the motor-cyclist did as he was asked without putting too many questions to his rather bad-tempered informant. Within the hour the police duly arrived to find the squat peasant-like man patiently waiting for them. He introduced himself as Gustave Dominici, the thirty-three-year-old son of Gaston Dominici, who owned the La Grande Terre farm nearby.

Gustave related his story curtly. While asleep at the farm he had been awakened during the night by the sound of gunfire. It had been fairly remote and meaningless, and he had done nothing about it. Later, around five-thirty, he had got up and walked over towards a railway cutting where there had been a landslide. Quite by chance he had come upon the brutally murdered body of a little girl. A little further on was a car, and close to the car he had also found the dead bodies of a man and a woman.

The police took over, sceptical at first, but what Gustave had said was true. Gustave led them away from the road in the direction of the nearby River Durance which flowed through a narrow ravine. About half-way they found the body of a young girl. She could not have been more than eleven years old, and her head had been violently beaten and crushed.

Not far away, on a level area of ground, was a green Hillman estate car with what appeared to be a British registration number. Alongside the car were two folding camp beds with travelling rugs, indicating that the occupants had evidently been camping for the night in the open air. Under one rug the police discovered the dead body of a woman in her late forties. She had been shot five times. Some distance away they came across the dead body of a man, aged about sixty, who had been shot in the back. It was quite obvious that the man, woman and child were a family, almost certainly British, and probably enjoying a camping holiday before violent death had overtaken them during a warm, starlit Provencal night.

The police examined the bodies and the contents of the clothing, and sifted the scene in minute detail. There was no apparent motive for the triple murder. Money and traveller's cheques had not been touched, and no sign that articles in the pockets of the victims had been tampered with or even looked at. The car had not been interfered with or even opened. There was no obvious indication of sexual assault. The only missing articles, so far as could be ascertained, were watches—but here it was necessary to assume that a touring family would be unlikely not to have at least one wrist-watch between them. But this was a hypothetical point—and would a murderer simply take a watch and not money?

During the course of the long day the police, suitably reinforced, examined every inch of the scene of the crime and the local environment. In due course they found the murder weapon. It was an automatic carbine, a relic of World War II, of the type that had been issued to the U.S. Army and had also been used by the French Resistance. The carbine was discovered at the bottom of the Durance river in the ravine. At that time of the year it was little more than a shallow stream, but there were occasional deep pools. The weapon was recovered from one of the deepest of the pools—and this suggested that it had been thrown there by someone with detailed local knowledge, and not just carelessly cast into the ravine by a stranger. Therefore the obvious focus of police suspicion was the Dominici family itself in the La Grande Terre farm nearby.

The Dominici family, as subsequent investigation revealed, proved to be more of a tribe—or perhaps a clan. Old Gaston Dominici, aged seventy-six, had nine grown-up children and sixteen grandchildren, but they did not all live at the farm. The family was of independent peasant stock, inward-turned psychologically and very bloody-minded; during the German occupation they were reputed to have been stubbornly active in the Resistance and the Maquis. They tended to be uncommunicative, and very much united among themselves against the outside world, in a manner characteristic of the southern Latins. The police quickly realized that the Dominicis, as witnesses, would be obstructive rather than co-operative, even though there was no evidence to show that any one of them was involved in the triple murder.

The investigation was taken over by Commissaire Edmond Sebeille, an experienced and thorough officer of the Marseilles Sûreté. It soon became apparent to him that the Dominicis were behaving in a taciturn and secretive fashion, which, even allowing for their natural reticence, suggested that they knew far more than they were prepared to divulge.

Meanwhile, the bodies of the murdered family were removed and identified. They were Sir John Drummond, his wife, Lady Drummond, and their daughter Elizabeth. It was confirmed that they had been on holiday in France, as the guests of Professor Guy Marrian and his wife, who had rented a villa at Villefranche for the month of August.

Sir John Drummond was a biochemist who had received his knighthood during the war for his advisory services to the then Ministry of Food. His first childless marriage had been dissolved, and later he had married his secretary, who had become Lady Drummond. Elizabeth was their daughter. Guy Marrian, their host, was Professor of Medical Chemistry at the University of Edinburgh, and a close colleague of Drummond.

Sebeille's enquiries showed that the first stage of the Drummonds' holiday had passed quietly and uneventfully at the villa. Then the family had decided to visit Digne, some seventy miles away in the mountains, where a local festival involving a mock bull-fight was about to take place. They set off in their estate car, taking camping gear with them as it was to be a leisurely trip involving one or two overnight stops. Although the distance was not great, the road was twisting and difficult, winding through a desolate mountainous region inhabited mainly by dour and clannish peasant families working the land for a meagre living. Speed of travel was not easy to attain, and, in fact, night overtook them before they reached their destination. Being self-contained, they decided to camp until morning—but for them morning never came.

There was plenty of investigation, but no leads. As a result a great deal of speculation arose in general gossip and the press. The case was widely reported. Cloak-and-dagger guesswork hinted at political and even British intelligence involvement. It was rumoured that Drummond had been killed because of wartime activity in the area—that the murders were some kind of obscure reprisal. In support of these rather wild assertions, it was learned that French and American Intelligence were taking an active interest in the police investigation—and public interest increased to a new pitch of intensity when it was discovered that Sir John Drummond had, during his holiday, been making his own private inquiries locally about a certain British officer who had been parachuted into the area during the war with money for the

Resistance leaders. The officer was found dead, and the money was never received. It seemed possible, therefore, that the killing of the Drummond family was an assassination rather than a murder, but the theory was not fully supported by hard fact.

There was the curious incident of a diary found in Nottingham which recorded that Drummond had, in fact, been in Lurs in 1947. The diary had belonged to a man who had himself been murdered in the Alpes Maritimes of Southern France. For a reason never properly explained, the diary was destroyed, apparently by the police, at the request of Drummond's relatives.

All in all, a sinister atmosphere of intrigue began to condense justifiably around the Drummond case. It possessed the hallmarks of secret-service machinations, with the truth hinted at but never revealed. The French newspapers openly anticipated sensational disclosures of a political or partisan nature, with a point of origin in wartime Maquis activities and perhaps connected with the spate of "liquidations" which had followed the liberation of France.

Whatever may have been the truth of the matter, and despite imaginative rumour and speculation, nothing sensational emerged from what was regarded as a deliberate conspiracy of silence. If the local people of Lurs knew the identity of the killer, they were keeping it to themselves, and the Dominici family in particular remained arrogantly and even defiantly uncommunicative.

Commissaire Sebeille, patiently pursuing his methodical investigation but getting nowhere, but convinced in his own mind that the Dominicis were the key to the solution of the enigma, decided to apply the full treatment of continuous interrogation to the limits permitted by French law. Only in such a way could variations and discrepancies in statements be detected. The truth remains the same, but lies, being artifacts of invention and memory, tend to vary in points of detail, since it is more difficult to recall the sum total of a contrived lie than it is to remember a true and real experience.

Consequently, on 3 September, a month after the murder, Gustave Dominici was taken to the Forcalquier police station for questioning. He was the key witness; it was he who had found the bodies in the first instance and who had called in

the police with the help of the motor-cyclist. Sebeille decided
to go back to square one and cover the ground in more
ruthless detail.

For two days Gustave was questioned unceasingly by a
team of detectives, and the pattern of questioning was repeated over and over again, and compared with his original
statement. This long interrogation produced only two discrepancies: one concerned a minor matter of the precise path
which he had taken after finding the dead body of the child
(this did not seem particularly significant, since the terrain
was wild open country), and the other was an inadvertent admission by Gustave that he had actually noticed Lady Drummond's body under a rug shortly after finding the little girl's
body—a fact which he had not mentioned previously. Either
his memory was improving or his invention was crumbling—
but there was still no evidence that would justify an arrest.
Sebeille retired, temporarily defeated but prepared to wait.
He knew very well that with the passage of time lies decay
more rapidly than the truth.

Another month went by. It was now October, and the
tourist season was coming to an end. Sebeille decided on a
further bout of intensive interrogation, and once more
Gustave was taken to the police station for a two-day session
of non-stop questioning. Again he managed to keep accurately
to the details of his original statements, but as before, under
the stress of interrogation, introduced a new admission which
had not been mentioned previously.

This time he confessed that the little girl, Elizabeth Drummond, had actually been still alive when he had first seen her
lying on the ground. She had moaned and moved one arm.
He had observed this, but nevertheless had done nothing to
help her. He had left her to die and had returned to the
farm-house.

Now, at last, Sebeille was able to take some action within
the framework of the law. He arrested Gustave on a charge,
under French law, of failing to aid a person in danger. It was
not a major indictment, but it was a step in the right
direction, and Sebeille felt that a taste of prison might help to
loosen Gustave's tongue. The Commissaire was still taking a
long-term view.

In due course Gustave came up for trial. He was convicted
and jailed for two months. But during the course of the trial

various items of conflicting evidence were presented in court—in particular, questions of time. It seemed strange that Gustave claimed to have found the girl's body around five-thirty a.m., after dawn, when witnesses had heard shots fired at about one-thirty. Yet Gustave had stated previously that he had gone out from the farm-house after hearing the shots. Why the four-hour time lapse? Or, if he had found the body after hearing the shots, why had he gone back to the farm to await dawn before taking any action? Gustave proved to be evasive on this issue, but on the evidence it looked as if he had in fact been callous enough to return to the farm after finding the dying girl, but was now ashamed and reluctant to admit it.

Statements made by Gustave's wife and his brother, Clovis, confirmed that Gustave had said that the girl had not actually been dead when he had found her, but he had been afraid to tell the police the truth in case it caused trouble. But trouble for whom? Sebeille was convinced that Gustave was covering up for somebody else, and that he was prepared to go to jail rather than reveal what he knew. And, of course, to jail he went.

That was the end of the case for a year. Even the newspapers forgot about it. But Commissaire Sebeille did not. There were too many loose threads to satisfy his methodical mind, and so far as he was concerned the imprisonment of Gustave on a minor charge was irrelevant to the main issue. He pursued his inquiries with patient single-mindedness. He called regularly on the Dominici family to ask more and more questions, but always meeting the same sullen barrier of indifference and noncommunication. In the long run it was Gustave again, after he had served his sentence and been released from prison, who in his characteristic way added new fragments of information to the ever-changing story.

Questioned by Sebeille on one occasion he said that on the evening before the murders, eleven-year-old Elizabeth had called at the farm to fill a kettle with water. He also admitted in a confused way that at some time during that fatal night he had, after finding the girl's dead body and returning to the farm, made a second visit to the Drummond camp, and had even examined the woman's body to see if she was still alive.

To Sebeille it was clear that Gustave was the weak link in the Dominici chain, and that sooner or later he would break down under rigorous questioning. So he pursued the interrogation in a stubborn unrelenting way. And in the end his judgment proved to be right. Gustave, unable to stand the strain any longer, and not able clearly to remember what he had said and what he had not said, accused his aged father, Gaston, of the triple murder. It was Gaston, he declared, who had shot the man and the woman, and had clubbed the little girl to death. He, Gustave, and most of the family, were well aware of the truth, and had tried to cover up for the old man—but there had to be a limit. So far as Gustave was concerned, he had already served a jail sentence on behalf of his father and was not prepared to make any further sacrifices.

It was now Sebeille's turn to tighten the screw on Gaston himself. He was a sly, cynical, taciturn old man in his late seventies—a kind of homespun rural philosopher with a cruel aggressive streak which made him a tyrant among his own family, with whom he enjoyed a kind of love-hate relationship.

Sebeille went to the farm-house and talked to Gaston over a bowl of soup. Gustave, he said, had finally told the whole story, and Gaston might just as well speak the truth. Surprisingly, Gaston very quickly confessed; it was as though the betrayal by his son had completely shattered his defiance. The confession, which was later produced at the trial, said:

"It was a crime of love. I watched the woman camper for about twenty minutes. Then I crept close and whispered to her.

"Then the Englishman rose and jumped on me. I picked up the carbine from the floor and I went crazy and shot at him. He ran away and I shot him twice more. The Englishwoman was screaming so I turned round and shot her once.

"Then the girl ran out from the car and I ran after her and gave her a blow on the head with the butt of the gun."

The case again became headline news throughout the world. But Gaston, having made his confession, withdrew it with equal facility and denied everything. At the same time, to make Sebeille's task more difficult, Gustave also withdrew his allegations against Gaston. The rest of the family played safe and said nothing at all.

Nevertheless, Sebeille felt that there was sufficient evidence to proceed with the case. Gaston Dominici was arrested and charged with murder, and brought to trial in November,

1954. As was to be expected, he revoked all confessions, claiming that they had been forced out of him under duress. He proclaimed his innocence very positively, but under examination went so far to admit that: "It was an accident. They attacked me. They took me for a marauder."

The only possible witnesses were members of his own family, but under French law they were not required to give evidence on oath. The testimony of some of them proved to be so conflicting and so full of contradictions and denials that it was of little value. Gaston accused them, and they in turn accused him and each other.

At one point, in a bitter tirade against his relatives, he said he loved his dog "more than all my family".

Sebeille, in court, described the key members of the Dominici family in this way: Gaston, head of the family—hard, severe, without heart, brutal; Marie, Gaston's wife—a good woman, bowing to the authority of her tyrant husband; Gustave—a liar, but he had the key to the mystery; Yvette, Gustave's wife—a dominant woman, with her husband under her thumb.

The most puzzling factor in the case was the lack of an adequate motive. The Drummonds had been murdered for neither robbery nor rape. The elusive hint of some obscure Maquis intrigue was discounted.

Gaston was convicted of murder and sentenced to death. But because of his old age and infirm health he was transferred from the death cell to a prison hospital in Marseilles.

The French Government considered the case so important and controversial that an official inquiry was instigated. The Sûreté Nationale after a long investigation prepared a detailed report of over a quarter of a million words—without reaching a positive conclusion.

The end of the affair was undramatic. After languishing in the prison hospital until the age of eighty-one, Gaston was reprieved, and life imprisonment was substituted for the death penalty. He spent the remaining few years of his life behind bars.

Chapter 23

THE FANTASIA
FANTASY

SOME criminal cases resemble an iceberg in that the greater part remains beneath the surface and is never revealed to the public eye, particularly if there is a hint of scandal involving the "Establishment". The case is tried and disposed of on a superficial level, even though the police and press suspect, or even know, that there is a great deal more behind the scenes which cannot be disclosed. Of course, when scandal is involved, the individuals concerned may not necessarily have committed an offence in law, and an exposure can only be justified if it is in the public interest to do so—subject to pressures applied in the interests of national security, politics and sometimes national morality.

A typical case of this kind occurred in Italy just after the end of World War II. At that time there had been a wave of murders in Rome which had baffled the police. In the late afternoon of 21 June, 1945, the Rome police received a telephone call from a young lady who said she was very concerned about the safety of a girl friend named Maria Laffi who lived in the apartment below. Nothing very dramatic had happened. She had called on Maria during that same afternoon, but when she rang the bell and then knocked there was no reply, even though Maria had been expecting her. That in itself was unusual, but not necessarily sinister. However, during the morning she had heard strange sounds in Maria's flat, and adding the two incidents together she now felt uneasy.

The police arrived a few minutes later. The door to the flat was still locked, and no key was readily available, so they broke in by force. They found Maria Laffi lying face down on a bloodsoaked carpet, close to a grand piano. She had been stabbed nine times in the back and had been dead for some hours. Blood had splashed on to the keys of the piano and on to a sheet music copy of Beethoven's "Moonlight Sonata" on the music ledge.

Maria, a pretty blonde girl, petite and of slight build, was wearing only a thin summer dress, with no underclothes of any kind. This was her professional uniform, for she was known to operate in the higher echelons of the call-girl business, and she was also the mistress of Count Cerretani whenever he happened to be in Rome. Consequently she was well established, and her apartment was in the luxury category.

The police made a meticulous search of the flat and eventually found the murder weapon in the bathroom. It was a hunting knife, but it had been carefully washed to remove all traces of blood. Not a single fingerprint was found on the handle or the blade. It was identified as the murder weapon because the shape of the incisions in the body of Maria corresponded with the shape of the blade.

As in the case of the previous murders in the recent spate of crime, the police made little apparent progress. They went through the obvious routine of investigation. The first line of enquiry was into Maria's male clientele, and among them was a certain Signor Alfio Fantasia, an antique dealer who was already known to the police for other reasons—for instance, his antique shop was actually a cover for a gambling saloon at the rear. In addition, Fantasia was on record in the police files as a "failed gunman" from Southern Italy, suspected of having connections with the Mafia.

Inevitably Signor Fantasia was required to answer a number of rather pointed questions—but when the police called he was not at home. A man-hunt operation was set up, and he was quickly traced to a hospital into which he had successfully contrived to gain admission during the murder hunt. He was to have an operation for piles.

But Fantasia's ingenuity failed him when the police duly arrived at his bedside. They asked questions, and he, in alarm and self-defence, gave what were probably truthful answers—at least to the extent that they resulted in the arrest and imprisonment of three young men. And at this point a simple murder case centred on a better-class prostitute began to assume submerged iceberg depths.

The Italian newspapers took up the story in a big way, and the chronicle of the crime and its subsequent investigation and ramifications is principally that presented by the press, who began to scent a hidden sensational scandal which was slowly emerging from an examination of the backgrounds of the three young men who had been imprisoned.

There seems little doubt, in retrospect, that behind the superficial story lay a much more complex tale of political intrigue which, if it was known to the police (and there seems little reason to suppose not), was carefully suppressed. It should be remembered that at this time, just after the war, Italy was in a chaotic state in the cross-currents of post-fascist politics. There was the cloak-and-dagger atmosphere of re-crimination and high-level wire pulling, the jockeying for position, which was seen in France after the liberation, and later in Germany after the unconditional surrender. In such an environment an apparently straightforward murder could well be a cover for something much more devious.

*　　　*　　　*

The Fantasia case, as reported in the Italian press, was crystallizing into what seemed to be a conventional pattern for that particular era. Fantasia turned out to be something of a "wide boy". In addition to running his antiques and gambling saloon business, he was involved in the black market and had also been making money by extortion and fraud. A friend of his named Alberto Gallupi put to him a scheme whereby he could extract "protection" money from a Signora Rossi whose absent husband was being sought by the police on a charge of being a former agent of O.V.R.A., the Fascist secret police organization. Signora Rossi, terrified as to her husband's fate, paid over the blackmail money. The accusation proved to be totally untrue. Signor Rossi had never had any connection with O.V.R.A., and when he eventually came home to Rome he made a point of seeking out Fantasia and threatening to denounce him to the police unless he immediately returned the money. The answer to the obvious question—why Rossi did not go straight to the police as soon as he learned of the blackmail—is that he wanted first and foremost to recover the money, which amounted to one million lire. Since it is virtually impossible to recover money from a convicted and imprisoned blackmailer, he used Fantasia's own weapon—threat and coercion.

Fantasia could not return the money because he had spent it, and his urgent problem was to find another source of supply. He knew that Rossi could send him to jail without any difficulty, but that Rossi would rather have his million lire back at the price of Fantasia's liberty. Fantasia could see the point; his freedom was worth more than a million spent lire. The only trouble was that money of that kind was in short supply.

Being a regular client of Maria Laffi, Fantasia knew from his frequent visits to her flat that she possessed a well-stocked jewel-case. Most of the contents had been provided by Count Cerretani, her principal admirer. The jewels could solve his problem, but he was not prepared to steal them himself.

Instead, he put the proposition to Alberto Gallupi, the friend who had involved him in the Signora Rossi extortion which was the direct cause of his present dilemma. Alberto rather reluctantly appreciated the justice of the arrangement— one good crime deserves another—and agreed to relieve Maria of her jewels which, after all, were merely the wages of sin.

But Alberto had no intention of doing the job himself—and here the first element of fantasy begins to enter the plot. He decided to use two accomplices—Renato Piacente, a 22-year-old undergraduate, and Luigi Tirone, a 25-year-old army officer. This was indeed a strange liaison. Both young men came from good families, and their fathers were respectively a senior civil servant and a colonel. Luigi, the officer, was on leave in Rome at the time; his unit was in the north of Italy, attached to the U.S. Army. Both agreed to lend their services under Alberto's supervision.

The three men called on Maria at nine o'clock in the morning on the day she was due to die. She was still in bed when the doorbell rang. She got up, slipped on a thin dress as a substitute for a négligée, not really expecting professional clients so early in the day, and admitted the callers, who were unknown to her. They said they had news of Count Cerretani. She served drinks and in a mood of hospitality, perhaps anticipating business, began to play the piano.

That was the moment when Luigi took out the hunting knife and stabbed her nine times in the back, while Renato went into the bedroom to pocket the contents of the jewel-case.

When arrested by the police in due course, all three men openly admitted their parts in the crime, as did Fantasia when he was interrogated—and this in itself was sufficient to arouse the suspicion of the press, for criminals seldom admit guilt and liability unless it is as a cover for some other unexposed activity.

In court, Luigi and Renato both confessed to the actual killing, and it was established that both were young men with an excellent family background and no previous record of crime. Alberto, the "sharp" friend of Fantasia, admitted to organizing the murder and theft, although he protested that the original plan had been only robbery; murder had not been on the agenda.

In any case, he had been cheated, he claimed. The stolen jewels had not brought more than one hundred pounds in the receiver market—about one-tenth of their real value. This was no use whatever, so far as he was concerned; he needed the equivalent of a thousand pounds to pay off Rossi. He stated, in fact, that he had given the paltry one hundred pounds to Luigi and Renato as a fee for their trouble.

If the police were satisfied with this story, the press was not. Journalists did their own investigations, and one newspaper reported that a neighbour had heard Maria cry out for "pardon" on the fatal morning of the murder. Other newspapers would not accept that two young men of impeccable record and background could so easily, for motives of petty robbery—and all that to assist a shabby and shifty character like Fantasia—allow themselves to become so easily and voluntarily involved in a brutal murder. Ancillary questions were asked: why nine stabbings when one would have been sufficient? What could a slight and helpless girl have done to trigger off such a vicious attack? And, the sixty-four-thousand-dollar question—what was the *real* motive behind the murder, when any professional criminal would have known that Maria's modest and pathetic collection of jewellery would not have brought much in the way of money in the frugal receiver market?

The newspapers rightly posed the questions, but the answers were not forthcoming. The trial, set down for July, was awaited with impatient interest and curiosity. Everybody felt that there was more behind the scenes than had been released to the public.

And then, by a strange coincidence—almost the day before the start of the trial—the judge appointed to try the case was knocked down by a car in Rome and was taken to hospital. It seems odd, looking back, that another judge was not appointed, and that the Ministry of Justice saw fit to postpone the trial until the judge had recovered, rather than find a substitute. The net result of this curious delaying action was that the trial was put back for another six months.

In the intervening period the newspapers investigated the various people involved in the case with a kind of dedicated enthusiasm. Journalists dug up a mass of background information, and some of it turned out to be quite strange and possibly significant material.

Take the killer himself, for instance—Luigi Tirone. During the German occupation of Rome in 1943-44 he had started as a member of the Underground resistance movement, but later had changed his allegiance to become a collaborationist and a Nazi informer. He was therefore a natural target for the anti-Fascist and anti-Nazi factions which gained ascendancy after the surrender of Italy. Yet, although he was denounced as a Nazi sympathizer after the liberation of Rome, no action was taken by authority. By this time Luigi was posing as a partisan again, and was apparently accepted at face value—so much so that he soon obtained a commission as an officer in the Italian Liberation Army, which was controlled by the Committee of National Liberation and the United States Fifth Army.

Luigi's behaviour in action was so bad that he was court-martialled for cowardice—and acquitted. His colonel protested to the Minister of War against the acquittal, but the protest was ignored. It was beginning to look as though Luigi had influential friends in high places.

Other odd incidents came to light. Luigi Tirone's dossier vanished from the filing cabinet at the Ministry of Justice shortly after his arrest for the murder of Maria. And it was discovered that while in custody awaiting trial he had been allowed to spend two days at home with his family, in civilian clothes and without guard or escort. This had happened during his transfer from one prison to another.

The press, sensing subtler manoeuvrings and mysteries behind the scenes, began to dig deeper and to shed any polite reticence where important public figures were involved. Journalists found themselves on the fringe of scandal. They discovered and announced in print that Luigi Tirone's uncle was none other than Signor Spataro, Under-Secretary of State for Home Affairs, and a member of the right-wing Christian Democrat Party. His Ministry was responsible for State security and the administration of prisons, and it looked as if Luigi's two-day unofficial parole to visit his family had been arranged by some discreet political wire-pulling.

The newspapers, particularly the left-wing and Communist ones, went gunning for Spataro in a big way, accusing him of corruption and demanding his resignation—but nothing happened, even though the predominantly left-wing government might reasonably have welcomed the opportunity to get rid of an embarrassing right-wing minister. Spataro remained in office.

It also seemed odd to the press that Luigi, well connected as he was, should after his two days of unguarded freedom have voluntarily and without apparent pressure returned to jail to await trial for murder when, with the aid of influential friends, he might well have escaped permanently and perhaps fled the country.

On his return to jail, however, after consultation with his family and advisers during his unofficial parole, Luigi withdrew his admission of murder. He now said that he had not really killed Maria at all, but was merely covering up for the real murderer who had killed her in order to recover secret documents in her possession.

Needless to say, this pronouncement was received by the press with extreme scepticism, and it merely started a new hare, which the journalists pursued with unflagging energy and enthusiasm.

*   *   *

In an Italy just emerging from the ravages of war and the shadow of many years of totalitarian fascism, the idea of political murder was by no means fanciful, and for many it must have seemed only too plausible.

New facts emerged and were duly published and commented on in the papers—and generally speaking they were facts which must have been known already to the police, although they had not been divulged at this stage. For example, it was learned that Maria Laffi had kept a diary, but several pages had been torn from it. By whom, and how significant were those pages?

Furthermore, two previous victims of unsolved murders had been friends of Maria. Both had been boarding-house keepers, and in both cases pages were found to have been torn out of their respective hotel registers when the bodies had been discovered. The police had been unable to find any logical motive for the murders—not even theft. By drawing a rather strained parallel, some newspapers suggested that the theft of Maria's jewels (which had brought so little reward in the receiver market) might well have been a subterfuge to cover the real reason for the killing. But the real reason for the killing remained an enigma, and no sensible suggestions were put forward. The press operated on the old and well-established principle of asking the questions without being able to provide the answers. It was the question-mark approach to journalism—building up a story in which the questions imply the answers, whether they are correct or not. And every minor crawling incident which was revealed by turning up a stone became sensational headline material. Such is the cavalier press fashion with stories which appear to involve political scandal.

The next significant event was the discovery of a link (albeit an obscure one, but good for the press headlines) between the murdered Maria Laffi and General Mario Roatta—a Fascist army officer who had disappeared the previous March while being tried for treason and murder. The tenuous link was embodied in the fact that a previous murder victim, a chauffeur, had frequently been required to drive an officer who was an aide-de-camp of General Roatta to Maria's flat for the usual services.

When Roatta disappeared during his trial, so did all the documentary evidence in the case, which was alleged to implicate many top Establishment people in Italy, from the king down to allied officers. The entire business had been well organized and executed, and from the point of view of the press the speculative possibilities now opened up even more. Could it be that Maria had known something about the General Roatta documentation? Had Roatta been kidnapped and spirited away and murdered as some part of a Royalist plot? And had Maria been eliminated because she was in possession of some knowledge or papers which could prove damaging to the conspirators? Finally, had Maria's killers been highly paid to stand the rap for what amounted to political assassination?

One final coincidental fact emerged which seemed to clinch the suggestion of political intrigue, and that was the arrest of a nobleman named Max Capuano on charges involving the extortion of money from none other than Signor Rossi—the same Rossi who had been, through his wife, an extortion victim of Alfio Fantasia. It was this previous incident, and Fantasia's urgent need for money to repay Rossi, which had set in motion the whole mysterious train of events that led to the murder of Maria Laffi.

Max Capuano, an executive of one of Italy's big chemical concerns, was found on investigation to have embezzled some sixty million lire from the company, and was blackmailing members of the management who were alleged to have sold metallurgical secrets to both the Germans and the Americans. Further inquiries revealed that among Capuano's associates were Alfio Fantasia, Alberto Gallupi (who had originally suggested to Fantasia that he could extract money from Rossi's wife by blackmail), and an unidentified "Maria" who, it was thought, could only have been Maria Laffi.

Here then was another possibility—that Maria had been murdered, not for money, but because she was in possession of papers or evidence implicating Capuano and his colleagues (including Fantasia and Gallupi) in international blackmail and even treason.

Wherever the truth lay among the tortuous twisted threads of the case, it seemed certain that the Maria Laffi murder trial would lift the lid off a hotbed of cloak-and-dagger intrigue involving politics, high finance, and very important people in Italy and other countries. There were too many interwoven strands to permit any facile explanation, and by this time the original suggestion that Maria had been murdered for the theft of a mere one hundred pounds worth of jewels was the most improbable theory of all. The world awaited the full denouement with intense interest and an almost greedy anticipation.

The trial, when it came, after many postponements, brought the press and the public in Italy and elsewhere down to earth with a disappointing thud. The case was treated within the original terms of reference as simply the murder of a prostitute for motives of theft, and not one of the related matters which had aroused such exotic speculations in the newspapers were referred to by either the prosecution or the defence. Luigi Tirone, presented as a crazy mixed-up victim of Fascist youth, was sentenced to life imprisonment, as were Fantasia and Gallupi. Renato Piacente, the young undergraduate, was sentenced to thirty years' imprisonment. Max Capuano, the embezzling businessman, whom many considered to be the key figure in this baffling intrigue, was fined a modest 30,000 lire and sent to prison for nine years.

And that was the end of that. Whatever secrets or conspiracies lay behind the superficial facts of murder, they were never brought to light. All that remains is the smoke of speculation and imaginative guesswork based on unremitting investigation by Italian and foreign journalists. Were they so wide of the mark as the trial judge implied when he described newspaper hints of political intrigue as "a ludicrous hoax"?

Twenty years have gone by since the trial. If there ever was more to the case than the simple surface facts, then people in the know, and there must have been quite a few of them quite apart from the principals who were jailed, have maintained a discreet silence for a long time.

Chapter 24

THE ODD PROPHET

In the early nineteenth century a wealthy New York businessman named Elijah Pierson experienced a revelation while riding on a bus. He claimed that an angel appeared before him and told him that he was a reincarnation of Elijah the Tishbite, and that his task in life was to prepare for the coming of the Prophet. Pierson took the angel's message very much to heart, and told his wife and daughter and friends that he had been commanded by God to await the Prophet who would come to take over the world in the name of the Lord. What his wife thought about it is not recorded—in any case, she died soon afterwards, leaving Pierson and his daughter to wait alone for the Prophet to turn up.

While we leave Pierson waiting, we must now take a look at a handsome young man named Robert Mathews, who started his career in 1804 as apprentice to a carpenter. He was then sixteen years old, and possessed an intense interest in the scriptures, large parts of which he could quote by heart. He moved from Hudson to New York, earning a living by doing casual work as a carpenter, and spending his spare time in churches and at prayer meetings—where he frequently caused trouble by interrupting to state his own rather forceful views. Because of his arrogant attitude, Mathews became very unpopular in religious circles, and he in turn grew more and more hostile to orthodox religion. He became known as "Jumping Jesus". Then, unexpectedly, he married and in due course produced two sons and a daughter.

His domestic responsibilities seem to have held his religious obsession in abeyance for a long time, but the breakout when it finally came was all the more dramatic. One day, after several years of uneventful marriage, he took his three young children away from home and "into the wilderness". Three or four days later he was tracked down in the woods near Albany, sheltering in a crude hut made from tree branches. The children were starving, as was Mathews himself; but while he allowed the children to be taken back to their mother, he himself refused to return. He insisted on staying in the "wilderness", starving or not. There was a parallel in his mind to Jesus Christ, who had also been a carpenter and had stayed in the wilderness alone.

During Mathews's sojourn in idle isolation a great revelation came to him—he was no longer Robert Mathews, the carpenter, but St Matthew, or Matthias, the Prophet. In order to fit himself for his new role in life he grew a long dense beard that suited his tall lean figure, and deserted his family.

After his return from the "wilderness", Matthias, the new Prophet, devoted his time to preaching at religious meetings in various places. He was a fluent and impressive speaker, with an encyclopaedic memory of the scriptures, and he began to attract followers. But Matthias was not enamoured of his nomadic and austere way of life; as a Prophet he felt that he was entitled to more civilized amenities, such as a nice home in New York, surrounded by a few faithful disciples who would be a captive audience for his religious harangues.

In New York, Matthias met a prosperous businessman named Mr Mills and talked him into providing financial support to further the good works of the Prophet. The support included the purchase of valuable silver plates and chalices engraved with the Lion of Judah to enhance the Prophet's religious ceremonies, and a luxurious royal purple robe and a gold watch for the Prophet to wear in order to maintain his proper dignity. But Mr Mills's family were most uncharitable about the whole business, and after a long dispute managed to have both the Prophet and his benefactor committed to a lunatic asylum. At this point Mr Mills, too, lost faith in the Prophet, and gave him no further support. But he had given him one valuable item of information—the name and address of a religious man who believed himself to be Elijah and professed to be waiting for the coming of the Prophet, as commanded by an angel. Matthias needed no second invitation. The paths of Elijah and the Prophet were destined to cross at long last.

On his release from the asylum he called on Elijah Pierson, and very quickly convinced him that he, Matthias, was the long awaited Prophet as foretold by the angel. Overjoyed by his good fortune, Pierson begged Matthias to do him the honour of staying and living in his house. Matthias accepted the invitation with alacrity, and rewarded Pierson by telling him that he was not Elijah but was really a reincarnation of John the Baptist, which pleased Pierson very much.

Matthias began to enjoy home comforts. He used the house as a base to widen his circle of disciples. Pierson introduced him to Mr Benjamin Folger, another rich New York businessman, who though at first sceptical soon fell under the Prophet's hypnotic spell. He, too, became a disciple and contributed more purple robes and a jewelled ceremonial sword.

In 1822 the Prophet visited the summer house of Mr and Mrs Folger, and liked it very much. He decided that Folger had been moved by the spirit and had, without knowing it, really bought the house under divine guidance as an abode for the Prophet. If Folger was not aware of this, he was not left long in ignorance. Matthias lost no time in persuading him that, as with Pierson, it was his duty to support the Prophet and provide him with a home—this particular home, in fact. For his foresight and generosity Folger would receive the blessing of the Almighty and a guarantee of forgiveness for all his sins, but he was reminded that any non-compliance with the wishes of the Prophet would incur the wrath of God, which would be most unpleasant. Such was the hold of this man upon his disciples that not only did Folger make over his house to Matthias, but so did Pierson, and both gave him ten thousand dollars each in cash. The kingdom of the Prophet was expanding rapidly.

Matthias accepted these offerings with patronizing indulgence—they were no more than his right. Folger's house he named "Mount Zion". In a patriarchal fashion he ruled his small flock, which consisted of Mr and Mrs Folger, Pierson and his daughter, and a devout coloured servant. Life at Mount Zion revolved entirely around the Prophet. He would preach to his assembled disciples for hours, and occasionally would carry out a "purification" ceremony he had devised, in which they all stripped to the nude while he sprinkled them with "holy water".

This nude ritual may well have triggered the Prophet's next divine revelation. An inner voice told him that Mrs Folger (a mother of two children) was his spiritual partner and must ceremonially consummate the unity required by such an esoteric affinity. With no audible protest from Mr Folger, the Prophet took Mrs Folger to his bed.

But Folger's reluctant acquiescence was to be rewarded. The Prophet decided that his own daughter, Isobelle, was Folger's spiritual partner, and he sent for her to come to Mount Zion. There was a little trouble with Isobelle's husband, but he was silenced by the gift of a gold watch, and Isobelle duly joined the Prophet's flock to sleep with Mr Folger while Mrs Folger continued to sleep with the Prophet. Isobelle did not much care for the arrangement, however, and she soon left. Her place was taken by another recruit to the movement, a young widow named Catherine. She was ceremoniously given to Folger by Matthias, even though Pierson rather fancied her for himself, thinking it was about time that he, too, was awarded a female spiritual partner.

Pierson had been feeling for some time that he was getting a raw deal. He was a sick man, and the Prophet always seemed to assign to him the most menial tasks. And he had to sleep alone while the others communed in bed with their spiritual partners. He began to grow disenchanted with the Prophet, and decided he wanted his house back—at least, he wanted the lease transferred from Matthias to his daughter Elizabeth. If he could not out-talk and dominate the Prophet's powerful personality, at least he could try a little quiet blackmail. Even the Prophet had to recognize that certain spiritual matters at Mount Zion conflicted with the law. Pierson, ill and not caring much whether he lived or died, made his point and recovered his own house, but not with the Prophet's blessing. He deserted the flock and went back home.

A few days later he was followed by the Prophet, accompanied by Mrs Folger, Catherine and Matthias's two sons, who decided to be unwanted guests. Pierson was unable physically to throw them out of the house and was probably too afraid to call the police. The unwanted guests stayed.

The next day, shortly after a meal, Pierson became violently ill and partly paralysed. Matthias solemnly announced that he was possessed by devils, and that anyone who tried to help him would be assisting the devil in his evil work and suffer eternal damnation. Pierson, alone and unattended in his room, managed to live for several days. When he fell from the bed to the floor he was forced to stay there, for the greater discomfort of the devils in possession of him. Eventually he died.

This incident came as rather a shock to the disciples. Their faith in the Prophet began to founder. Even the most fervent believer could not help connecting Pierson's death with the fact that he had so recently taken his house back from Matthias, and the sick man had the symptoms of poisoning rather than possession by devils. After all, devils affected the mind rather than the stomach. To make matters worse, Mr Folger went bankrupt, and the house and other assets he had bestowed upon the Prophet became in law the property of Folger's creditors. The disenchantment grew and hostility replaced adulation. Very soon the Prophet thought it expedient to go away for a while to meditate.

The meditation lasted a week, and then he was back at the Folgers's house to meet with an ice-cold reception and very reluctant hospitality. He was asked to leave at the earliest possible moment, as soon as he had secured accommodation elsewhere. It would have been better for the Folgers if the Prophet had not been allowed to set foot over the door, but he was a man of very dominating personality. He stayed at what had once been Mount Zion for a few days, warning his hosts that only sickness and death could follow such a satanic inhospitable attitude to a Prophet.

On the morning of his departure, Matthias took no breakfast and drank no coffee—but the rest of the family did. Soon after the Prophet had left the house the entire Folger family became violently sick, but fortunately nobody died. There was no positive proof that they had been poisoned by Matthias, but Folger was determined that he should not get away scot-free. He managed to get a warrant issued for Matthias's arrest on a charge of theft.

The police, when they caught the Prophet, were astonished at the contents of his cases: rich purple robes, a ceremonial sword, a large key to the Gate of Heaven, a night-cap embroidered with the names of the twelve apostles—and the gold watch and a sum of money which Folger alleged had been stolen from him.

Meanwhile the police were acting in another direction. They had received information that Pierson had died, not from epilepsy as had been suggested, but from poisoning. The body was exhumed and the stomach removed for inspection. The police pathologist found evidence of poison. The lesser charge of theft was dropped in favour of the more serious charge of murder.

Matthias, the Prophet, was brought to trial in New York in 1835 at the age of forty-seven, and put on a histrionic performance which would have been comic had not the circumstances been so tragic. Elegantly dressed, with luxuriant wavy greying hair and a long full beard, he dominated the court-room, and roundly cursed the judge, jury and witnesses, threatening damnation for them all. Evidence was brought to demonstrate that the Prophet was insane, but other evidence proved his shrewd business acumen, and he was adjudged sane enough to stand trial.

The medical evidence on Pierson, based on an examination of the stomach and oesophagus after exhumation, indicated arsenical poisoning, but this was in the days before positive tests for arsenic had been discovered, and the presence of arsenic did not rule out the possibility of death from another cause. It was revealed that Pierson had suffered from epilepsy for a long time, and this could well have been an important contributory factor if not the actual cause of his death. A great deal of the evidence was circumstantial, and the Prophet's eccentricities did not necessarily show murderous intent. The prosecution failed to dispel an element of doubt and the jury, perhaps a little concerned that there might after all be something in the question of eternal damnation, returned a verdict of Not Guilty. The Prophet was acquitted—but not for long.

He was promptly arrested on another charge—one of assault, brought by the husband of his own daughter whom he had "donated" for a while to Folger as his spiritual partner. On this charge the Prophet was convicted and sentenced to three months' imprisonment, plus another month for contempt of court in respect of curses directed at the judge and jury. Matthias learned the hard way that temporal law has to be obeyed just as much as spiritual law.

When Matthias was released from jail, he travelled west and attempted to resume his preaching and perhaps recruit some new disciples in areas where he was relatively unknown. But he was now a discredited prophet. His kingdom had collapsed and his divine authority had evaporated. Nobody took him seriously any more. There were other prophets who were far more influential, such as Joseph Smith and Brigham Young, who were founding the Mormon religion. Matthias was no longer regarded as a prophet, but simply a con man.

It is said that while he was in Utah he visited Joseph Smith, perhaps because of some sense of affinity, and perhaps to find out the qualities that went to make up a successful prophet. Smith's comment on Matthias was that he had a "brilliant intellect but a mind full of darkness". And that seems to be about as generous a summing-up as the Prophet, Matthias, could reasonably expect.

Chapter 25

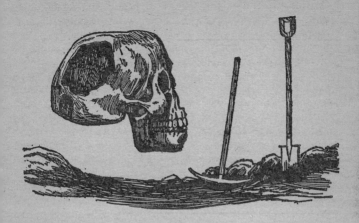

THE MISSING LINK

NOT all crimes are of the type that break a clearly defined law and therefore invoke the attention of the police and the judiciary. They may involve dishonesty and even fraud, but without any financial motive. It is more usual to think of such misdemeanours in terms of scandal, particularly when they question the integrity of somebody of standing in society, or of eminence in the arts and sciences. It was a scandal of this kind which blew like a tornado through the reputation of Charles Dawson, solicitor and amateur archaeologist, nearly half a century after his death. For Dawson was the discoverer of the Piltdown Man, who, after some forty years of respectability in scientific circles, turned out to be a hoax.

Dawson lived at Lewes, Sussex. As a man of law he was a respected member of the community, and his hobby of archaeology conferred on him an intellectual cachet. He was a very active archaeologist (indeed, palaeontologist) and spent his spare time roaming the countryside in search of prehistoric flints and fossils, and with much success. His collection included many unusual specimens—even relics of a dinosaur and bones of a new unclassified prehistoric animal which was duly named after him. He was well known at the British Museum, where he used to send many of his finds for inspection and identification, for his indefatigable enthusiasm. He was regarded as quite an expert in his own right.

In 1908, at the age of forty-four, Dawson was the steward of Barkham Manor at Piltdown in Sussex. A nearby gravel-pit, close to Piltdown Common, particularly interested him because of the unusual colour and nature of the gravel. He did some digging in the pit himself, and asked the estate workmen to bring to him any curious pieces of bone or gravel they happened to find when working in the pit.

During the next few years they found a great deal. Dawson took a series of more than twenty specimens of flint, bones and teeth to the British Museum. So impressed were the Museum authorities that one of their senior palaeontologists personally took part in diggings at the Piltdown site.

Among these finds were fragments of a very old skull—pieces of a fossilized cranium, and an ape-like section of jawbone complete with teeth, but with the molars worn flat. In addition there were animal fossils dating back half a million years to the early Ice Age. As all the finds were roughly in the same level of the gravel pit, it was logical to assume that they had approximately the same point of origin in time.

The piece of jaw and the small fragments of skull, on close examination, appeared to be more human than simian. The flattened molars were undeniably characteristic of the swinging motion of the human jaw as compared with the less flexible animal jaw.

The remains were scrutinized by experts, who decided that the skull fragments—neither fully simian nor fully human—were probably relics of a "Piltdown Man". He had been a prehistoric ancestor of *homo sapiens* today, was almost certainly half a million years old, and could well be the "missing link" between monkey and man. The Piltdown Man was a scientific discovery of major importance, and he took his place alongside the Neanderthal Man, the Heidelberg Man and the Peking Man as one of the honourable ancestors of mankind, in its several forms, as we know it today.

There were, of course, sceptics and critics, but on the whole the Piltdown Man was accepted and respected as a tangible "missing link", and proof of the Darwinian theory of evolution. His reputation survived virtually untarnished for forty years. Plaster casts of the jaw and the skull fragments were sent to museums all over the world to be put on display in glass cases. Dead as he was, the Piltdown Man outlived his discoverer by many years, for Charles Dawson died in 1916 at the age of fifty-two. The Piltdown Man had several decades of vicarious life ahead of him in academic minds before he was finally destroyed.

With a reputed age of about half a million years, the Piltdown Man was virtually the father of all human beings (perhaps mother—the sex was never determined). There were no relics which pre-dated him, and therefore he was unique. In honour of the man who had discovered him he was given the Latin name of *Eoanthropus Dawsoni*. He had arrived, and was presumably here to stay. But in learned anthropological circles argument and controversy continued behind the scenes.

The Piltdown Man might have passed into history and become a basic ingredient of education, like the Battle of Hastings and the French Revolution, had it not been for the inexorable progress of science, particularly in the fields of chemical analysis and spectrography, and in measurement techniques using X-rays and radio-activity—the measurement of the concentration of radio-active Strontium 90 in bones, for example.

After World War II the attention of the scientific world was drawn once more to the relics of the Piltdown Man when, in 1950, Dr Kenneth Oakley, a British Museum geologist, used a new system of chemical dating by measuring the amount of fluorine in the bones. Buried bones absorb fluorine from the soil; the longer they have been in the ground, the more fluorine they contain. The process is very slow, and therefore the timescale is long. If the Piltdown bones were really half a million years old then they would show an appreciable fluorine content. But, in fact, they did not. Dr Oakley's careful tests revealed that the Piltdown remains could not possibly be half a million years old, and were certainly not more than 50,000 years of age. He had not at this stage tested the jawbone, but had assumed that it came from the same point in time as the fragments of cranium and certain other genuine fossils.

This discovery put paid to the "missing link" theory that

Eonthropus Dawsoni, the Piltdown Man, represented the evolutionary stage of development between monkey and man. A missing link half a million years old was feasible, but a mere 50,000 years was far too recent for such a pronounced evolutionary change to have taken place.

The debunking of the Piltdown Man now began in earnest. The next step was conducted by Dr J. S. Weiner, an anthropologist at Oxford University, with the aid of Dr Oakley himself, and a colleague, Professor Wilfred le Gros Clark. All three men were experts, and they set out to analyse certain points of detail which seemed inconsistent with the "missing link" theory.

Weiner, for instance, was puzzled by the flat-topped teeth set in the undoubtedly ape-like jaw. While the flat molars were more characteristic of the human, they were flat in an odd way, and the edges of the flat area were sharper than one would expect. He carried out meticulous tests on the jawbone and teeth, using the most up-to-date electronic equipment available at that time. As a result, a series of harsh facts came to light.

In the first place, microscopic scratches on the flat tops of the molars suggested that they had been filed down, and chemical analysis showed that the filed surface had been stained with a brown oil paint. But the next discovery was even more sensational—the jawbone itself, including the teeth, was not even 50,000 years old. It was contemporary. Chemical and radio-activity tests demonstrated beyond all doubt that it was part of the jaw of a modern ape (an orang-outang, it was thought) which had been cleverly doctored by chemical staining to resemble a genuine fossil.

The three scientists then turned their attention to the other remains found in the gravel in the Piltdown pit. Some of the items, including fragments of cranial bone, were genuine enough and about 50,000 years old, but the remainder, including all the principal specimens, were fakes. They were pieces of modern bone discoloured by chemical stains, in particular bichromate of iron. The Piltdown Man was undoubtedly an outrageous fraud.

The cat was out of the bag with a vengeance, but Dawson himself was above suspicion. He had been dead for a long time, and his reputation was such that one did not—indeed, dared not—question his integrity. The culprit obviously lay elsewhere.

It was known that Dawson used to pay the estate workmen for any flints and fossils they handed over to him, and the amount paid would vary with the apparent age and importance of the specimen. Consequently there was an obvious temptation for the workmen to "salt" the gravel with faked fossils, in particular specimens which would appear to have pre-historic significance—and would therefore earn a bigger fee. It was assumed that those fossils which had been shown to be genuinely 50,000 years old were true Piltdown finds (but they were very much in the minority), while the remainder, consisting of stained contemporary bones—including the ape's jawbone with the filed teeth—had been put into the gravel as a hoax or fraud to extract money out of poor old gullible Charles Dawson.

This theory, however, could not stand up to critical examination. It pre-supposed, for a start, that the workmen concerned with the gravel-pit possessed sufficient palaeontological knowledge to be able to stain bones and teeth with enough expertise to deceive an expert like Dawson, and that they were informed enough about evolutionary anatomy to take the trouble to file the molars in the ape's jawbone flat enough to suggest human origin—and, indeed, that they were able to obtain an ape's jawbone at all (it is not the kind of thing one can readily buy in a shop). It also pre-supposed that they had planted the jawbone to match the genuine pieces of fossiled cranium which they had discovered in the pit, and even more unlikely that they had recognized the skull fragments for what they were. Such a theory credited the Piltdown labourers with as much expert knowledge of fossils as Dawson himself—or the British Museum for that matter. As a theory it was untenable.

Even worse, it was easily confirmed that no further prehistoric relics had ever been found at Piltdown after Dawson's death, and to clinch the argument it was eventually discovered that even the genuine animal fossils, those which had been proved to be 50,000 years old, had come from elsewhere. The genuine fossils had, of course, given credence to the spurious antiquity of the faked relics—but not one of them, whether genuine or false, was of true Piltdown origin. They had all been put into the gravel by hand.

While one might just conceivably believe that a skilled and competent labourer might, given the know-how, be capable of staining modern bone fragments with bichromate chemicals and planting them in the gravel, it was surely asking too much to accept that the same workman would also have access to genuine fossils dating back 50,000 years (including a pre-historic elephant tooth from Tunisia) and use these as props to be able to pass off the doctored modern bones as antiques.

The man who possessed a large collection of fossils, including some pre-historic skull fragments, was Dawson himself. And it was known that Dawson had carried out experiments in staining bones with various chemicals—partly to "find a way of staining bones in order to preserve them", and partly "to discover the way in which natural staining occurred".

Finally, as a matter of interest, some three years after the discovery and launching upon the world of the Piltdown Man, the remains of a second "missing link" were unearthed by Dawson at a site some two miles away from the original Piltdown gravel-pit. These relics, when examined, were also shown to be chemically stained fakes.

There we have most of the evidence in the case of Dawson versus the world of modern science. Dawson is long dead, and most of the evidence is circumstantial and therefore inconclusive. The only tangible evidence remains in the fossils and flints, genuine and fraudulent, which have yielded their secrets to modern methods of analysis. All that is left are the questions. Was it a hoax or a fraud? And was Dawson guilty? If so, why did he do it and what did he hope to gain from it? There was certainly no question of financial gain—indeed, Dawson spent money in paying for specimens found by workmen in the gravel. Was it a case of an amateur desperately in search of professional recognition? If so, he achieved it for a while.

It is simple enough to assume that Charles Dawson's enthusiasm for fossil collecting ran away with him, and that, not content with acquiring a miscellaneous collection of relatively insignificant flints and bones, he wished to be known and perhaps become famous for a really important find. He wanted to be a big fish in the small pond of fossil collectors.

On the other hand, it should be remembered that Dawson was a reputable member of his community, and by profession a solicitor—and that he was assisted in his diggings at the site by one of the British Museum's eminent palaeontologists. Does it seem likely that Dawson, who during his life was never regarded as a rogue or a cheat, would implicate an expert who was very much of a personal friend in a brash and rather naïve attempt to hoax the entire scientific world?

Was Dawson himself the victim of another hoaxer who, in addition to having the ability to stain bones so that they resembled fossils, had access to an impressive number of genuine fossils? And if so, bearing in mind Dawson's experience and expertise, would he be likely to be taken in? There is no evidence that Dawson was as gullible as those who accepted the fact of the Piltdown Man.

On balance, it rather looks as though Charles Dawson himself was the hoaxer. His motives will never be known. His hoax, despite his many doubters and opponents, survived for forty years, and was finally demolished by science.

Poor old "missing link"! When the fraud was finally exposed in 1953 there must have been many who were genuinely sorry to witness the annihilation of the Piltdown Man—the erasing of a remote and completely fictitious phase in the history of human evolution. One can't help feeling that there was a definite niche and need for the Piltdown Man in history—had he been genuine!

Chapter 26

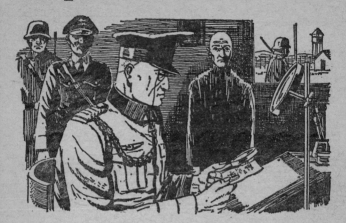

OPERATION INFLATION

WARFARE is not exclusively a matter of force of arms. While basically it may be necessary to demolish the military strength of an enemy as a prelude to invasion and occupation, other measures can be equally effective in shortening the period of hostilities before surrender—attacks on the economy of a country, for example, by blockade and sanctions. But there are other more subtle means. One which has a certain wry appeal in that it depends on the cupidity of human nature for its success is to forge the enemy's currency in vast amounts, distribute it as widely as possible, and hope that people will be dishonest and greedy enough to hoard it and spend it. Such a flood of useless paper money passing into circulation would cause a galloping inflation and undermine the economy almost overnight.

It was Heinrich Himmler, in the early years of World War II, who decided that an attack of acute inflation might very rapidly persuade Britain to give up the struggle and negotiate peace terms. After Dunkirk, when the blitz-krieg was in full swing, German Intelligence gained an erroneous impression that the British people had reached a final stage of desperation. The blockade, the air-raids and the stringent rationing had produced, it was thought, a tense situation in which a sudden inflationary economic crisis on top of all the other hardships would almost certainly bring about the fall of the government, which would be replaced by Nazi sympathizers and result in conditional surrender and an end of fighting. Himmler thought that the quickest and most effective way of achieving the total collapse of the British economy, which was already under strain, was to forge and print millions of British banknotes and distribute them throughout the United Kingdom from aircraft during bombing raids.

It was not a new idea. It had been tried before as a tactical weapon in military confrontations, with notable lack of success. But previous attempts had lacked the German thorough and methodical approach to the technical details of the problem. The forgeries had to be good. They had to be so good that nothing short of an intensive scientific examination would distinguish between a genuine note and a bad one. They had to be of a quality worthy of the Bank of England itself.

An officer named Captain Friedrich Kruger was appointed by Himmler to set up this highly specialized operation. He was an able administrator. His first move was to recruit a team of experts in art, draughtsmanship, process engraving, colour printing and paper technology. Very shrewdly he selected most of his experts from among Jewish prisoners detained by the Gestapo, inviting their willing co-operation as an alternative to the gas-oven. Naturally enough, they were prepared to co-operate; while it might not alter their ultimate fate in the long term, assuming Germany won the war, at least it meant a postponement of the death sentence and an improvement of living conditions to something more tolerable.

Bank-notes are printed by what are called "security printers". For obvious reasons the companies engaged in such printing take every possible precaution to make sure that not a single note or printing plate, or even a sheet of blank bank-note paper, can be stolen from the fenced-off security area. But in the case of the German essay in forgery an even greater degree of security was called for, because the operation had also to be kept top secret. If British agents were to learn what the Germans were doing, the entire project would inevitably fail. The Bank of England could very quickly issue newly designed bank-notes and withdraw the old.

The counterfeiting factory was therefore established in what could be regarded as one of the most secure sites in Nazi Germany—the middle of a concentration camp. A special block in Sachsenhausen concentration camp was allocated to the task. It was surrounded by a high electrified fence and patrolled by S.S. guards. Here, in this concentration camp within a concentration camp, Captain Kruger set his team of experts to work, under the general management of a man named Oskar Stein. The key member of his staff was one of the prisoners, an experienced "professional" forger who for many years had made a good private living by forging Swiss, British and American currency. He was nothing if not a perfectionist.

Although the project sounded simple enough, given modern photographic, engraving and colour-printing equipment—and the Germans were always accomplished in the graphic sciences—great difficulties arose in practice. The first major obstacle was paper—the special linen paper used for British bank-notes which at that time was manufactured by only one company in the world. As there was no possible way of obtaining supplies of this exclusive paper, the only thing Kruger could do was to arrange to have it analysed and then synthesized by Germany's highly proficient chemists.

At first linen imported from the Middle East was used, but the finished product was not quite good enough. The paper lacked the crisp resilience of the genuine article. It felt wrong to the touch, and this alone would create suspicion in a bank clerk accustomed to handling notes all day long. A great deal of research was expended on improving the quality of the paper, and the problem was finally solved by using old linen cloth and reprocessing it. The fibres were drier and more brittle, and produced a paper which was virtually indistinguishable from the real thing. The watermark impression was a relatively minor challenge.

Getting the paper exactly right was perhaps the biggest hurdle to be overcome, but many difficulties still lay ahead. The next step was the photographing of genuine British bank-notes and the production of engraved plates for colour process printing, not to mention the difficulties of selecting the precise grades and colours of the printing inks, and the introduction of security "traps" during the actual printing. Here the counterfeiter's skill proved to be invaluable. There was more to forgery than merely copying genuine bank-notes. In the printing of bank-notes anti-forgery tricks are introduced by the security printers during the actual printing—slight modifications of colour blending or register or actual design intended to deceive the naïve or unobservant counterfeiter. But the experienced eye could detect what the colour camera might easily overlook. The British bank-notes which in due course began to roll off the printing presses in Germany were very good forgeries indeed.

There was, however, one fundamental snag which had nothing to do with the quality of the forged notes. They were all of high denomination, mainly £5, with a sprinkling of higher values such as £10 and £20, and at that period in wartime Britain high-denomination notes were seldom if ever used by the ordinary people. With wages at less than half of what they are today, a fiver was about the highest value of bank-note in general public circulation, and even they tended to be few and far between. The man who flashed a fiver was regarded as affluent as compared with the man who produced five one-pound notes from his wallet, mainly because fivers were not in wide general use. It was, therefore, a major error of psychology for Germany to forge high-denomination bank-notes for "free" distribution to the British public. Pound notes and ten-shilling notes might have made some impact, for they were the common currency of the day, but what was a man to do with a bunch of fivers, tenners or twenty-pound notes found lying in a street or a field after an air-raid?

From the German point of view, of course, the high-denomination notes would, in theory, speed the inflationary process. To print the equivalent amount of one-pound notes and ten-shilling notes would have added enormously to the bulk of paper to be "air-dropped", and put up the cost of the whole operation. One twenty-pound note would theoretically do the job of twenty one-pound notes or forty ten-shilling notes with a considerable saving in printing costs, but it overlooked the fact that the average British citizen did not, and probably would not, dare to spend a twenty-pound note in a shop or change it in a bank. The fiver was marginally acceptable, but a sudden spate of fivers in a particular area could only give rise to suspicion, and a very close inspection of each note presented to a retailer or bank clerk. The forgeries were perfect, but the basic psychological premises were wrong.

However, the operation was not yet ready for launching. The new notes coming off the printing-machines were splendid, but they had to be aged and given a soiled, creased appearance as if they had been well used. A special machine was invented, with the forger's aid, to convert the new notes into well-worn but serviceable specimens, and various handwritten marks were added to some of them—the kind of marks and figures which bank clerks write on the top note of a bundle to check on the number of notes remaining.

Great care had been taken to make sure that the serial numbers on the notes were within the range of serial numbers in use on genuine British notes, and in this respect German agents operating in Britain rendered a complete and accurate information service.

By the beginning of 1944 all was ready. The bank-notes were superficially as good as any issued by the Bank of England, and unlikely to be detected as forgeries for a long time. Distribution commenced, by air-drops during air-raids and through agents operating in neutral countries. A massive fortune in counterfeit notes was flung into the German war effort, and the British economy should in theory have collapsed like the South Sea Bubble. In fact, nothing happened at all. Several factors contributed to the futility of the exercise, quite apart from the psychological error of forging high-denomination notes.

First, the British Government very quickly learned that counterfeit currency was being dropped from aircraft, and the public were alerted to the fact and asked to hand in such currency to the nearest police-station. Second, the British, being inherently a law-abiding and generally honest people, did exactly what they were asked to do. They picked up the forged fivers and tenners and the rest and handed them over to the police. To have made use of the forged money out of mercenary greed would have been tantamount to collaborating with the enemy, and there were very few Britishers who were prepared to risk a taint of that kind. Fiddle the Inland Revenue, by all means—that's an honourable occupation—

but never give comfort to the enemy, fivers for the taking or not.

If Hitler's intelligence agents had been a little more observant they might have noticed the peculiar British habit of always paying for a newspaper at an unattended street newspaper-stall when they could help themselves, unobserved—and further, of always taking the correct change for silver from the coins spread on the top of such an unattended stall. If this small but significant symptom of British insanity (which is to be seen nowhere else in the world) had been noted and reported by German spies, Himmler might well have realized the futility of his "operation inflation" and not bothered to waste so much time, effort and expense on the production of such elegant but unmarketable forgeries. The truth is that the British, in a masochistic sort of way, prefer to organize their own inflationary spirals, and what's more, they succeed where the Germans failed.

At this time the war was beginning to go badly for the Germans. North Africa was lost, Italy and Russia were almost lost, German cities and industry were experiencing thousand-bomber air-raids, and the allied invasion of Europe was imminent. Kruger abandoned his unsuccessful effort to undermine the British economy; in any case, the Bank of England was now withdrawing high-denomination notes from circulation and replacing them with notes of a new design. It was too late to start again from the beginning. Moreover, it was only too apparent that at this stage in the war the important national economy was that of the Americans, and not the British.

In a last-ditch attempt to salvage something from the wasted operation, Captain Kruger and his forgery experts at Sachsenhausen began to forge American dollars, again in notes of high denomination. Whether the ultimate intention was seriously to undermine the American economy is a matter for speculation; even Hitler himself could hardly believe in such a possibility. More likely it was an act of self-preservation conforming to a kind of Parkinsonian law—when an organization fails in one direction, it seeks another direction in which to fail in order to survive at all.

This was certainly true of the dollar forgery operation. The programme called for the printing of massive quantities of counterfeit dollars, but somehow the production line seemed to slow down. Very few dollars ever got as far as distribution. The truth was that Oskar Stein and his staff of Jewish experts, realizing only too well that the Germans were losing the war, started a deliberate go-slow policy—even to the point of sabotaging the printing machines in order to hold up production. With the possibility of liberation by the allied troops now beginning to assume reality, they were making amends for the long period of enforced co-operation in forging British currency.

The beginning of the end followed a characteristic pattern. One day, early in 1945, Captain Kruger loaded a suit-case with several thousands of forged British fivers, left the concentration camp and disappeared. Shortly afterwards, orders were received to destroy the machinery and burn all forged bank-notes and anything that might be used as evidence. The Americans had almost arrived, and the Germans were departing at high speed.

For the prisoners, escape was not so easy—at least not until the American troops had actually entered the camp. And then the others lost no time in vanishing into the German landscape with a liberal supply of counterfeit money.

They were all arrested in due course. Captain Kruger was picked up in Hamburg, but his cache of forged notes was never found. Stein, when arrested, was able to produce a note-book listing the serial numbers of many of the forged notes, which helped the authorities in rounding up the bad money. And the professional counterfeiter was discovered in Rome, where he had set up in business making counterfeit lire.

None of the men was charged with any criminal offence. Kruger had been obeying orders and was not by any stretch of imagination a war criminal—in fact, by his shrewd employment policy he had (perhaps unintentionally) saved a number of skilled Jewish craftsmen and artisans from an almost certain death. The forgers had been forced to co-operate under duress. They were interrogated, then set free.

Chapter 27

THE POSTHUMOUS GANGSTER

PERHAPS one aspect of fame which even the most notorious gangster would hardly seek is to be pursued posthumously by the police for crimes which took place after his death. Madman Pete achieved such a dubious distinction. As long as three years after he was dead and buried he was named by newspapers and the police as the man behind a series of armed robberies in France, while his best friend, who had no connection with these criminal activities, was hounded by the law as "second-in-command" to the dead gangster. If that sounds strange enough, the full story of guilty Pete and his innocent friend is even stranger. It began in the Sahara desert just before World War II.

Tataouine was a disciplinary camp of the French Foreign Legion in North Africa—a hell-hole that was in many respects worse than a prison, with appalling conditions and punishments that could turn even the toughest delinquent soldier into a human wreck. Among the offenders sent to this baking, stinking establishment in the middle of the hot desert in 1938 were Pierre Loutrel and Jo Attia, a couple of hard-bitten rebellious soldiers who were destined to become firm friends.

While they were sweating out their military service at Tataouine, France fell to the Germans. The Nazi occupation of the homeland delayed their return from North Africa, but they eventually returned to France in 1941 after a rigorous and brutal disciplinary training in the desert. At this point their careers separated for a while, and what they chose to do is perhaps the best indication of their respective characters.

Loutrel, always an opportunist, joined the infamous French Gestapo, which was a collaborative French organization whose personnel included gangsters, criminals and thugs, and whose main task it was to hunt down, interrogate, torture and kill members of the French Resistance. Jo Attia was also invited to join the Gestapo, but declined. Instead, he decided to work for the Resistance movement.

Both men were "dur"—tough and ruthless after their harrowing service in the Foreign Legion. Loutrel found no difficulty in applying his acquired brutality in the interests of Gestapo policy. He was reputed to have killed some eighty members of the French Resistance movement. Jo Attia used his toughness in a different way. In 1943 he was caught by the Gestapo, tortured, sentenced to death, reprieved, and finally sent to Mauthausen concentration camp in Austria. There he became a hero and leader of his fellow-prisoners because of his stubborn defiance of the Nazi guards, and because of his successful efforts to steal food in sufficient quantities to save many of his fellow-inmates from a sure death by starvation. He was continually risking his own life on behalf of the others.

In 1945 came D-day and the Allied landings in Normandy. The Germans were on the run, and were soon to surrender unconditionally. Jo Attia survived a forced "march of death" in which emaciated and dying prisoners were made to walk ninety miles from the concentration camp by their Nazi guards to keep them out of the hands of the advancing Allies. He was duly liberated after an experience that must have been tougher than his service at Tataouine.

For Loutrel, on the other side of the fence and a marked *collaborateur*, the situation was quite different. He had become known as Pierrot le Fou, or "Madman Pete", because of the savage and sadistic way in which he had pursued his

Gestapo duties, and with an Allied victory imminent it was clearly time for him to change his allegiance, as did so many other pro-Nazi gangsters. He decided to join the Resistance, but in an unobtrusive way. He went to the south of France and became a member of the F.F.I. (French Forces of the Interior) under an assumed name, and blandly set about killing his former Nazi associates with the same ruthlessness as he had used to murder Resistance fighters.

But it was not long before he was recognized. One day, while drinking in a bar, he was identified and challenged by a man who had known him only too well in the Gestapo phase of his career. Madman Pete could not afford to argue the point. He shot his accuser dead, claiming that the man had unjustly and maliciously insulted him by charging him with collaboration with the enemy. He evaded the police and disappeared into the underworld.

It should be remembered that France in the immediate post-war era was a haven for gangsters of all kinds. Guns abounded; they could be bought openly in bars and on the streets. Many criminals were armed with automatic weapons—a legacy of the German occupation and the Resistance. There was also a psychological climate conducive to violence which was a hangover from the Nazi reign of terror. Life had been cheap, and it was still cheap. Revaluation took time. So the gangsters did not hesitate to use their guns.

At the same time the French police and judiciary were, in the early years of the peace, more obsessed with exacting political vengeance against former Nazi sympathizers and collaborators than with suppressing ordinary non-political crime. For a time France was in the grip of a major crime wave reminiscent of Chicago in the thirties.

Madman Pete, now on the run from the police, went to Marseilles, which was one of the easiest towns in France for a criminal to sink himself without trace. He joined forces with a well-known gangster based in the town, and together they decided to exploit the possibilities of armed robberies while the police were still concerned with other more political matters. They started operations in Nice, where the biggest "job" was a hold-up in the main Post Office. That netted a quick, safe £70,000 which could be invested in expanding operations. They moved elsewhere, and eventually started on Paris. There, in 1946, they carried out three of the biggest armed robberies known in the city, including the theft of £40,000 in wages for the entire staff of the Paris Metro.

This period of intensive armed robbery was compressed into a period of one year. During this time Madman Pete met his old friend Jo Attia again, but Jo was now known as Jo le Moko. Despite their bitterly opposed activities during the German occupation—French Gestapo versus the Resistance— Pete and Jo were still firm friends, with brotherly bonds that went back to the Foreign Legion. There was never any evidence to show that Jo was concerned in crime, but his friendship with Pete did him no good, and put him under the shadow of suspicion. The newspapers, with no justification whatever, referred to him as a murderer, overlooked his splendid record in Mauthausen concentration camp, and described him as the chief lieutenant of Madman Pete, and a dangerous gangster. The police, too, regarded him as an active member of Madman Pete's hold-up gang, but this speculation was never supported by fact, except of the most circumstantial kind. Both the police and the press seemed to consider it highly unlikely that a criminal such as Madman Pete could have an old and faithful friend who was not also a criminal, particularly as one had been with the Gestapo and the other with the Resistance. No friendship could survive such a rift, and therefore it was assumed that the only interest they had in common was crime.

The incursions of the Marseilles gang into the Paris territory annoyed the local gangsters, who regarded it as poaching, and contrary to the spirit of the trade unionism of villainy. Gangs tend to be parochial in outlook, and there is no doubt that the organized professional criminals in Paris resented the only too successful intrusion of a gang from the provinces. As is usual in such situations, the Paris police began to receive hints and tips from underworld informers concerning the movements and location of the gangsters from Marseilles.

One of these tip-offs hinted to the police that the two principal characters—Madman Pete and Jo le Moko—could be found at the Hotel de Marroniers at Saint Maur, on the banks of the Marne. This was a quiet, picturesque spot much favoured by week-end trippers from Paris. Police Commissaire Casanova of the Brigade des Agressions (a kind of anti-gangster unit) decided to act on the tip on the scale of what was virtually a military operation. He planned to strike with a massive force of police and gardes mobiles, plus a tear-gas squad. In all some fifty vehicles were involved. Like a flashback to Chicago during the gang warfare days of the thirties, this vast flying squad went into action, with sirens wailing and guns at the ready.

The police surrounded the Hotel de Marroniers, but were immediately fired on by an armed guard who had been posted outside the hotel by Madman Pete. The guard was shot dead, as were a number of other more innocent people who were careless enough to show themselves, including the hotel manager. The trigger-happy police even wounded some of their own colleagues. Meanwhile the gangsters, unscathed and unseen, escaped in a fast car, driving straight through a section of the police cordon under the protective screen of machine-gun bursts. Jo le Moko always maintained that he was at the hotel purely as a friend and guest of Madman Pete's, and it is true that when Jo was later arrested on a different charge the magistrate decided that allegations that he had been implicated in previous crimes were "not proven".

The Hotel de Marroniers incident took place in 1946 at roughly the peak of Madman Pete's anti-social career. There was not much longer to go. After lying low for two months, Pete returned to Paris to resume his professional activities in the art of armed robbery. Although he did not realize it, his luck, which had never deserted him even though he had shot four policemen and a number of innocent civilians during his raids, was about to fail.

The final hold-up was in a jeweller's shop in Rue Boissiere, Paris. Unfortunately for Pete the jeweller happened to be a Judo expert and was not very impressed by the gun. He tackled Pete with skilful competence, and Pete fired his gun—only to discover that he had shot himself in the stomach and was splashing blood all over the place. Pete's friend, who was in on the raid, promptly shot the jeweller dead. He quickly dragged his seriously wounded friend to the car and rushed him to a clinic where no questions would be asked. The emergency treatment was more emergency than treatment. The bullet had severed a main artery and there was little that could be done without rushing the gangster to a hospital where he would certainly be identified. Pete, in any case, realized that he was dying, and he insisted in being taken from the clinic direct to his best friend, Jo le Moko.

And there Madman Pete died, his fingers clutching a tiny golden image of the Holy Virgin. He died cradled in the strong arms of his old comrade Jo le Moko, who was unable to control his tears. But before he died Pete made Jo promise that he would never allow the police to find his body, for they would send it to the Police School of Pathology for dissection. The mere idea of this horrified him, hardened killer though he was.

Pete, dressed in his best suit with a black tie, was buried secretly on a tiny island in the Seine near Mantes, close to Versailles, and not far from the home of a friend of Jo's named Henri Courtois. The latter, having assisted Jo in the macabre burial of Madman Pete, swore that he would never reveal the site of Pete's last resting place, nor the manner in which he met his death. And Jo, for his part, kept up the pretence that Pete was still very much alive and actively engaged in his métier of armed robbery. Nobody outside of Courtois and Jo le Moko knew that Pete was dead—least of all the police—and because of this a very odd situation arose which was to embarrass Jo le Moko and threaten his liberty for several years to come.

Madman Pete, though lying quietly in his grave on an island in the Seine, continued to hit the newspaper headlines and form the focus of police pursuit. For a period of three years, every major hold-up and armed robbery was attributed to Pete who, so far as authority was concerned, was adept at lying low between raids, and had never been more elusive. But if the police could not trace Madman Pete, at least they could pick up Jo le Moko, who was still regarded as Pete's lieutenant and known to be his good friend. But Jo kept his secret and insisted, quite truthfully, that he had not seen Pete for a long time, and that he had never been even remotely connected with any of the robberies under investigation. The police were never able to prove otherwise.

As the search for Madman Pete intensified, Jo became the subject of almost continuous police surveillance and interrogation. They were certain that he knew where Pete was to be found, and could be made to talk. Jo knew well enough, but he had made a solemn promise to his friend on his death-bed, and was not prepared to talk. This promise was to earn him a savage jail sentence in due course, but Jo was not the type to go back on his word.

The persistence of the police became so embarrassing that Jo was forced to move to Marseilles and change his name to Marcel Deloffre, but this provided only a temporary respite. In 1947, the year after Pete's death, he was picked up by the police in a casual check which was part of a "clean up Marseilles" campaign. Although his true identity was unknown, he was detained when he was found to be carrying a loaded revolver. To carry a gun was not in itself an offence, provided the calibre did not exceed 0.32. Only the police and other officials were allowed to carry heavier-calibre weapons. This particular gun happened to be a 0.45, which was therefore illegal. During a long interrogation by the police he was recognized by a detective as Jo le Moko, and was promptly arrested.

The police pursued their questioning with the persuasion of some strong-arm treatment and beating-up. They wanted to know where Madman Pete was hiding, but all Jo would say was that so far as he knew Pete had gone to South America. He could have saved himself a great deal of trouble and discomfort by revealing that Pete was dead. In the event, nine charges were brought against him, none of which could be made to stick, but he was nevertheless imprisoned to await trial while investigations proceeded. Under French law this could mean imprisonment for two years or more before a case came into court—and this was exactly what happened to Jo le Moko, simply because he would not admit that his friend was dead and buried.

While Jo kept his secret, Henri Courtois did not. Perhaps he believed that if the truth were told Jo might be released from prison. After two years, during which time Jo was in jail first in Paris and finally in Marseilles, Courtois talked too much. The Paris police learned that the much sought-after Madman Pete, far from being in South America, was buried on a small island in the Seine not far from Paris.

Courtois revealed the site of the grave and Pete's remains were carefully exhumed and handed over to the pathologists and scientists. The skeleton was accurately measured and checked against photographs of Pete, and a transparency of the skull was superimposed on a picture of his face. They matched well enough. The evidence was sufficient to convince a coroner's court that the skeleton was that of Madman Pete, and that he had been dead for about three years. And this was the man who for those three years had been accused of organizing a series of successful robberies and hold-ups!

The police were naturally embarrassed, but they still had Jo le Moko—the man who if he had told the truth in the first place could have saved them a great deal of useless work and effort, not to mention the final embarrassment. Jo obviously had to pay the penalty. True, they had tried unsuccessfully for a long time to find a charge against Jo that would stick, but had failed. Now, however, they had got him—under an ancient statute which had been framed in the days when body-snatching for dissection was a common practice.

Having nailed their man on a charge, and by this time it was a case of "any charge will do", the judiciary convicted him of "illegal detention of a corpse"—this being the technical definition under the ancient and obsolete statute of secretly burying the body without notifying the authorities, even though it had been at Pete's own dying request. He was then sentenced to a vicious seven years in solitary confinement. It was clear to many people that Jo le Moko was being severely punished, not for the "illegal detention of a corpse", but for alleged criminal activities of which he had been suspected as a friend of Pete's, but never convicted, and, perhaps in greater measure, as a reprisal for the three years in which the French police had wasted time and manpower in trying to trap and arrest a gangster who was already dead and buried. The police had the last laugh, and the joke was on Jo le Moko.

He served his full sentence in Fresne prison, near Paris, and was released at the end of 1953. His former fellow-inmates of Mauthausen concentration camp celebrated his release by holding a special dinner in his honour in a plush restaurant near the Champs Elysees. Jo le Moko was still their hero.

It was not quite the end of the story. Jo settled down to a life of quiet respectability, running a small bar in Montmartre with the aid of a girl friend named Carmen. For three or four years he was out of the news. And then, suddenly, he became inexplicably involved in a gun-running incident in Tangiers and was jailed on suspicion pending investigation by the Spanish police. Jo found that Spanish jails were even worse than French jails, and that was saying something! He made up his mind not to accept Spanish hospitality any longer than could be helped.

The plan which he put into effect was as ingenious as it was cynical, and it called ironically for the unwitting co-operation of the French police in securing his escape from Spanish jurisdiction. It also called for a knowledge of international law and, in particular, extradition treaties, which proved that Jo was no fool.

He was allowed to read newspapers in prison, and with a shrewd sense of timing he put his plan into action when he read one day about a sensational murder at Montfort-l'Amaury, near Paris, which was rumoured to be connected with a major political scandal. Assessing nicely the predictable reaction of the French police, Jo le Moko told the Spanish prison governor that he was implicated in the Montfort murder. This information was relayed to Paris, and in no time at all the French had obtained an extradition warrant, despite opposition from the Spanish authorities, who were more concerned with the gun-running charge. Jo le Moko found himself once more in solitary confinement in a French prison, which was only a marginal improvement on a Spanish jail. There was no reason why he should have been in solitary confinement; it was just that the French police had not forgiven him for those three wasted years spent in pursuing a dead man. They had no sense of humour. But Jo le Moko knew what he was doing.

In a very short space of time police investigations into the Montfort murder proved that Jo le Moko could not possibly have been involved. He had not even been in France at the time. Consequently he was released—with bad feeling and ill grace. The police now knew precisely why he had confessed to involvement in a crime with which he could have no possible connection.

The position was that the Spanish authorities in Tangiers had collected sufficient evidence to show that Jo had definitely been involved in the gun-running escapade, and they wanted him back for trial. But it could not be done. The legal position between France and the Tangiers Free Zone was that the Spanish police could not extradite him from France, even though the French police had been able to do so in the reverse direction. Jo le Moko had played his cards well, and no doubt he believed he had finally got his own back on the French police for the seven years of solitary confinement he had suffered for "illegal detention of a corpse".

Apart from the gun-running incident, and even that was

inconclusive, there was never any acceptable evidence that Jo le Moko was involved at all in any armed robbery or crime generally. Despite police and juridical hostility, a conviction was never obtained against him. As an intimate friend of Madman Pete, an admitted bandit, he naturally attracted the full force of police suspicion, but it is significant that no charge could ever be substantiated against him apart from the dubious one of concealing the death and secret burial of his friend, Madman Pete, and that is, perhaps, a charge which the French police would prefer to forget about.

Pete enjoyed the distinction (although he was never aware of it) of posthumously being accused of committing crimes for some three years after his violent death.

After his final successful bout with the French police, Jo le Moko returned to Carmen and his small bar in Montmartre to find the peace and quiet which had eluded him for so long. And so far as is known he is still there to this day.